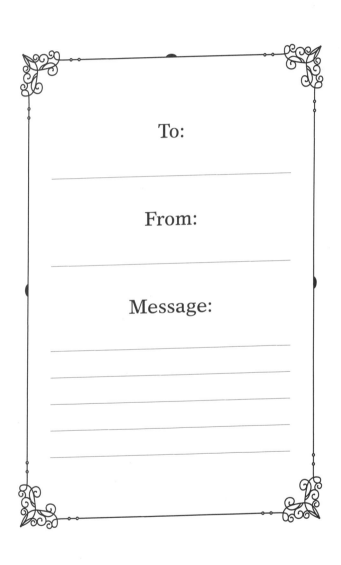

To:

_____

From:

_____

Message:

_____

_____

_____

_____

_____

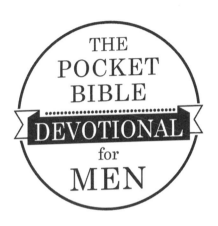

# Stephan Joubert

*The Pocket Bible Devotional for Men*

Published by Christian Art Publishers
PO Box 1599, Vereeniging, 1930, RSA

© 2017
First edition 2017

Cover designed by Christian Art Publishers

Images used under license from Shutterstock.com

Printed in China

ISBN 978-1-4321-1924-9

22  23  24  25  26  27  28  29  30  31  –  33  32  31  30  29  28  27  26  25  24

# Introduction

Men face battles of many kinds on a daily basis. Do you sometimes wish you had a wise mentor to offer a fresh perspective on the challenges you face at home, work and in the community? God's eternal Word is the starting point to find guidance and renewed vision to face these challenges head on. If you seek to become a man after God's own heart, you'll find the encouragement and wisdom you need in the pages of this Pocket Bible Devotional.

The 366 devotions arranged alphabetically according to the topics, candidly address the struggles and trials men face in their everyday lives. You'll also find a collection of specially-selected Scripture verses under each topic. They offer real answers to life's tough issues at your fingertips. The handy format makes it perfect to carry along. So whether in your car or on your desk, you will want to keep this Pocket Bible Devotional close at hand.

You'll be challenged to become a man of courage, as the book gives you the tools you need from the Word to develop a powerful and productive life of faith in Christ. The thematic index at the back of the book is helpful to instantly find what the Word says about a specific topic.

It is a spiritual resource offering a fresh perspective on the issues you grapple with. The wide and varied topics put today's troubles and triumphs into eternal perspective. Day by day, you'll learn a bit more of what it means to be a man of God.

The biblical insights from Scripture will impact your life, deepen your understanding of God and give you the wisdom you need to live courageously, knowing where you're headed – God's way.

JANUARY

May the **Lord** **BLESS YOU** & PROTECT YOU

Numbers 6:24

# Discovering God's Abundance

"Watch out! Be on your guard against all kinds of greed; life does not consist in an abundance of possessions." Luke 12:15 NIV

"The thief does not come except to steal, and to kill, and to destroy. I have come that they may have life, and that they may have it more abundantly." John 10:10 NKJV

May God give you heaven's dew and earth's richness – an abundance of grain and new wine. Genesis 27:28 NIV

So I have reason to be enthusiastic about all Christ Jesus has done through me in my service to God. Romans 15:17 NLT

But the meek shall inherit the land and delight themselves in abundant peace. Psalm 37:11 ESV

For as we share abundantly in Christ's sufferings, so through Christ we share abundantly in comfort too. 2 Corinthians 1:5 ESV

You prepare a table before me in the presence of my enemies. You anoint my head with oil; my cup overflows. Psalm 23:5 NIV

God is able to bless you abundantly, so that in all things at all times, having all that you need, you will abound in every good work. 2 Corinthians 9:8 NIV

God does everything abundantly. He doesn't measure His grace with a dropper. When God gives life, He does so abundantly. He grants eternal life to every beggar of godly grace. You and I should also forgive and be abundantly gracious to everyone around us. Not to mention our finances. We have received so abundantly from the Lord that we won't be able to use it up in our lifetime. Let's share what we have!

# Accept Others in Love

"For you will be treated as you treat others. The standard you use in judging is the standard by which you will be judged. And why worry about a speck in your friend's eye when you have a log in your own? How can you think of saying to your friend, 'Let me help you get rid of that speck in your eye,' when you can't see past the log in your own eye? Hypocrite! First get rid of the log in your own eye; then you will see well enough to deal with the speck in your friend's eye."
**Matthew 7:2-5 NLT**

Accept the one whose faith is weak, without quarreling over disputable matters
**Romans 14:1 NIV**

"I have come in My Father's name, and you do not receive Me; if another comes in his own name, him you will receive."
**John 5:43 NKJV**

Therefore, accept each other just as Christ has accepted you so that God will be given glory.
**Romans 15:7 NLT**

Put on then, as God's chosen ones, holy and beloved, compassionate hearts, kindness, humility, meekness, and patience.
**Colossians 3:12 ESV**

To accept each other is not only a kind gesture, it's also a heavenly instruction. God expects it from us. The reason why? He accepts us unconditionally, and therefore we owe it to our fellow men. Strangers, friends, colleagues, acquaintances, family, believers and the likes, we must strive to make them feel welcome ... and safe in our presence. We should radiate the Lord's caring and warm heart to the world. Accept people as they are, without trying to change them all the time. Leave that part to God.

# You Can Accomplish Much Through Him

But God was fulfilling what all the prophets had foretold about the Messiah – that He must suffer these things.
**Acts 3:18 NLT**

If you really fulfill the royal law according to the Scripture, "You shall love your neighbor as yourself", you do well.
**James 2:8 NKJV**

"Humanly speaking, it is impossible. But not with God. Everything is possible with God." **Mark 10:27 NLT**

The Lord has fulfilled the promise He made.
**2 Chronicles 6:10 NLT**

For I can do everything through Christ, who gives me strength.
**Philippians 4:13 NLT**

"Do not think that I have come to abolish the Law or the Prophets; I have not come to abolish them but to fulfill them."
**Matthew 5:17 NIV**

Again Jesus spoke to them, saying, "I am the light of the world. Whoever follows Me will not walk in darkness, but will have the light of life."
**John 8:12 ESV**

Bear one another's burdens, and so fulfill the law of Christ.
**Galatians 6:2 ESV**

Fulfillment has to do with making promises come true. Jesus made the biblical promises true through His life, death and resurrection. But the fulfillment in the Bible also has to do with something that was finalized. You and I are busy fulfilling the Bible by obeying it on a daily basis. Fulfillment is a continuous process. We are living fulfillers of God's eternal Word.

# Glorious Achievements

"You are the light of the world. A city set on a hill cannot be hidden. Nor do people light a lamp and put it under a basket, but on a stand, and it gives light to all in the house. In the same way, let your light shine before others, so that they may see your good works and give glory to your Father who is in heaven."
**Matthew 5:14-16 ESV**

"But when you give to someone in need, don't let your left hand know what your right hand is doing. Give your gifts in private, and your Father, who sees everything, will reward you."
**Matthew 6:3-4 NLT**

Those who do well as deacons will be rewarded with respect from others and will have increased confidence in their faith in Christ Jesus.
**1 Timothy 3:13 NLT**

Through the proof of this ministry, they glorify God for the obedience of your confession to the gospel of Christ, and for your liberal sharing with them and all men. **2 Corinthians 9:13 NKJV**

I don't mean to say that I have already achieved these things or that I have already reached perfection. But I press on to possess that perfection for which Christ Jesus first possessed me. **Philippians 3:12 NLT**

Achievement relates to the moments where we excel in life. A trophy, a certificate, a medal, public recognition – all these things are proof of good performance. It's good that we use our talents for the Lord, and excel. We must just remember to give Him all the glory and not take the recognition for ourselves in thinking we're the best thing that happened to planet earth. True achievers know to whom the glory belongs.

# The Problem with Addiction

No temptation has overtaken you that is not common to man. God is faithful, and He will not let you be tempted beyond your ability, but with the temptation He will also provide the way of escape, that you may be able to endure it. **1 Corinthians 10:13 ESV**

In the same way, deacons must be well respected and have integrity. They must not be heavy drinkers or dishonest with money. **1 Timothy 3:8 NLT**

Since an overseer manages God's household, he must be blameless – not overbearing, not quick-tempered, not given to drunkenness, not violent, not pursuing dishonest gain. **Titus 1:7 NIV**

Older women likewise are to be reverent in behavior, not slanderers or slaves to much wine. They are to teach what is good. **Titus 2:3 ESV**

For we ourselves were also once foolish, disobedient, deceived, serving various lusts and pleasures, living in malice and envy, hateful and hating one another. But when the kindness and the love of God our Savior toward man appeared, not by works of righteousness which we have done, but according to His mercy He saved us, through the washing of regeneration and renewing of the Holy Spirit. **Titus 3:3-5 NKJV**

Addiction abounds. Alcohol, drugs, pornography and food are but a few of the destructive addictions that can ensnare. Addictive behavior can be destructive. It consumes your whole life and makes you a slave. The Lord is the only One who sets people truly free. He breaks the bonds of addiction. But sometimes He also uses people in the process, like therapists, doctors, friends and pastors. Be such a friend to an addict.

# Our Advocate

For Mordecai the Jew was second to King Ahasuerus, and was great among the Jews and well received by the multitude of his brethren, seeking the good of his people and speaking peace to all his countrymen.
**Esther 10:3 NKJV**

Even now my witness is in heaven. My advocate is there on high.
**Job 16:19 NLT**

My little children, I am writing these things to you so that you may not sin. But if anyone does sin, we have an advocate with the Father, Jesus Christ the righteous.
**1 John 2:1 ESV**

"I will ask the Father, and He will give you another advocate to help you and be with you forever."
**John 14:16 NIV**

"It is best for you that I go away, because if I don't, the Advocate won't come. If I do go away, then I will send Him to you."
**John 16:7 NLT**

Whatever city you enter, and they do not receive you, go out into its streets and say, "The very dust of your city which clings to us we wipe off against you. Nevertheless know this, that the kingdom of God has come near you."
**Luke 10:10-11 NKJV**

Jesus had to return to heaven after He completed His earthly mission, otherwise the Spirit would not have come to all of us as believers. The Holy Spirit fulfills the work of Jesus all over the world. He is omnipresent. Unlike Jesus when He was on earth and could only be at one place at a time. The Spirit is everywhere. After all, He is our Advocate who intercedes for us before the Father. He pleads for us all the time.

# Fear, Worry and the God of Rest

When they saw Him walking on the water, they cried out in terror, thinking He was a ghost. They were all terrified when they saw Him. But Jesus spoke to them at once. "Don't be afraid," He said. "Take courage! I am here!"
**Mark 6:49-50 NLT**

Even when I walk through the darkest valley, I will not be afraid, for You are close beside me. Your rod and Your staff protect and comfort me.
**Psalm 23:4 NLT**

"Come to Me, all you who labor and are heavy laden, and I will give you rest."
**Matthew 11:28 NKJV**

"Do not be afraid, little flock, for your Father has been pleased to give you the kingdom."
**Luke 12:32 NIV**

God gave us a spirit not of fear but of power and love and self-control.
**2 Timothy 1:7 ESV**

"Have I not commanded you? Be strong and of good courage; do not be afraid, nor be dismayed, for the LORD your God is with you wherever you go."
**Joshua 1:9 NKJV**

"My presence will go with you, and I will give you rest." **Exodus 33:14 ESV**

When God is near, there is no place for fear. Well, there is no place for fear of danger. We just fall down at His feet, because we know that He is so much greater than the gravest danger. Our only legitimate fear is that of God. It is holy reverence for the Lord. Without such reverence for God we become too familiar with Him. Then we don't know our place in God's presence.

# Age Is Just a Number

The glory of young men is their strength. And the splendor of old men is their gray head.
**Proverbs 20:29 NKJV**

You have made known to me the paths of life; You will make me full of gladness with Your presence.
**Acts 2:28 ESV**

Older women likewise are to be reverent in behavior, not slanderers or slaves to much wine. They are to teach what is good.
**Titus 2:3 ESV**

It is not only the old who are wise, not only the aged who understand what is right.
**Job 32:9 NIV**

"Listen to Me, you descendants of Jacob, all the remnant of the people of Israel, you whom I have upheld since your birth, and have carried since you were born. Even to your old age and gray hairs I am He, I am He who will sustain you. I have made you and I will carry you. I will sustain you and I will rescue you."
**Isaiah 46:3-4 NIV**

Gray hair is a crown of glory; it is gained by living a godly life.
**Proverbs 16:31 NLT**

So teach us to number our days that we may get a heart of wisdom.
**Psalm 90:12 ESV**

Age matters. We measure people against their years. God doesn't. He says little children aren't too young to work for Him, and that the elderly is not too old because they're retired. In fact, the New Testament doesn't really refer to age. We are permanently in service of God. Our value and purpose don't decrease as we grow older. We are precious, no matter our age.

# Standing Up for God

Let God arise, let His enemies be scattered, and let those who hate Him flee before Him.
**Psalm 68:1 NKJV**

Behold, I make you this day a fortified city, an iron pillar, and bronze walls, against the whole land, against the kings of Judah, its officials, its priests, and the people of the land.
**Jeremiah 1:18 ESV**

Brothers and sisters, I want to remind you of the gospel I preached to you, which you received and on which you have taken your stand.
**1 Corinthians 15:1 NIV**

Oh, the joys of those who do not follow the advice of the wicked, or stand around with sinners, or join in with mockers. **Psalm 1:1 NLT**

"Now will I arise," says the LORD. "Now will I be exalted; now will I be lifted up."
**Isaiah 33:10 NIV**

Therefore submit to God. Resist the devil and he will flee from you. **James 4:7 NKJV**

Be shepherds of God's flock that is under your care, watching over them – not because you must, but because you are willing, as God wants you to be; not pursuing dishonest gain, but eager to serve. **1 Peter 5:2 NIV**

To stand up for something or someone is to take a stand for it. To stand up for the Lord means to have the courage to swim upstream, and to say and do things that are unpopular. It is to truly rise up for the Lord and start living a holy life, as we're taught in Psalm 1. When we're not sitting down, standing or walking with the wicked, then we're standing up for God. Then we make His heart glad.

# Spiritual Authority

Jesus called His twelve disciples to Him and gave them authority to drive out impure spirits and to heal every disease and sickness.
**Matthew 10:1 NIV**

The people were amazed at His teaching, for He taught with real authority – quite unlike the teachers of religious law.
**Mark 1:22 NLT**

For the Lord's sake, submit to all human authority – whether the king as head of state. **1 Peter 2:13 NLT**

"But I want you to know that the Son of Man has authority on earth to forgive sins." **Matthew 9:6 NIV**

Let every person be subject to the governing authorities. For there is no authority except from God, and those that exist have been instituted by God.
**Romans 13:1 ESV**

"Yet it shall not be so among you; but whoever desires to become great among you shall be your servant. And whoever of you desires to be first shall be slave of all."
**Mark 10:43-44 NKJV**

There is no authority except from God.
**Romans 13:1 ESV**

God has full authority in heaven and on earth. Yet He shares His power with people in leadership positions. Authority according to the Bible, when given to people, is never bossy or authoritarian. The Lord's leaders serve others with their spiritual gifts. They shift the spotlight to Jesus, where our focus needs to be. They use their authority to uplift the weak, lonely and outcast. They serve while they lead.

# True Authority Comes from God

One day Jesus called together His twelve disciples and gave them power and authority to cast out all demons and to heal all diseases.
**Luke 9:1 NLT**

Obey those who rule over you, and be submissive, for they watch out for your souls, as those who must give account.
**Hebrews 13:17 NKJV**

Wives, submit yourselves to your husbands, as is fitting in the Lord. Husbands, love your wives and do not be harsh with them.
**Colossians 3:18-19 NIV**

But I want you to realize that the head of every man is Christ, and the head of the woman is man, and the head of Christ is God.
**1 Corinthians 11:3 NIV**

An oracle is on the lips of a king; his mouth does not sin in judgment. A just balance and scales are the LORD's; all the weights in the bag are His work.
**Proverbs 16:10-11 ESV**

Submit to God and be at peace with Him; in this way prosperity will come to you.
**Job 22:21 NIV**

We should never confuse biblical authority with some sort of obsession with power. Authority, when applied to people in the church or in marriage, is always functional. Not hierarchically. It means certain forms of authority are given to some people by God to help and serve others in love. And so that there can be healthy order. Such authority serves. It's not bossy. It creates spaces and doesn't demand attention or recognition.

# Getting Back in the Race

Timothy, guard what has been entrusted to your care. Turn away from godless chatter and the opposing ideas of what is falsely called knowledge, which some have professed and in so doing have departed from the faith. Grace be with you all.
1 Timothy 6:20-21 NIV

Dear brothers and sisters, if another believer is overcome by some sin, you who are godly should gently and humbly help that person back onto the right path. And be careful not to fall into the same temptation yourself.
Galatians 6:1 NLT

But if we confess our sins to Him, He is faithful and just to forgive us our sins and to cleanse us from all wickedness. 1 John 1:9 NLT

Avoid irreverent babble, for it will lead people into more and more ungodliness, and their talk will spread like gangrene. Among them are Hymenaeus and Philetus, who have swerved from the truth, saying that the resurrection has already happened. They are upsetting the faith of some.
2 Timothy 2:16-18 ESV

Why then has this people turned away in perpetual backsliding? They hold fast to deceit; they refuse to return.
Jeremiah 8:5 ESV

Sometimes people forsake their faith. They just stop believing, and fall back into their old way of living. Or they are worse off than before. Paul referred to a few examples when he wrote to Timothy. Backsliding happens when people don't put their faith in Christ as the only Rock. They give up hope somewhere along the steep way. Stay close to the Lord. Walk close enough to Him so that you don't get lost when life gets tough.

# A Sign of the New Covenant

I baptize you with water for repentance. But after me comes one who is more powerful than I, whose sandals I am not worthy to carry. He will baptize you with the Holy Spirit and fire.
**Matthew 3:11 NIV**

"Therefore, go and make disciples of all the nations, baptizing them in the name of the Father and the Son and the Holy Spirit."
**Matthew 28:19 NLT**

For as many of you as were baptized into Christ have put on Christ.
**Galatians 3:27 ESV**

Yes, I also baptized the household of Stephanas. Besides, I do not know whether I baptized any other. For Christ did not send me to baptize, but to preach the gospel, not with wisdom of words, lest the cross of Christ should be made of no effect.
**1 Corinthians 1:16-17 NKJV**

Baptism, which corresponds to this, now saves you, not as a removal of dirt from the body but as an appeal to God for a good conscience, through the resurrection of Jesus Christ.
**1 Peter 3:21 ESV**

Being baptized is a ritual that shifts boundaries. It symbolizes dying to self and living a new life in Christ. It is not an isolated event. People are always incorporated into the community of believers by being baptized. That is why families were baptized together in the New Testament. But being baptized alone doesn't save you. It is also not more important than spreading the gospel.

# Bargaining with God

And so it was that all who saw it said, "No such deed has been done or seen from the day that the children of Israel came up from the land of Egypt until this day. Consider it, confer, and speak up!"
Judges 19:30 NKJV

"Come now, let us reason together," says the LORD, "though your sins are like scarlet, they shall be as white as snow; though they are red like crimson, they shall become like wool."
Isaiah 1:18 ESV

For the word of the LORD is upright, and all His work is done in faithfulness.
Psalm 33:4 ESV

LORD, You always give me justice when I bring a case before You. So let me bring You this complaint; Why are the wicked so prosperous? Why are evil people so happy? Jeremiah 12:1 NLT

The people were all so amazed that they asked each other, "What is this? A new teaching – and with authority! He even gives orders to impure spirits and they obey Him."
Mark 1:27 NIV

For it is by grace you have been saved, through faith – and this is not from yourselves, it is the gift of God.
Ephesians 2:8 NIV

We have nothing to bargain with God. We have nothing to offer that He needs. In fact, we are beggars of grace. It doesn't mean that we can't talk to Him or direct our requests to Him. We can and we should ask questions and bring our worries and doubts and struggles to Him. He can handle it. He is never discouraged by our questions. But we need to wrestle through our problems at His feet.

# The Beauty of God

One thing have I asked of the LORD, that will I seek after: that I may dwell in the house of the LORD all the days of my life, to gaze upon the beauty of the LORD and to inquire in His temple.
**Psalm 27:4 ESV**

Stolen water is sweet, and bread eaten in secret is pleasant.
**Proverbs 9:17 NKJV**

He has made everything beautiful in its time. He has also set eternity in the human heart; yet no one can fathom what God has done from beginning to end.
**Ecclesiastes 3:11 NIV**

She will place a lovely wreath on your head; she will present you with a beautiful crown.
**Proverbs 4:9 NLT**

But reject profane and old wives' fables, and exercise yourself toward godliness. For bodily exercise profits a little, but godliness is profitable for all things, having promise of the life that now is and of that which is to come.
**1 Timothy 4:7-8 NKJV**

Queen Vashti, wearing her royal crown, in order to display her beauty to the people and nobles, for she was lovely to look at.
**Esther 1:11 NIV**

Beauty is usually a topic for women. We don't think in such terms about ourselves. But beauty and grandeur are also characteristics of God. His holiness and purity are so overwhelming that we fall down before Him in awe and worship. We are overcome by His holy beauty. It lets us draw near to Him with respect and joy. See Him in this way, and serve Him as the Lord of all beauty.

# You Belong to God

For you are a holy people, who belong to the LORD your God. Of all the people on earth, the LORD your God has chosen you to be His own special treasure.
**Deuteronomy 7:6 NLT**

"Do not fear, for I have redeemed you; I have summoned you by name; you are Mine."
**Isaiah 43:1 NIV**

Be not far from me, for trouble is near and there is none to help.
**Psalm 22:11 ESV**

For we are God's fellow workers. You are God's field, God's building.
**1 Corinthians 3:9 ESV**

Rejoice, you nations, with His people, for He will avenge the blood of His servants; He will take vengeance on His enemies and make atonement for His land and people.
**Deuteronomy 32:43 NIV**

But you are a chosen generation, a royal priesthood, a holy nation, His own special people, that you may proclaim the praises of Him who called you out of darkness into His marvelous light. **1 Peter 2:9 NKJV**

So you are no longer a slave, but God's child; and since you are His child, God has made you also an heir.
**Galatians 4:7 NIV**

All of us want to belong somewhere. Our family, friends and local community are places where we want to feel welcome and loved. The most important thing is to know that we always belong to God. The fact that He made us His children in Christ is the greatest comfort and certainty in our lives. In life and death we are part of his brand-new nation. We are His people, His co-heirs, and His treasured possessions.

# Bowed Down in Worship

Oh come, let us worship and bow down; let us kneel before the LORD, our Maker!
**Psalm 95:6 ESV**

For this reason I kneel before the Father.
**Ephesians 3:14 NIV**

At the name of Jesus every knee should bow, in heaven and on earth and under the earth.
**Philippians 2:10 NIV**

The LORD will be awesome against them; for He will famish all the gods of the earth, and to Him shall bow down, each in its place, all the lands of the nations.
**Zephaniah 2:11 ESV**

"I have sworn by Myself; the word has gone out of My mouth in righteousness, and shall not return, that to Me every knee shall bow, every tongue shall take an oath."
**Isaiah 45:23 NKJV**

Then I bowed low and worshiped the LORD. I praised the LORD, the God of my master, Abraham, because He had led me straight to my master's niece to be his son's wife.
**Genesis 24:48 NLT**

Worship the LORD in the splendor of His holiness; tremble before Him, all the earth. **Psalm 96:9 NIV**

To bow our knees before God, as Paul literally puts it in Ephesians 3:14, is to know our place before Him. His holiness wills us to bow down low before Him. Our own unworthiness makes us crumble before God. We are like dust to the heavenly scales, yet God has compassion on us. He sees us through His grace when we're humble and small before Him. Then God, in turn, bows down to us.

# Hope after Betrayal

Jesus said to him, "Assuredly, I say to you that today, even this night, before the rooster crows twice, you will deny Me three times."
**Mark 14:30 NKJV**

Then He said to the crowd, "If any of you wants to be My follower, you must give up your own way, take up your cross daily, and follow Me." **Luke 9:23 NLT**

Don't love money; be satisfied with what you have. For God has said, "I will never fail you. I will never abandon you." **Hebrews 13:5 NLT**

The fear of the Lord is true wisdom; to forsake evil is real understanding. **Job 28:28 NLT**

A servant girl saw him seated there in the firelight. She looked closely at him and said, "This man was with Him." But he denied it. "Woman, I don't know Him," he said. A little later someone else saw him and said, "You also are one of them." "Man, I am not!" Peter replied.
**Luke 22:56-58 NIV**

"And then many will fall away and betray one another and hate one another."
**Matthew 24:10 ESV**

Jesus said to him, "Judas, would you betray the Son of Man with a kiss?"
**Luke 22:48 ESV**

Peter is notorious for it … betrayal I mean! Who will ever forget how he denied three times that he knew Jesus or had any connection to Him. It was when he was there in the courtyard of the high priest's home during Jesus' trial. Confess that you know Jesus, don't deny Him. Acknowledge Him everywhere, and don't pretend not to know Him. Because then you'll miss God's awesome grace and love.

# God's Wonderful Blessings

May the LORD bless you and protect you. May the LORD smile on you and be gracious to you. May the LORD show you His favor and give you His peace.
**Numbers 6:24-26 NLT**

Now behold, Boaz came from Bethlehem, and said to the reapers, "The LORD be with you!" And they answered him, "The LORD bless you!" **Ruth 2:4 NKJV**

All praise to God, the Father of our Lord Jesus Christ, who has blessed us with every spiritual blessing in the heavenly realms because we are united with Christ.
**Ephesians 1:3 NLT**

All the saints greet you. The grace of the Lord Jesus Christ and the love of God and the fellowship of the Holy Spirit be with you all.
**2 Corinthians 13:13-14 ESV**

Surely You have granted him unending blessings and made him glad with the joy of Your presence. For the king trusts in the LORD; through the unfailing love of the Most High He will not be shaken.
**Psalm 21:6-7 NIV**

Every good and perfect gift is from above, coming down from the Father of the heavenly lights, who does not change like shifting shadows.
**James 1:17 NIV**

Blessings indicate God's mercy and grace in the lives of the recipients. In the Old Testament, fathers used to give a blessing to their firstborn son. In the New Testament, the Triune God's favor and blessings are bestowed on all His children. Live a life based on these blessings. Receive it, and be blessed by Him. Also bless others by serving and loving them in His name.

# The Blood and the Glory

"Whoever eats My flesh and drinks My blood has eternal life, and I will raise them up at the last day."
**John 6:54 NIV**

In Him we have redemption through His blood, the forgiveness of sins, according to the riches of His grace.
**Ephesians 1:7 NKJV**

"You are worthy to take the scroll and break its seals and open it. For You were slaughtered, and Your blood has ransomed people for God from every tribe and language and people and nation."
**Revelation 5:9 NLT**

He then would have had to suffer often since the foundation of the world; but now, once at the end of the ages, He has appeared to put away sin by the sacrifice of Himself. **Hebrews 9:26 NKJV**

For God's will was for us to be made holy by the sacrifice of the body of Jesus Christ, once for all time.
**Hebrews 10:10 NLT**

How much more, then, will the blood of Christ, who through the eternal Spirit offered Himself unblemished to God, cleanse our consciences from acts that lead to death, so that we may serve the living God!
**Hebrews 9:14 NIV**

Blood must flow in order to reconcile us with God. For this purpose, Jesus' blood that was shed has been more than enough. On the cross He made atonement for all our sins and flaws once and for all. God has also accepted His offering on our behalf. To believe in Him as our Lord and Savior, is to be set free by God. Jesus made the way to God perfect for us. He is our peace, our advocacy and redemption.

# The Real Me

Do you not know that your bodies are temples of the Holy Spirit, who is in you, whom you have received from God? You are not your own.

1 Corinthians 6:19 NIV

The human body has many parts, but the many parts make up one whole body. So it is with the body of Christ.

1 Corinthians 12:12 NLT

For as we have many members in one body, but all the members do not have the same function, so we, being many, are one body in Christ, and individually members of one another.

Romans 12:4-5 NKJV

He is the head of the body, the church, who is the beginning, the firstborn from the dead, that in all things He may have the preeminence.

Colossians 1:18 NKJV

Since therefore the children share in flesh and blood, He Himself likewise partook of the same things, that through death He might destroy the one who has the power of death, that is, the devil.

Hebrews 2:14 ESV

Let the peace of Christ rule in your hearts, since as members of one body you were called to peace. And be thankful.

Colossians 3:15 NIV

One of the most powerful images used for the church of the Lord is the body. We are all part of His earthly body. In the same way a body has many limbs and parts, each with its own different function, the church also consists of people with many different gifts and talents to fulfill different roles. Some preach, others sing, encourage, support, guide, reprimand, teach or manage the administration. No matter what role or function you have to fulfill, make sure it's always constructive and uplifting.

# Bold and Fearless

Our actions will show that we belong to the truth, so we will be confident when we stand before God. Even if we feel guilty, God is greater than our feelings, and He knows everything. Dear friends, if we don't feel guilty, we can come to God with bold confidence. And we will receive from Him whatever we ask because we obey Him and do the things that please Him. And this is His commandment: We must believe in the name of His Son, Jesus Christ, and love one another, just as He commanded us.
**1 John 3:19-23 NLT**

In whom we have boldness and access with confidence through our faith in Him. **Ephesians 3:12 ESV**

Let us then approach God's throne of grace with confidence, so that we may receive mercy and find grace to help us in our time of need. **Hebrews 4:16 NIV**

For You have been my hope, Sovereign Lord, my confidence since my youth. **Psalm 71:5 NIV**

But blessed is the one who trusts in the Lord, whose confidence is in Him. **Jeremiah 17:7 NIV**

To come to God confidently and boldly are to approach Him with a conscience that is at peace. When we live close to the Lord, our conscience is finely tuned-in by the Holy Spirit. Then we are sensitive for His guidance in our lives. Then we're directed and guided by the constant inner conviction of the Spirit. When our conscience is at peace, then we can approach God's throne with confidence. Then we can bow before Him in joy.

# Living a Mundane Life?

A wise man fears and departs from evil, but a fool rages and is self-confident. **Proverbs 14:16 NKJV**

Whoever keeps the commandment keeps his life; he who despises his ways will die. **Proverbs 19:16 ESV**

Remember me for this, my God, and do not blot out what I have so faithfully done for the house of my God and its services. **Nehemiah 13:14 NIV**

I want you to remember what the holy prophets said long ago and what our Lord and Savior commanded through your apostles. **2 Peter 3:2 NLT**

Then you will not become spiritually dull and indifferent. Instead, you will follow the example of those who are going to inherit God's promises because of their faith and endurance. **Hebrews 6:12 NLT**

Besides that, they learn to be idlers, going about from house to house, and not only idlers, but also gossips and busybodies, saying what they should not. **1 Timothy 5:13 ESV**

What holds your attention? When do you become bored? Fact is, if something doesn't captivate you, your mind wanders. Then you become restless. Boredom can change into a don't-care attitude. Don't let this happen to you. Practice to find the beauty in everything and everyone around you. See people as God's handiwork. Then you will never be bored in their company.

# Finally Alive

The priests and Levites brought up the Ark of the LORD along with the special tent and all the sacred items that had been in it.
**1 Kings 8:4 NLT**

"The time promised by God has come at last!" he announced. "The Kingdom of God is near! Repent of your sins and believe the Good News!" **Mark 1:15 NLT**

"Therefore bear fruits worthy of repentance, and do not begin to say to yourselves, 'We have Abraham as our father.' For I say to you that God is able to raise up children to Abraham from these stones."
**Luke 3:8 NKJV**

"Those who are well have no need of a physician, but those who are sick. I came not to call the righteous, but sinners." **Mark 2:17 ESV**

Truly, these times of ignorance God overlooked, but now commands all men everywhere to repent.
**Acts 17:30 NKJV**

"Even now," declares the LORD, "return to Me with all your heart, with fasting and weeping and mourning. Rend your heart and not your garments. Return to the LORD your God, for He is gracious and compassionate, slow to anger and abounding in love."
**Joel 2:12-13 NIV**

Metanoia or spiritual conversion is to follow a new way of thinking and living. It is to experience a radical life transformation as a result of an encounter with the living God. To be converted changes your way of thinking, doing and believing. The result is that we start living differently with regards to all our relationships. Jesus calls us to continuous repentance and transformation. He asks that we live brand-new lives in His presence.

# Bought at a Price

Flee from sexual immorality. Every other sin a person commits is outside the body, but the sexually immoral person sins against his own body. Or do you not know that your body is a temple of the Holy Spirit within you, whom you have from God? You are not your own, for you were bought with a price. So glorify God in your body. **1 Corinthians 6:18-20 ESV**

For He has rescued us from the dominion of darkness and brought us into the kingdom of the Son He loves, in whom we have redemption, the forgiveness of sins.
**Colossians 1:13-14 NIV**

He gave His life to free us from every kind of sin, to cleanse us, and to make us His very own people, totally committed to doing good deeds.
**Titus 2:14 NLT**

He sent redemption to His people; He has commanded His covenant forever. Holy and awesome is His name!
**Psalm 111:9 ESV**

For He who is called in the Lord while a slave is the Lord's freedman. Likewise He who is called while free is Christ's slave. You were bought at a price; do not become slaves of men.
**1 Corinthians 7:22-23 NKJV**

When someone buys out a business, the business probably went bankrupt. In fact, the same thing happened to us when Jesus met us on the market place of sin and death. He alone was able, but also loved us enough, to buy us out of the eternal mess. He alone has the power and strength to convert bankrupt lives into temples of the living God.

# Faithful Worship

"You shall not bow down to them nor serve them. For I, the LORD your God, am a jealous God, visiting the iniquity of the fathers upon the children to the third and fourth generations of those who hate Me."
**Exodus 20:5 NKJV**

Come, let us worship and bow down. Let us kneel before the LORD our Maker.
**Psalm 95:6 NLT**

"Let us go to His dwelling place; let us worship at His footstool!"
**Psalm 132:7 ESV**

With what shall I come before the LORD and bow down before the exalted God? Shall I come before Him with burnt offerings, with calves a year old?
**Micah 6:6 NIV**

At the name of Jesus every knee should bow, in heaven and on earth and under the earth.
**Philippians 2:10 ESV**

Thus the secrets of his heart are revealed; and so, falling down on his face, he will worship God and report that God is truly among you.
**1 Corinthians 14:25 NKJV**

To bow down before God is to confirm His authority and omnipotence visibly. To bow before Him doesn't only concern our words, but our whole bodies. It is a symbolic act of complete surrender where we confess and acknowledge our dependence on God. To bow before Christ is also to recognize Him as the only Lord who offers true deliverance. A true encounter with the living God always leads to such worship.

# Stay Away from Bribes

You shall take no bribe, for a bribe blinds the clear-sighted and subverts the cause of those who are in the right.
**Exodus 23:8 ESV**

You must never twist justice or show partiality. Never accept a bribe, for bribes blind the eyes of the wise and corrupt the decisions of the godly.
**Deuteronomy 16:19 NLT**

Extortion turns a wise person into a fool, and a bribe corrupts the heart.
**Ecclesiastes 7:7 NIV**

Be careful that no one entices you by riches; do not let a large bribe turn you aside.
**Job 36:18 NIV**

Now therefore, let the fear of the LORD be upon you; take care and do it, for there is no iniquity with the LORD our God, no partiality, nor taking of bribes.
**2 Chronicles 19:7 NKJV**

The wicked accept bribes in secret to pervert the course of justice.
**Proverbs 17:23 NIV**

Whoever is greedy for unjust gain troubles his own household, but he who hates bribes will live.
**Proverbs 15:27 ESV**

Bribery doesn't go down well with God. He doesn't like it one bit when people do shady business dealings under the table. God expects integrity from His children. They need to be transparent. They don't bribe people, and they don't have two sets of rules – one for church and one for work! In fact, their lives and their business are left in plain sight before God and others.

# Build Others Up

Encourage one another and build each other up, just as in fact you are doing.
**1 Thessalonians 5:11 NIV**

Let us consider one another in order to stir up love and good works, not forsaking the assembling of ourselves together, as is the manner of some, but exhorting one another, and so much the more as you see the Day approaching.
**Hebrews 10:24-25 NKJV**

So then, let us aim for harmony in the church and try to build each other up.
**Romans 14:19 NLT**

Now these are the gifts Christ gave to the church: the apostles, the prophets, the evangelists, and the pastors and teachers. Their responsibility is to equip God's people to do His work and build up the church, the body of Christ. This will continue until we all come to such unity in our faith and knowledge of God's Son that we will be mature in the Lord, measuring up to the full and complete standard of Christ. **Ephesians 4:11-13 NLT**

For one who speaks in a tongue speaks not to men but to God. On the other hand, the one who prophesies speaks to people for their upbuilding and encouragement and consolation. **1 Corinthians 14:2-3 ESV**

The Lord's church needs to build up. He uses people to do this work. The calling on ministers is to equip believers with the right knowledge from God's Word, but also to inspire and teach them to practically care for others. The church also teaches us how to spread the gospel. Building up of the church is therefore vitally important. Use your gifts and talents to support fellow believers, and to strengthen their faith. Then you're using your gifts wisely.

# When You Feel Like Giving Up

I am feeble and severely broken; I groan because of the turmoil of my heart. Lord, all my desire is before You; and my sighing is not hidden from You. **Psalm 38:8-9 NKJV**

"Come to Me, all you who are weary and burdened, and I will give you rest. Take My yoke upon you and learn from Me, for I am gentle and humble in heart, and you will find rest for your souls." **Matthew 11:28-29 NIV**

"Only in returning to Me and resting in Me will you be saved. In quietness and confidence is your strength." **Isaiah 30:15 NLT**

Even youths will become weak and tired, and young men will fall in exhaustion. But those who trust in the LORD will find new strength. They will soar high on wings like eagles. They will run and not grow weary. They will walk and not faint. **Isaiah 40:30-31 NLT**

We are pressed on every side by troubles, but we are not crushed. We are perplexed, but not driven to despair. **2 Corinthians 4:8 NLT**

So let's not get tired of doing what is good. At just the right time we will reap a harvest of blessing if we don't give up. **Galatians 6:9 NLT**

When I've reach the end of my physical strength, as well as that of my soul, I tend to suffer from burnout. Then I'm running on empty. Then I'm stealing from my reserves that are already depleted. To sidestep burnout, you have to learn to rest well, and say no. You don't have to be everything to everyone. You're nobody's servant, only God's.

# A Caring Heart

We hear that some among you are idle and disruptive. They are not busy; they are busybodies. Such people we command and urge in the Lord Jesus Christ to settle down and earn the food they eat.
**2 Thessalonians 3:11-12 NIV**

He must manage his own family well, having children who respect and obey him. For if a man cannot manage his own household, how can he take care of God's church?
**1 Timothy 3:4-5 NLT**

With all humility and gentleness, with patience, bearing with one another in love.
**Ephesians 4:2 ESV**

Cast all your anxiety on Him because He cares for you.
**1 Peter 5:7 NIV**

Know the state of your flocks, and put your heart into caring for your herds.
**Proverbs 27:23 NLT**

You are being faithful to God when you care for the traveling teachers who pass through, even though they are strangers to you.
**3 John 1:5 NLT**

For God is not unjust. He will not forget how hard you have worked for Him and how you have shown your love to Him by caring for other believers, as you still do. **Hebrews 6:10 NLT**

To care for your family is a biblical command. Paul taught the elders that they can't care for God's house or His church if they can't care for and control their own house. To care for them is more than merely putting bread on the table. It is to pray for your family and to intercede for them before God. It is also to read to them from the Word, and to guide them in shaping their faith.

# Truly Carefree

I was thrust into Your arms at my birth. You have been my God from the moment I was born.

**Psalm 22:11 NLT**

"That is why I tell you not to worry about everyday life – whether you have enough food and drink, or enough clothes to wear. Isn't life more than food, and your body more than clothing? Look at the birds. They don't plant or harvest or store food in barns, for your heavenly Father feeds them. And aren't you far more valuable to Him than they are? Can all your worries add a single moment to your life?"

**Matthew 6:25-27 NLT**

"So don't worry about these things, saying, 'What will we eat? What will we drink? What will we wear?' These things dominate the thoughts of unbelievers, but your heavenly Father already knows all your needs. Seek the Kingdom of God above all else, and live righteously, and He will give you everything you need. So don't worry about tomorrow, for tomorrow will bring its own worries. Today's trouble is enough for today."

**Matthew 6:31-34 NLT**

"I have made you and I will carry you."

**Isaiah 46:4 NIV**

Being carefree flows from the right kind of faith. It definitely doesn't mean being irresponsible. It is to believe God's Word that He will provide bread when you need it. And that He will care for us like a Father cares for His family. If you believe this, your life becomes carefree. Then you trust the Lord with the small detail in your life, and with the big things.

FEBRUARY

# He Cares for Us

"Come to Me, all you who are weary and burdened, and I will give you rest."
**Matthew 11:28 NIV**

Blessed be the Lord God of Israel, for He has visited and redeemed His people.
**Luke 1:68 NKJV**

See then that you walk circumspectly, not as fools but as wise. **Ephesians 5:15 NKJV**

Give all your worries and cares to God, for He cares about you. **1 Peter 5:7 NLT**

He will feed His flock like a shepherd. He will carry the lambs in His arms, holding them close to His heart.
**Isaiah 40:11 NLT**

Therefore if there is any consolation in Christ, if any comfort of love, if any fellowship of the Spirit, if any affection and mercy, fulfill my joy by being like-minded, having the same love, being of one accord, of one mind. **Philippians 2:1-2 NKJV**

"If God cares so wonderfully for wildflowers that are here today and thrown into the fire tomorrow, He will certainly care for you.
**Matthew 6:30 NLT**

Let us think of ways to motivate one another to acts of love and good works.
**Hebrews 10:24 NLT**

The Lord cares about us. He cares about His people all the time and everywhere. He is never far removed from His children. Never is He deaf to our prayers. Never is God busy with more important things when we call out to Him. He cares for us so much that we can give our burdens completely over to Jesus. He is strong enough to carry every load, even that of the whole world.

# A God Who Provides

Then the LORD God took the man and put him in the garden of Eden to tend and keep it.
**Genesis 2:15 NKJV**

For God is the one who provides seed for the farmer and then bread to eat. In the same way, He will provide and increase your resources and then produce a great harvest of generosity in you.
**2 Corinthians 9:10 NLT**

The LORD is my shepherd, I lack nothing.
**Psalm 23:1 NIV**

For if a man cannot manage his own household, how can he take care of God's church? **1 Timothy 3:5 NLT**

"I am the good shepherd; I know My own sheep, and they know Me." **John 10:14 NLT**

Let us consider how to stir up one another to love and good works. **Hebrews 10:24 ESV**

It is the LORD who provides the sun to light the day and the moon and stars to light the night, and who stirs the sea into roaring waves. His name is the LORD of Heaven's Armies. **Jeremiah 31:35 NLT**

For no one ever hated his own flesh, but nourishes and cherishes it, just as the Lord does the church. For we are members of His body, of His flesh and of His bones.
**Ephesians 5:29-30 NKJV**

Care is the Father's heart in action. He looks after us as a Shepherd cares for His sheep. He knows you by name. He leads you to quiet waters. He carries us through the valley of the shadow of death. He is our Father. In His name we have to accept responsibility for our own homes. We have to cherish them. We must lead our loved ones in our dedication to God and service in His Kingdom.

# God Will Carry You

I can't carry all these people by myself! The load is far too heavy!
**Numbers 11:14 NLT**

"After He has suffered, He will see the light of life and be satisfied; by His knowledge My righteous servant will justify many, and He will bear their iniquities."
**Isaiah 53:11 NIV**

Christ was offered once to bear the sins of many. To those who eagerly wait for Him He will appear a second time, apart from sin, for salvation.
**Hebrews 9:28 NKJV**

Share with the Lord's people who are in need. Practice hospitality.
**Romans 12:13 NIV**

Then Jesus said, "Come to Me, all of you who are weary and carry heavy burdens, and I will give you rest. Take My yoke upon you. Let Me teach you, because I am humble and gentle at heart, and you will find rest for your souls."
**Matthew 11:28-29 NLT**

Bear one another's burdens, and so fulfill the law of Christ.
**Galatians 6:2 ESV**

When you carry someone, you feel his or her weight. The Bible tells us that Christ carried the heaviest burden in the universe – all our sins. He carried it by Himself on the cross. It weighed so heavily on Him that He eventually died. Our sins caused His death. As the Resurrected Lord He asks of us to also carry each other's burdens. No, not each other's hang-ups or sinful practices, but each other's pain and distress.

# A Sure Certainty

And Jesus said to them, "I am the bread of life. He who comes to Me shall never hunger, and he who believes in Me shall never thirst."
John 6:35 NKJV

"This is the will of God, that I should not lose even one of all those He has given Me, but that I should raise them up at the last day. For it is My Father's will that all who see His Son and believe in Him should have eternal life. I will raise them up at the last day." John 6:39-40 NLT

This hope we have as an anchor of the soul, both sure and steadfast.
Hebrews 6:19 NKJV

I am sure of this, that He who began a good work in you will bring it to completion at the day of Jesus Christ.
Philippians 1:6 ESV

"Very truly I tell you, the one who believes has eternal life."
John 6:47 NIV

For I am sure that neither death nor life, nor angels nor rulers, nor things present nor things to come, nor powers, nor height nor depth, nor anything else in all creation, will be able to separate us from the love of God in Christ Jesus our Lord.
Romans 8:38-39 ESV

Nobody likes uncertainty. In fact, we know today that the adult brain especially manages three fears, namely fear of public speaking, fear of the unknown and fear of being rejected. We like familiar things and certainty. Life can never offer security and certainty all the time, only God can! Christ grants us the surety of eternal life for each one who believes in Him. He guarantees it personally. He is our only surety.

# Face Challenges Head On

"You have heard that it was said, 'Eye for eye, and tooth for tooth.' But I tell you, do not resist an evil person. If anyone slaps you on the right cheek, turn to them the other cheek also. And if anyone wants to sue you and take your shirt, hand over your coat as well. If anyone forces you to go one mile, go with them two miles. Give to the one who asks you, and do not turn away from the one who wants to borrow from you." **Matthew 5:38-42 NIV**

We know that God causes everything to work together for the good of those who love God and are called according to His purpose for them. **Romans 8:28 NLT**

Consider Him who endured such opposition from sinners, so that you will not grow weary and lose heart. **Hebrews 12:3 NIV**

"Because he has set his love upon Me, therefore I will deliver him; I will set him on high, because he has known My name. He shall call upon Me, and I will answer him; I will be with him in trouble; I will deliver him and honor him." **Psalm 91:14-15 NKJV**

Instead, be very glad – for these trials make you partners with Christ in His suffering, so that you will have the wonderful joy of seeing His glory when it is revealed to all the world. **1 Peter 4:13 NLT**

When someone challenges you to do something, it's usually a matter of honor. An insult or a raised finger in traffic hurt your feelings. Then you want to act out in anger to protect your own honor. Remember Jesus' words that walking the second mile is walking on the right route. Rather be the least, than losing your dignity in life. That's foolishness.

# Cultivating a Christian Character

As iron sharpens iron, so a friend sharpens a friend.
**Proverbs 27:17 NLT**

For we all stumble in many ways. And if anyone does not stumble in what he says, he is a perfect man, able also to bridle his whole body.
**James 3:2 ESV**

Show me Your ways, O LORD; teach me Your paths. Lead me in Your truth and teach me, for You are the God of my salvation; on You I wait all the day.
**Psalm 25:4-5 NKJV**

Honesty guides good people; dishonesty destroys treacherous people. **Proverbs 11:3 NLT**

May you always be filled with the fruit of your salvation – the righteous character produced in your life by Jesus Christ – for this will bring much glory and praise to God.
**Philippians 1:11 NLT**

Endurance develops strength of character, and character strengthens our confident hope of salvation.
**Romans 5:4 NLT**

Make every effort to respond to God's promises. Supplement your faith with a generous provision of moral excellence, and moral excellence with knowledge.
**2 Peter 1:5 NLT**

Character is the internal, moral characteristics that influence people's daily way of living on a continuous basis. Believers' characters are shaped by God. It becomes evident through the way we use our words; how we behave and how we live our lives. Our character is not a state secret; it always gets exposed – even a lack thereof. Character growth happens when we allow the Spirit to continuously shape and reshape us according to God's image and likeness.

# Choosing Not to Cheat

"If you sell anything to your neighbor or buy from your neighbor's hand, you shall not oppress one another. According to the number of years after the Jubilee you shall buy from your neighbor, and according to the number of years of crops he shall sell to you. According to the multitude of years you shall increase its price, and according to the fewer number of years you shall diminish its price; for he sells to you according to the number of the years of the crops. Therefore you shall not oppress one another, but you shall fear your God; for I am the LORD your God."
**Leviticus 25:14-17 NKJV**

A merchant, in whose hands are false balances, he loves to oppress.
**Hosea 12:7 ESV**

Don't cheat your neighbor by moving the ancient boundary markers; don't take the land of defenseless orphans. For their Redeemer is strong; He Himself will bring their charges against you.
**Proverbs 23:10-11 NLT**

The LORD detests dishonest scales, but accurate weights find favor with Him. When pride comes, then comes disgrace, but with humility comes wisdom.
**Proverbs 11:1-2 NIV**

To be cheated is to be treated unfairly. It's to lose your money, possessions, or investments. Be careful of cheaters and tricksters who want to sell great profit investments to you. Protect the rights of the poor and vulnerable who often fall victim to sly, hungry wolves. Warn people against profiteering … and against those who wants to steal the hard-earned money and possessions of others. Tricksters stand in God's way. They draw heavenly fire to themselves.

# Be Like a Child

Then He put a little child among them. Taking the child in His arms, He said to them, "Anyone who welcomes a little child like this on My behalf welcomes Me, and anyone who welcomes Me welcomes not only Me but also My Father who sent Me." Mark 9:36-37 NLT

Have you forgotten the exhortation that addresses you as sons? My son, do not regard lightly the discipline of the Lord, nor be weary when reproved by Him. For the Lord disciplines the one He loves, and chastises every son whom He receives.
Hebrews 12:5-6 ESV

When Jesus saw this, He was indignant. He said to them, "Let the little children come to Me, and do not hinder them, for the kingdom of God belongs to such as these. Truly I tell you, anyone who will not receive the kingdom of God like a little child will never enter it." And He took the children in His arms, placed His hands on them and blessed them.
Mark 10:14-16 NIV

For you did not receive the spirit of bondage again to fear, but you received the Spirit of adoption by whom we cry out, "Abba, Father." Romans 8:15 NKJV

To receive the kingdom of God like a child is to have faith like you should. Jesus doesn't only call us to believe like children, but to really change and become like a child. It supposes a backward growth process where all the certainties of adulthood, successes and routes are sacrificed for the sake of this one certainty – Jesus Christ. Being a child equals being small before Christ. It is to live with amazement in His presence.

# Making Godly Choices

"Cry out again, thus says the Lord of hosts: 'My cities shall again overflow with prosperity, and the Lord will again comfort Zion and again choose Jerusalem.'"
**Zechariah 1:17 ESV**

After much discussion, Peter got up and addressed them: "Brothers, you know that some time ago God made a choice among you that the Gentiles might hear from my lips the message of the gospel and believe."
**Acts 15:7 NIV**

Who, then, are those who fear the Lord? He will instruct them in the ways they should choose.
**Psalm 25:12 NIV**

Don't you realize that you become the slave of whatever you choose to obey? You can be a slave to sin, which leads to death, or you can choose to obey God, which leads to righteous living.
**Romans 6:16 NLT**

All things are lawful for me, but not all things are helpful; all things are lawful for me, but not all things edify. Let no one seek his own, but each one the other's well-being. **1 Corinthians 10:23-24 NKJV**

Direct your children onto the right path, and when they are older, they will not leave it.
**Proverbs 22:6 NLT**

Choices suppose different options. The more options we have, the more difficult it is to make a decision. To be able to choose correctly, the Lord's Word should be our guiding principle and signpost. When we read the way we're supposed to, we will be better able to distinguish between right and wrong, and good and evil. As believers we should also ask ourselves continuously if our choices are to the benefit and enhancement of others. After all, we don't live only for ourselves.

# The Voice of an Angel

"You are worthy to take the scroll, and to open its seals; for You were slain, and have redeemed us to God by Your blood. Out of every tribe and tongue and people and nation and have made us kings and priests to our God; and we shall reign on the earth."
**Revelation 5:9-10 NKJV**

Shout joyfully to the LORD, all the earth; break forth in song, rejoice, and sing praises. Sing to the LORD with the harp, with the harp and the sound of a psalm, with trumpets and the sound of a horn; shout joyfully before the LORD, the King.
**Psalm 98:4-6 NKJV**

For long ago in the days of David and Asaph there were directors of the singers, and there were songs of praise and thanksgiving to God.
**Nehemiah 12:46 ESV**

Always be full of joy in the Lord. I say it again – rejoice.
**Philippians 4:4 NLT**

David was dressed in a robe of fine linen, as were all the Levites who carried the Ark, and also the singers, and Kenaniah the choir leader. David was also wearing a priestly garment.
**1 Chronicles 15:27 NLT**

I can't sing. My forte is false notes. That is one reason I'm looking forward to heaven – to have a new voice with which I'll be able to glorify God forever and in tune with the music. Still, despite the false sounds, I can do it here and now too. On earth I get time to practice every Sunday when I praise and worship God and glorify His name with a few chords. Sing to God with all you've got!

# The Pursuit of Christ

"But what about you?" He asked. "Who do you say I am?" Peter answered, "You are the Messiah."
**Mark 8:29 NIV**

For everyone has sinned; we all fall short of God's glorious standard. Yet God, in His grace, freely makes us right in His sight. He did this through Christ Jesus when He freed us from the penalty for our sins.
**Romans 3:23-24 NLT**

For while we were still weak, at the right time Christ died for the ungodly.
**Romans 5:6 ESV**

This is a faithful saying and worthy of all acceptance, that Christ Jesus came into the world to save sinners, of whom I am chief.
**1 Timothy 1:15 NKJV**

Now He has made all of this plain to us by the appearing of Christ Jesus, our Savior. He broke the power of death and illuminated the way to life and immortality through the Good News.
**2 Timothy 1:10 NLT**

We are made right with God by placing our faith in Jesus Christ. And this is true for everyone who believes, no matter who we are.
**Romans 3:22 NLT**

Christ means the Anointed One. Jesus is God's Messiah. Jesus came to fulfill God's will on earth through His death and resurrection. Through faith in Him we share in the new life that God gives. Jesus is God's answer to all the sin, death, violence and chaos in the world. He is God's One-Man Army. He turns heaven and earth upside-down. Believe in Him!

# You Are the Church of God

"I also say to you that you are Peter, and on this rock I will build My church, and the gates of Hades shall not prevail against it."
Matthew 16:18 NKJV

Simon Peter replied, "You are the Christ, the Son of the living God." And Jesus answered him, "Blessed are you, Simon Bar-Jonah! For flesh and blood has not revealed this to you, but My Father who is in heaven. And I tell you, you are Peter, and on this rock I will build My church, and the gates of hell shall not prevail against it." Matthew 16:16-18 ESV

Now I rejoice in what I am suffering for You, and I fill up in my flesh what is still lacking in regard to Christ's afflictions, for the sake of His body, which is the church. I have become its servant by the commission God gave me to present to you the word of God in its fullness. Colossians 1:24-25 NIV

I am writing to God's church in Corinth, to you who have been called by God to be His own holy people. He made you holy by means of Christ Jesus, just as He did for all people everywhere who call on the name of our Lord Jesus Christ, their Lord and ours. 1 Corinthians 1:2 NLT

Church is not synonyms with a building, as many think. The church, first of all, consists of people who share one confession, namely that of Christ the Lord. As people in Christ, we carry and care for each other. If someone stumbles, he or she is taken aside and encouraged. Churchgoers are always there for each other. They lift each other up, pray for each other, forgive each other, care for and allow a place in the sun for each individual on this earth.

# Close to God

"Seek the Lord while He may be found; call upon Him while He is near."
**Isaiah 55:6 ESV**

We wipe even the dust of your town from our feet to show that we have abandoned You to Your fate. And know this – the Kingdom of God is near!
**Luke 10:11 NLT**

But without faith it is impossible to please Him, for he who comes to God must believe that He is, and that He is a rewarder of those who diligently seek Him.
**Hebrews 11:6 NKJV**

Come near to God and He will come near to you. Wash your hands, you sinners, and purify your hearts, you double-minded.
**James 4:8 NIV**

The Lord is close to all who call on Him, yes, to all who call on Him in truth. He grants the desires of those who fear Him; He hears their cries for help and rescues them.
**Psalm 145:18-19 NLT**

"I am in My Father, and you in Me, and I in you."
**John 14:20 NKJV**

God is never far from us. He is really close. He is as close as your next prayer. He is one call far ... or near! Call out to Him, and you will begin to understand this. Draw near to Him, and experience His closeness. Distance is irrelevant when you draw near to Almighty God in the name of Jesus. There is no rift between you and Him anymore.

# God at Work

You gave me life and showed me Your unfailing love. My life was preserved by Your care. **Job 10:12 NLT**

Fear God and keep His commandments, for this is man's all. For God will bring every work into judgment, including every secret thing, whether good or evil. **Ecclesiastes 12:13-14 NKJV**

When I came to the city of Troas to preach the Good News of Christ, the Lord opened a door of opportunity for me. **2 Corinthians 2:12 NLT**

In their hearts humans plan their course, but the LORD establishes their steps. **Proverbs 16:9 NIV**

Every good and perfect gift is from above, coming down from the Father of the heavenly lights, who does not change like shifting shadows. **James 1:17 NIV**

In Him we were also chosen, having been predestined according to the plan of Him who works out everything in conformity with the purpose of His will. **Ephesians 1:11 NIV**

"For I know the plans I have for you," declares the LORD, "plans to prosper you and not to harm you, plans to give you hope and a future." **Jeremiah 29:11 NIV**

The ancient Greeks had goddesses associated with coincidence and fate. One of them was called Tuchē and the other one Moira. Everything that the people didn't understand, they plainly ascribed to the intervention as "coincidental". We as Christians don't believe in coincidence. God is in control of everything. That is why we will have to give account of our lives before His throne one day. Forget about fate. Let your life be an open book before Him.

# The God of All Comfort

Blessed be the God and Father of our Lord Jesus Christ, the Father of mercies and God of all comfort, who comforts us in all our affliction, so that we may be able to comfort those who are in any affliction. For as we share abundantly in Christ's sufferings, so through Christ we share abundantly in comfort too. If we are afflicted, it is for your comfort and salvation; and if we are comforted, it is for your comfort, which you experience when you patiently endure the same sufferings that we suffer. Our hope for you is unshaken, for we know that as you share in our sufferings, you will also share in our comfort.
2 Corinthians 1:3-7 ESV

If we are distressed, it is for your comfort and salvation; if we are comforted, it is for your comfort, which produces in you patient endurance of the same sufferings we suffer. And our hope for you is firm, because we know that just as you share in our sufferings, so also you share in our comfort.
2 Corinthians 1:6-7 NIV

In Him we were also chosen, having been predestined according to the plan of Him who works out everything in conformity with the purpose of His will.
Ephesians 1:11 NIV

The Lord is the God of comfort. When we suffer, He comforts us. That is why we can comfort others in the same way that He has comforted us. We can extend His goodness to others. We are never the end users of God's heavenly handkerchief. We need to share it with others in His name. We encourage others with the same encouragement we receive from God.

# Our Great Comforter

"But the Advocate, the Holy Spirit, whom the Father will send in My name, will teach you all things and will remind you of everything I have said to you."
**John 14:26 NIV**

"But when the Helper comes, whom I shall send to you from the Father, the Spirit of truth who proceeds from the Father, He will testify of Me."
**John 15:26 NKJV**

"Blessed are those who mourn, for they shall be comforted."
**Matthew 5:4 ESV**

"Nevertheless, I tell you the truth: it is to your advantage that I go away, for if I do not go away, the Helper will not come to you. But if I go, I will send Him to you."
**John 16:7 ESV**

"When He, the Spirit of truth, comes, He will guide you into all the truth. He will not speak on His own; He will speak only what He hears, and He will tell you what is yet to come."
**John 16:13 NIV**

"I will ask the Father, and He will give you another advocate to help you and be with you forever."
**John 14:16 NIV**

Jesus calls the Holy Spirit God's special Comforter. This term can also refer to an Advocate, Intercessor or Helper. That is exactly what He does. He glorifies God in our midst. He is with us to guide us in all truth and to keep us on the right track. What a privilege to have such a special Helper with us 24 hours of every day, and to be guided by Him on the way to eternity.

# Communion with God

As they were eating, Jesus took bread, blessed and broke it, and gave it to the disciples and said, "Take, eat; this is My body."
**Matthew 26:26 ESV**

"Whoever eats My flesh and drinks My blood has eternal life, and I will raise him up at the last day. For My flesh is food indeed, and My blood is drink indeed."
**John 6:54-55 NKJV**

May the grace of the Lord Jesus Christ, and the love of God, and the fellowship of the Holy Spirit be with you all. **2 Corinthians 13:14 NIV**

For as often as you eat this bread and drink this cup, you proclaim the Lord's death till He comes. Therefore whoever eats this bread or drinks this cup of the Lord in an unworthy manner will be guilty of the body and blood of the Lord.
**1 Corinthians 11:26-27 NKJV**

He took some bread and gave thanks to God for it. Then He broke it in pieces and gave it to the disciples, saying, "This is My body, which is given for you. Do this in remembrance of Me."
**Luke 22:19 NLT**

The New Testament begins the exact moment Jesus replaced Passover with Holy Communion. God's new covenant came into full swing. A new meal symbolized it from that moment on. This plain meal of bread and wine symbolizes Jesus body that was broken and His blood that flowed for us on Golgotha's cross. Eat this meal with great reverence, but also tremendous joy. It's the meal of all meals!

# Companions in Christ

The LORD God said, "It is not good for the man to be alone. I will make a helper suitable for him."
**Genesis 2:18 NIV**

He who walks with wise men will be wise, but the companion of fools will be destroyed.
**Proverbs 13:20 NKJV**

Many will say they are loyal friends, but who can find one who is truly reliable?
**Proverbs 20:6 NLT**

Two are better than one, because they have a good return for their labor.
**Ecclesiastes 4:9 NIV**

I ask you also, true companion, help these women, who have labored side by side with me in the gospel together with Clement and the rest of my fellow workers, whose names are in the book of life.
**Philippians 4:3 ESV**

A friend loves at all times, and a brother is born for adversity. **Proverbs 17:17 NKJV**

If anyone asks about Titus, say that he is my partner who works with me to help you. And the brothers with him have been sent by the churches, and they bring honor to Christ.
**2 Corinthians 8:23 NLT**

A companion is someone who is connected to you in a special way. For example, we refer to our marriage partner as a companion. It includes good friends whom we trust. These companions on our journey through life fill our lives with goodness and enrich us. They encourage us when we become despondent, and they pick us up when we fall down. Are you also a companion to others? Do you try to make life easier for them?

# Curbing Comparison

They are upright, like a palm tree, and they cannot speak; They must be carried, because they cannot go by themselves. Do not be afraid of them, for they cannot do evil, nor can they do any good."
**Jeremiah 10:5 NKJV**

We do not dare to classify or compare ourselves with some who commend themselves. When they measure themselves by themselves and compare themselves with themselves, they are not wise. **2 Corinthians 10:12 NIV**

No one is like You, LORD; You are great, and Your name is mighty in power.
**Jeremiah 10:6 NIV**

Pay careful attention to your own work, for then you will get the satisfaction of a job well done, and you won't need to compare yourself to anyone else.
**Galatians 6:4 NLT**

Consider Him who endured from sinners such hostility against Himself, so that you may not grow weary or faint-hearted.
**Hebrews 12:3 ESV**

For I say, through the grace given to me, to everyone who is among you, not to think of himself more highly than he ought to think, but to think soberly, as God has dealt to each one a measure of faith.
**Romans 12:3 ESV**

Comparisons are a normal part of life. People compare. Sometimes in a negative way, and other times positively. When someone recently said to his friend: "It could have been worse!" the friend immediately answered, "In comparison to what?" Maybe it's time we stop comparing and just be the best version of ourselves that we can be. Then we're maintaining the right standard. Then we're measuring ourselves correctly, as God does.

# Compassion without Compromise

The faithful love of the LORD never ends! His mercies never cease.
**Lamentations 3:22 NLT**

May you be blessed by the LORD, for you have had compassion on me.
**1 Samuel 23:21 ESV**

He has made His wonderful works to be remembered; The LORD is gracious and full of compassion.
**Psalm 111:4 NKJV**

Be kind and compassionate to one another, forgiving each other, just as in Christ God forgave you.
**Ephesians 4:32 NIV**

When He saw the crowds, He had compassion for them, because they were harassed and helpless, like sheep without a shepherd.
**Matthew 9:36 ESV**

But whoever has this world's goods, and sees his brother in need, and shuts up his heart from him, how does the love of God abide in him?
**1 John 3:17 NKJV**

The LORD your God will restore your fortunes and have compassion on you and gather you again from all the nations where He scattered you.
**Deuteronomy 30:3 NIV**

God has a heart for people. He has a gentle heart. He does more than that, He shows His caring heart. Jesus, too. His heart broke for people, so much so that He increased the bread for the hungry, and healed the sick while He was on earth. He also laid down His life for us. Because Jesus' heart is now beating in our chests, we should also care for others, to the extent that our lives are open to them.

# The Competitive Edge

Then I observed that most people are motivated to success because they envy their neighbors. But this, too, is meaningless – like chasing the wind.
**Ecclesiastes 4:4 NLT**

If you have raced with men on foot, and they have wearied you, how will you compete with horses? And if in a safe land you are so trusting, what will you do in the thicket of the Jordan?
**Jeremiah 12:5 ESV**

Do you not know that in a race all the runners run, but only one gets the prize? Run in such a way as to get the prize.
**1 Corinthians 9:24 NIV**

Fight the good fight of faith, lay hold on eternal life, to which you were also called and have confessed the good confession in the presence of many witnesses.
**1 Timothy 6:12 NKJV**

An athlete is not crowned unless he competes according to the rules.
**2 Timothy 2:5 ESV**

If you think you are too important to help someone, you are only fooling yourself. You are not that important. Pay careful attention to your own work, for then you will get the satisfaction of a job well done, and you won't need to compare yourself to anyone else. **Galatians 6:3-4 NLT**

Competition is part of life. Almost every program on TV is about some or other competition. Who is the best chef? Who is the most talented? Who is the cleverest? Competition becomes unpleasant when it categorizes people as good or bad all the time. Don't get sucked into this way of doing things. Allow God to call you to higher grounds. Compete as a team. Run the race without getting weary. Then you'll outwit the big guns!

# Refuse to be a Moaner

In the desert the whole community grumbled against Moses and Aaron.
**Exodus 16:2 NIV**

Jesus was aware that His disciples were complaining, so He said to them, "Does this offend you?"
**John 6:61 NLT**

Be hospitable to one another without grumbling.
**1 Peter 4:9 NKJV**

Therefore it is against the LORD that you and all your company have gathered together. What is Aaron that you grumble against him?
**Numbers 16:11 ESV**

Do all things without complaining and disputing.
**Philippians 2:14 NKJV**

A cheerful heart is good medicine, but a broken spirit saps a person's strength.
**Proverbs 17:22 NLT**

Nor complain, as some of them also complained, and were destroyed by the destroyer.
**1 Corinthians 10:10 NKJV**

If I say, "'I will forget my complaint', I will change my expression, and smile."
**Job 9:27 NIV**

Complaining is a universal occurrence. Even religious people moan. When moaning and groaning become the norm of society, it's time to hit the road. Somewhere at some point, you have to get past the moaning. Refuse to be part of the department of complaints. Refuse to see others in a bad light. To constantly complain is a sin. It brings no glory to His name, because complaining people are discontented people. They are never satisfied with anything. Find contentment in the Lord.

# Compromises and Consequences

God stretches the northern sky over empty space and hangs the earth on nothing. **Job 27:6 NIV**

Do not be conformed to this world, but be transformed by the renewing of your mind, that you may prove what is that good and acceptable and perfect will of God. **Romans 12:2 NKJV**

"Whoever can be trusted with very little can also be trusted with much, and whoever is dishonest with very little will also be dishonest with much." **Luke 16:10 NIV**

You must show mercy to those whose faith is wavering. Rescue others by snatching them from the flames of judgment. Show mercy to still others, but do so with great caution, hating the sins that contaminate their lives. **Jude 22-23 NLT**

Therefore do not let sin reign in your mortal body so that you obey its evil desires. **Romans 6:12 NIV**

The servant girl at the door said to Peter, "You also are not one of this man's disciples, are you?" He said, "I am not." **John 18:17 ESV**

Compromising is a matter of conscience. To compromise is to violate your own principles. It is to sell out on yourself. It is to stop being who you are before God. Don't do this. Don't sell yourself out for the sake of popularity, money or temporary benefits. Be faithful until the end to Christ. Stay on His course. Hold on to His Word. Remember, He never compromises when it concerns you.

# Don't be Biased

He is the Rock; His deeds are perfect. Everything He does is just and fair. He is a faithful God who does no wrong; how just and upright He is! **Deuteronomy 32:4 NLT**

In the presence of God and of Christ Jesus and of the elect angels I charge you to keep these rules without prejudging, doing nothing from partiality.
**1 Timothy 5:21 ESV**

My brothers and sisters, believers in our glorious Lord Jesus Christ must not show favoritism.
**James 2:1 NIV**

If you show partiality, you commit sin, and are convicted by the law as transgressors.
**James 2:9 NKJV**

There is therefore now no condemnation for those who are in Christ Jesus.
**Romans 8:1 ESV**

For God did not send His Son into the world to condemn the world, but in order that the world might be saved through Him.
**John 3:17 ESV**

My dear brothers and sisters, stand firm. Let nothing move you.
**1 Corinthians 15:58 NIV**

God is not biased. He has no favorites. And He also doesn't discriminate. We have to learn this over and over from God. Otherwise we're quick to be prejudiced towards other people. Such a mindset is destructive. It causes us to be suspicious of the people against whom we foster prejudices. We owe people an open heart and mind, as God has done with us.

# Only God Can Judge

Therefore you have no excuse, O man, every one of you who judges. For in passing judgment on another you condemn yourself, because you, the judge, practice the very same things. **Romans 2:1 ESV**

He canceled the record of the charges against us and took it away by nailing it to the cross. **Colossians 2:14 NIV**

So why do you condemn another believer? Why do you look down on another believer? Remember, we will all stand before the judgment seat of God. **Romans 14:10 NLT**

For the word of God is living and powerful, and sharper than any two-edged sword, piercing even to the division of soul and spirit, and of joints and marrow, and is a discerner of the thoughts and intents of the heart. **Hebrews 4:12 NKJV**

"Judge not, and you shall not be judged. Condemn not, and you shall not be condemned. Forgive, and you will be forgiven." **Luke 6:37 NKJV**

"Do not judge others, and you will not be judged." **Matthew 7:1 NLT**

To condemn someone without having all the facts, and without talking with them personally about the things that worry you about their lives, is to pass false judgment. Don't do it. Take the plank out of your eye first, before speaking without thinking about your words. You're allowed to address people's wrong behavior, but you may not talk about them in a destructive way. Let the judgment over to God. Love others.

# Confessions of a Happy Christian

"But if they confess their iniquity and the iniquity of their fathers, with their unfaithfulness in which they were unfaithful to Me, and that they also have walked contrary to Me."
**Leviticus 26:40 NKJV**

"Whoever acknowledges Me before others, I will also acknowledge before My Father in heaven."
**Matthew 10:32 NIV**

If you confess with your mouth that Jesus is Lord and believe in your heart that God raised Him from the dead, you will be saved.
**Romans 10:9 ESV**

If we confess our sins to Him, He is faithful and just to forgive us our sins and to cleanse us from all wickedness. **1 John 1:9 NLT**

Acknowledge that the Lord is God! He made us, and we are His. We are His people, the sheep of His pasture.
**Psalm 100:3 NLT**

Finally, I confessed all my sins to You and stopped trying to hide my guilt. I said to myself, "I will confess my rebellion to the Lord." And You forgave me! All my guilt is gone.
**Psalm 32:5 NLT**

When we confess with our mouths that Christ is the Lord, and believe it in our hearts, it's the greatest confession we can ever make. We acknowledge Him as our Savior. But we also confess our trespasses before the Lord when we sin. To confess your sins is to repent and to turn away from them. We also confess our faith in Christ by never denying Him in public.

# A Confidence Boost

This is how we know that we belong to the truth and how we set our hearts at rest in His presence: If our hearts condemn us, we know that God is greater than our hearts, and He knows everything. Dear friends, if our hearts do not condemn us, we have confidence before God and receive from Him anything we ask, because we keep His commands and do what pleases Him. And this is His command: to believe in the name of His Son, Jesus Christ, and to love one another as He commanded us. **1 John 3:19-23 NIV**

For I fully expect and hope that I will never be ashamed, but that I will continue to be bold for Christ, as I have been in the past. And I trust that my life will bring honor to Christ, whether I live or die. **Philippians 1:20 NLT**

Let us therefore come boldly to the throne of grace that we may obtain mercy and find grace to help in time of need. **Hebrews 4:16 NKJV**

In Him and through faith in Him we may approach God with freedom and confidence.
**Ephesians 3:12 NIV**

To come to God confidently and boldly are to approach Him with a conscience that is at rest. When we live close to the Lord, our conscience is finely tuned-in to the Holy Spirit. Then we are sensitive for His guidance in our lives. Then we're directed and guided by the constant inner convictions of the Spirit. When our conscience is at peace, then we can approach God's throne with confidence. Then we can bow before Him with joy.

# Conflict Resolution

You have delivered me from the strivings of the people; You have made me the head of the nations; a people I have not known shall serve me. **Psalm 18:43 NKJV**

A hot-tempered man stirs up strife, but he who is slow to anger quiets contention. **Proverbs 15:18 ESV**

An employer who hires a fool or a bystander is like an archer who shoots at random. **Proverbs 26:20 NLT**

A gentle answer turns away wrath, but a harsh word stirs up anger. **Proverbs 15:1 NIV**

Alas, my mother, that you gave me birth, a man with whom the whole land strives and contends! I have neither lent nor borrowed, yet everyone curses me. **Jeremiah 15:10 NIV**

The beginning of strife is like letting out water, so quit before the quarrel breaks out. **Proverbs 17:14 ESV**

Hatred stirs up quarrels, but love makes up for all offenses. Wise words come from the lips of people with understanding, but those lacking sense will be beaten with a rod. **Proverbs 10:12-13 NLT**

Conflict happens. It happens all the time and everywhere. It happens all too often. You know what I'm talking about. Maybe you've experienced conflict today. Maybe you have to fight for your spot in the sun. Or for your rights. Don't let conflict get the better of you. It will make you callous and bitter. Learn to keep your mouth shut sometimes, and to put others before yourself. Endure suffering for the sake of Christ. It will save your soul.

# A Christian Conscience

Paul looked straight at the Sanhedrin and said, "My brothers, I have fulfilled my duty to God in all good conscience to this day."
**Acts 23:1 NIV**

To the pure, all things are pure, but to the defiled and unbelieving, nothing is pure; but both their minds and their consciences are defiled. **Titus 1:15 ESV**

The purpose of my instruction is that all believers would be filled with love that comes from a pure heart, a clear conscience, and genuine faith.
**1 Timothy 1:5 NLT**

By this we know that we are of the truth, and shall assure our hearts before Him. For if our heart condemns us, God is greater than our heart, and knows all things.
**1 John 3:19-20 NKJV**

With Christ as my witness, I speak with utter truthfulness. My conscience and the Holy Spirit confirm it.
**Romans 9:1 NLT**

Righteousness guards him whose way is blameless, but sin overthrows the wicked.
**Proverbs 13:6 ESV**

Your conscience is the inner conviction deep in your heart of right and wrong. As believers we should allow the Holy Spirit to shape and sharpen our conscience. It is our first warning system to indicate when things aren't running smoothly in our lives. We must listen to this inner voice, otherwise our conscience becomes numb. Then we tend to sin easily. We should never allow our conscience to become defiled.

MARCH

WHOEVER DWELLS IN THE SHELTER of the Most High will rest in the SHADOW OF THE Almighty.

Psalm 91:1

# More Stuff?

We are instructed to turn from godless living and sinful pleasures. We should live in this evil world with wisdom, righteousness, and devotion to God.
**Titus 2:12 NLT**

"For where your treasure is, there your heart will be also." **Luke 12:34 NIV**

Give thanks in all circumstances; for this is the will of God in Christ Jesus for you. **1 Thessalonians 5:18 ESV**

"Store up for yourselves treasures in heaven, where moths and vermin do not destroy, and where thieves do not break in and steal." **Matthew 6:20 NIV**

"Watch out! Be on your guard against all kinds of greed; life does not consist in an abundance of possessions." **Luke 12:15 NIV**

You are my God, and I will praise You; You are my God, and I will exalt You. Give thanks to the LORD, for He is good; His love endures forever. **Psalm 118:28-29 NIV**

There is one who makes himself rich, yet has nothing; and one who makes himself poor, yet has great riches. The ransom of a man's life is his riches, but the poor does not hear rebuke. The light of the righteous rejoices, but the lamp of the wicked will be put out. **Proverbs 13:7-9 NKJV**

Consumerism characterizes the Western world today. People use up everything that they have. They are addicted to have the latest of everything: phones, cars, clothes, tools, technology. People are unhappy until they have the latest gadgets. Be careful of such a mentality. Be thankful for what you have for a change. Count your blessings. Don't just want more stuff for the sake of wanting more. Test your heart before the Lord in this.

# The Unknown

They are like trees planted along the riverbank, bearing fruit each season. Their leaves never wither, and they prosper in all they do.
**Psalm 1:3 NLT**

I will consider all Your works and meditate on all Your mighty deeds.
**Psalm 77:12 NIV**

I remember the days of old; I meditate on all Your works; I muse on the work of Your hands. **Psalm 143:5 NKJV**

Remember, O LORD, what has befallen us; look, and see our disgrace!
**Lamentations 5:1 ESV**

And immediately the rooster crowed the second time. Suddenly, Jesus' words flashed through Peter's mind: "Before the rooster crows twice, you will deny three times that you even know Me." And he broke down and wept.
**Mark 14:72 NLT**

Keep this Book of the Law always on your lips; meditate on it day and night, so that you may be careful to do everything written in it. Then you will be prosperous and successful.
**Joshua 1:8 NIV**

Contemplation or reflection is vitally important. Psalm 1 teaches us not to only read the Bible, but to meditate on it day and night. We need to reflect in a focused way on the things God tells us in the Bible. We must move the other things to the background, and put His will in the foreground of our thoughts. To meditate on His Word, is to radically change the entire course of your life.

# The Secret of Contentment

Better is the sight of the eyes than the wandering of the appetite: this also is vanity and a striving after wind. **Ecclesiastes 6:9 ESV**

Then you will experience God's peace, which exceeds anything we can understand. His peace will guard your hearts and minds as you live in Christ Jesus. **Philippians 4:7 NLT**

I am not saying this because I am in need, for I have learned to be content whatever the circumstances. **Philippians 4:11 NIV**

Let your conduct be without covetousness; be content with such things as you have. For He Himself has said, "I will never leave you nor forsake you." **Hebrews 13:5 NKJV**

So if we have enough food and clothing, let us be content. **1 Timothy 6:8 NLT**

As for me, I shall behold Your face in righteousness; when I awake, I shall be satisfied with Your likeness. **Psalm 17:15 ESV**

To be content with who you are and what you have, is to master the art of life. Contentment is not only a virtue, God Himself expects us to be content. It means to make peace with our circumstances and to be grateful for every piece of bread, but also for food in abundance. Being content brings a deep stillness in our hearts before God.

# Constructive Conversations

Even in your thoughts, do not curse the king, nor in your bedroom curse the rich, for a bird of the air will carry your voice, or some winged creature tell the matter.
**Ecclesiastes 10:20 ESV**

So when I come, I will call attention to what he is doing, spreading malicious nonsense about us. Not satisfied with that, he even refuses to welcome other believers. He also stops those who want to do so and puts them out of the church.
**3 John 10 NIV**

Gracious words are a honeycomb, sweet to the soul and healing to the bones.
**Proverbs 16:24 NIV**

The mouths of the righteous utter wisdom, and their tongues speak what is just.
**Psalm 37:30 NIV**

Let all bitterness, wrath, anger, clamor, and evil speaking be put away from you, with all malice.
**Ephesians 4:31 NKJV**

So get rid of all evil behavior. Be done with all deceit, hypocrisy, jealousy, and all unkind speech.
**1 Peter 2:1 NLT**

But as He who called you is holy, you also be holy in all your conduct.
**1 Peter 1:15 ESV**

Words have great power. Therefore we need to think before we speak, sometimes even twice! We have to take our words captive before they escape our lips. When we talk to other people, we need to encourage and uplift them. Our conversations must always be filled with mercy and love. We should boast about God and have people's backs in their absence. Then our conversations are constructive and healthy.

# Complete Conviction

"When He comes, He will prove the world to be in the wrong about sin and righteousness and judgment."
**John 16:8 NIV**

He went into the synagogue and spoke boldly for three months, reasoning and persuading concerning the things of the kingdom of God. **Acts 19:8 NKJV**

Our actions will show that we belong to the truth, so we will be confident when we stand before God.
**1 John 3:19 NLT**

"This is the judgment: the light has come into the world, and people loved the darkness rather than the light because their works were evil. For everyone who does wicked things hates the light and does not come to the light, lest his works should be exposed. But whoever does what is true comes to the light, so that it may be clearly seen that his works have been carried out in God."
**John 3:19-21 ESV**

And some were convinced by what he said, but others disbelieved.
**Acts 28:24 ESV**

The Spirit is God's heavenly Advocate on earth. He convinces people of what is wrong and right, not us. We are mere witnesses for Christ. It doesn't mean that we don't participate in conversations with unbelievers. Take Paul for example. He was willing and open to reason with people, and tried to persuade them of the truth. Yet Paul knew that it was the Spirit alone who transformed hearts. While we are talking, He is persuading.

# Listen to Good Counsel

For instance, there was Joseph, the one the apostles nicknamed Barnabas (which means "Son of Encouragement"). He was from the tribe of Levi and came from the island of Cyprus. He sold a field he owned and brought the money to the apostles.

Acts 4:36-37 NLT

Better was a poor and wise youth than an old and foolish king who no longer knew how to take advice.

Ecclesiastes 4:13 ESV

Without counsel, plans go awry, but in the multitude of counselors they are established.

Proverbs 15:22 NKJV

To humans belong the plans of the heart, but from the LORD comes the proper answer of the tongue. All a person's ways seem pure to them, but motives are weighed by the LORD.

Proverbs 16:1-2 NIV

Here is my judgment about what is best for you in this matter. Last year you were the first not only to give but also to have the desire to do so. Now finish the work, so that your eager willingness to do it may be matched by your completion of it, according to your means.

2 Corinthians 8:10-11 NIV

We all need advice and wise counsel. We need good advisers. People do only put their hand on our shoulder like Barnabas, whose name means "son of consolation". Or we need a Paul in our lives to tell us which way to choose when we're not sure how to manage our money. Listen to good counsel. Take it to heart.

# A Man of Courage

But as for me, I am filled with power, with the Spirit of the LORD, and with justice and might, to declare to Jacob his transgression and to Israel his sin. **Micah 3:8 ESV**

"Now be strong, Zerubbabel," declares the LORD. "Be strong, Joshua son of Jozadak, the high priest. Be strong, all you people of the land," declares the LORD, "and work. For I am with you," declares the LORD Almighty. **Haggai 2:4 NIV**

After this prayer, the meeting place shook, and they were all filled with the Holy Spirit. Then they preached the word of God with boldness. **Acts 4:31 NLT**

"These things I have spoken to you, that in Me you may have peace. In the world you will have tribulation; but be of good cheer, I have overcome the world." **John 16:33 NKJV**

Now, Lord, look on their threats, and grant to Your servants that with all boldness they may speak Your word, by stretching out Your hand to heal, and that signs and wonders may be done through the name of Your holy Servant Jesus. **Acts 4:29-30 NKJV**

"Be strong and courageous! Do not be afraid or discouraged. For the LORD your God is with you wherever you go." **Joshua 1:9 NLT**

To take a stand against the popular opinion or majority, requires courage. Most people are not up for the task. They are scared. None of us likes rejection. Yet it is the group of courageous ones who manage to swim upstream, who change the universe for the good. When you risk something, make sure it happens in the name of the Lord. With Him, courageous people can accomplish much.

# Your Covenant with God

Rather, it was simply that the LORD loves you, and He was keeping the oath He had sworn to your ancestors. That is why the LORD rescued you with such a strong hand from your slavery and from the oppressive hand of Pharaoh, king of Egypt. **Deuteronomy 7:8 NLT**

The Israelites had moved about in the wilderness forty years until all the men who were of military age when they left Egypt had died, since they had not obeyed the LORD. For the LORD had sworn to them that they would not see the land He had solemnly promised their ancestors to give us, a land flowing with milk and honey. **Joshua 5:6 NIV**

But above all, my brothers, do not swear, either by heaven or by earth or by any other oath, but let your "yes" be yes and your "no" be no, so that you may not fall under condemnation. **James 5:12 ESV**

He remembers His covenant forever, the word that He commanded, for a thousand generations, the covenant that He made with Abraham, His sworn promise to Isaac, which He confirmed to Jacob as a statute, to Israel as an everlasting covenant, saying, "To you I will give the land of Canaan as your portion for an inheritance." **Psalm 105:8-11 ESV**

A covenant is an agreement between God and His people. The one who makes such a vow commits him or herself to the truth of their covenant directly to God, and not to people. Jesus and James were not overly excited about such agreements. Your yes should be yes, and your no, should be no. After all, we live in God's presence all the time and don't need a covenant to speak the truth.

# God's Precious Creation

In the beginning God created the heavens and the earth. **Genesis 1:1 NKJV**

I consider that our present sufferings are not worth comparing with the glory that will be revealed in us. For the creation waits in eager expectation for the children of God to be revealed. **Romans 8:19-20 NIV**

Let all creation rejoice before the LORD, for He comes, He comes to judge the earth. He will judge the world in righteousness and the peoples in His faithfulness. **Psalm 96:13 NIV**

You created north and south. Mount Tabor and Mount Hermon praise Your name. **Psalm 89:12 NLT**

God blessed them and said to them, "Be fruitful and increase in number; fill the earth and subdue it. Rule over the fish in the sea and the birds in the sky and over every living creature that moves on the ground." **Genesis 1:28 NIV**

Every creature which is in heaven and on the earth and under the earth and such as are in the sea, and all that are in them, I heard saying: "Blessing and honor and glory and power be to Him who sits on the throne, and to the Lamb, forever and ever!" **Revelation 5:13 NKJV**

God is the Creator of heaven and earth. He doesn't only save our souls, He also saves the entire universe. In fact, God's creation is so precious to Him that He created a new heaven and earth. In the meantime, we should look after the Creation. We shouldn't watch rivers being polluted or toxic gasses pumped into the atmosphere without protesting against it in God's name.

# Take God's Hand in Times of Crises

But now the LORD my God has given me peace on every side; I have no enemies, and all is well.
**1 Kings 5:4 NLT**

The LORD is my light and my salvation – whom shall I fear? The LORD is the stronghold of my life – of whom shall I be afraid?
**Psalm 27:1 NIV**

Do not be afraid of sudden terror, nor of trouble from the wicked when it comes.
**Proverbs 3:25 NKJV**

You are a hiding place for me; You preserve me from trouble; You surround me with shouts of deliverance.
**Psalm 32:7 ESV**

God has said, "Never will I leave you; never will I forsake you." **Hebrews 13:5 NIV**

No temptation has overtaken you except what is common to mankind. And God is faithful; He will not let you be tempted beyond what you can bear. But when you are tempted, He will also provide a way out so that you can endure it.
**1 Corinthians 10:13 NIV**

But immediately Jesus spoke to them, saying, "Take heart; it is I. Do not be afraid."
**Matthew 14:27 ESV**

One of my friends believes that if you can handle a crisis well, then you're in trouble. Because you're not supposed to be able to handle it well. It is, after all, known as a crisis. Crises happen outside of your comfort zone. You can't handle it with your normal human abilities, insight and strength. That's why you always need to take refuge in the Lord in crisis. He wants to help you. Surround yourself with good friends also in such times.

# Constructive Criticism

Better is open rebuke than hidden love. Faithful are the wounds of a friend; profuse are the kisses of an enemy.
**Proverbs 27:5-6 ESV**

The heartfelt counsel of a friend is as sweet as perfume and incense.
**Proverbs 27:9 NLT**

A fool vents all his feelings, but a wise man holds them back.
**Proverbs 29:11 NKJV**

Whoever heeds life-giving correction will be at home among the wise.
**Proverbs 15:31 NIV**

Accept other believers who are weak in faith, and don't argue with them about what they think is right or wrong.
**Romans 14:1 NLT**

Therefore let us stop passing judgment on one another. Instead, make up your mind not to put any stumbling block or obstacle in the way of a brother or sister. **Romans 14:13 NIV**

Let a righteous man strike me – it is a kindness; let him rebuke me – it is oil for my head; let my head not refuse it. Yet my prayer is continually against their evil deeds.
**Psalm 141:5 ESV**

Being easily offended is a characteristic of many people. They get hurt very easily and are sometimes overly sensitive. They bleed when others just look at them the wrong way. Make sure that you don't become so sensitive to criticism. Also, don't live a life motivated by criticism. Make sure that when you are the one to criticize, that it's always constructive. Let your correcting of others be to the glory of God, and the benefit of them. Then you're speaking the truth in love.

# A Place of Hope

So when we preach that Christ was crucified, the Jews are offended and the Gentiles say it's all nonsense. But to those called by God to salvation, both Jews and Gentiles, Christ is the power of God and the wisdom of God.
1 Corinthians 1:23-24 NLT

For I determined not to know anything among you except Jesus Christ and Him crucified.
1 Corinthians 2:2 NKJV

For the message of the cross is foolishness to those who are perishing, but to us who are being saved it is the power of God.
1 Corinthians 1:18 NIV

May the God of hope fill you with all joy and peace as you trust in Him, so that you may overflow with hope by the power of the Holy Spirit.
Romans 15:13 NIV

When you were dead in your sins and in the uncircumcision of your flesh, God made you alive with Christ. He forgave us all our sins, having canceled the charge of our legal indebtedness, which stood against us and condemned us; He has taken it away, nailing it to the cross. Colossians 2:13-14 NIV

The Lord has risen indeed, and has appeared to Simon!
Luke 24:34 ESV

The cross is not a romantic symbol. It is the place of death and disdain. It is the place where our Lord and Savior died on our behalf. The cross is where Jesus traded places with us, and took our sins on Him. He, who knew no sin, took the status of a sinner. That's why the cross with all its terrors is also the place of hope and life.

# A Crown of Victory

I have fought the good fight, I have finished the race, I have kept the faith. Finally, there is laid up for me the crown of righteousness, which the Lord, the righteous Judge, will give to me on that Day, and not to me only but also to all who have loved His appearing.

**2 Timothy 4:7-8 NKJV**

Fixing our eyes on Jesus, the pioneer and perfecter of faith. For the joy set before Him He endured the cross, scorning its shame, and sat down at the right hand of the throne of God.

**Hebrews 12:2 NIV**

The twenty-four elders fall down and worship the one sitting on the throne (the one who lives forever and ever). And they lay their crowns before the throne and say, "You are worthy, O Lord our God, to receive glory and honor and power. For You created all things, and they exist because You created what You pleased."

**Revelation 4:10 NLT**

For You have made him most blessed forever; You have made him exceedingly glad with Your presence. For the king trusts in the LORD, and through the mercy of the Most High he shall not be moved.

**Psalm 21:6-7 NKJV**

Crowns are signs of authority. Kings wear crowns. We are also going to receive a heavenly crown one day because God changed our status to kings and priests. We are going to reign the earth together with Christ. Therefore we live with our eyes fixed on Jesus, as the Author and Perfecter of our faith. He has a crown of victory ready for each of us. He lets us stand with Him in first place on the winning podium, forever!

# Jesus Wept

"Yet even now," declares the LORD, "return to Me with all your heart, with fasting, with weeping, and with mourning."
**Joel 2:12 ESV**

The second thing you do: You cover the altar of the LORD with tears, with weeping and crying; so He does not regard the offering anymore, nor receive it with goodwill from your hands.
**Malachi 2:13 NKJV**

Then she knelt behind Him at His feet, weeping. Her tears fell on His feet, and she wiped them off with her hair. Then she kept kissing His feet and putting perfume on them. **Luke 7:38 NLT**

"He will wipe every tear from their eyes. There will be no more death or mourning or crying or pain, for the old order of things has passed away."
**Revelation 21:4 NIV**

And he fixed his gaze and stared at him, until he was embarrassed. And the man of God wept.
**2 Kings 8:11 ESV**

Because of this I will weep and wail; I will go about barefoot and naked. I will howl like a jackal and moan like an owl.
**Micah 1:8 NIV**

To cry is to be deeply moved. Tears are the language of grief and intense joy. In God's presence, it is equal to great sorrow about what we've done wrong. Fortunately, God can dry every tear from our eyes. He also assures us that in His new heaven there will be no more mourning and tears. Then sorrow and suffering are forever a thing of the past.

# Safe in the Arms of God

The LORD is my light and my salvation; whom shall I fear? The LORD is the strength of my life; of whom shall I be afraid? **Psalm 27:1 NKJV**

A quick-tempered person does foolish things, and the one who devises evil schemes is hated. **Proverbs 14:17 NIV**

I long to dwell in Your tent forever and take refuge in the shelter of Your wings. For You, God, have heard my vows; You have given me the heritage of those who fear Your name. **Psalm 61:4-5 NIV**

Watch your tongue and keep your mouth shut, and you will stay out of trouble. **Proverbs 21:23 NLT**

In peace I will lie down and sleep, for You alone, LORD, make me dwell in safety. **Psalm 4:8 NIV**

Who shall separate us from the love of Christ? Shall tribulation, or distress, or persecution, or famine, or nakedness, or danger, or sword? **Romans 8:35 ESV**

LORD, You are my strength and fortress, my refuge in the day of trouble! **Jeremiah 16:19 NLT**

God is a shield to those who take refuge in Him. **Proverbs 30:5 NIV**

Danger is all around us. Wise people know how to avoid it. They think before they speak and avoid foolish conversations. But believers also know that no danger or fear can separate them from the Lord's presence. Nothing or no one can pull us from His hand. In times of great danger, the Lord is our Rock and Fortress. We can take refuge in Him. We are safe in His arms.

# Light in the Darkness

Even though I walk through the darkest valley, I will fear no evil, for You are with me; Your rod and Your staff, they comfort me. **Psalm 23:4 NIV**

The earth was formless and empty, and darkness covered the deep waters. And the Spirit of God was hovering over the surface of the waters.
**Genesis 1:2 NLT**

But their evil intentions will be exposed when the light shines on them, for the light makes everything visible. This is why it is said, "Awake, O sleeper, rise up from the dead, and Christ will give you light."
**Ephesians 5:13-14 NLT**

He has delivered us from the power of darkness and conveyed us into the kingdom of the Son of His love.
**Colossians 1:13 NKJV**

To open their eyes, in order to turn them from darkness to light, and from the power of Satan to God, that they may receive forgiveness of sins and an inheritance among those who are sanctified by faith in Me.
**Acts 26:18 NKJV**

But you are a chosen race, a royal priesthood, a holy nation, that you may proclaim the excellencies of Him who called you out of darkness into His marvelous light.
**1 Peter 2:9 ESV**

Darkness is a daily reality. Or should I rather say a nightly one! God expelled the darkness right at the beginning of Creation by making light. But the Bible also knows about the great darkness when people live far-removed from God. Not to believe in Him means to get lost in the darkness. Only God can drive out this darkness, because He is the true Light of Life. He pulls us from the kingdom of darkness to True Light.

# Every Day Is in God's Hand

God called the light Day, and the darkness He called Night. So the evening and the morning were the first day. **Genesis 1:5 NKJV**

This Book of the Law shall not depart from your mouth, but you shall meditate on it day and night, so that you may be careful to do according to all that is written in it. For then you will make your way prosperous, and then you will have good success. **Joshua 1:8 ESV**

Yours is the day, Yours also the night; You have established the heavenly lights and the sun. **Psalm 74:16 ESV**

"For no one can come to Me unless the Father who sent Me draws them to Me, and at the last day I will raise them up." **John 6:44 NLT**

He who began a good work in you will carry it on to completion until the day of Christ Jesus. **Philippians 1:6 NIV**

He made the Pleiades and Orion; He turns the shadow of death into morning and makes the day dark as night; He calls for the waters of the sea and pours them out on the face of the earth; the LORD is His name. **Amos 5:8 NKJV**

Every day counts. When God created time right at the beginning, He divided it into day and night rhythms. He also grants us life on the basis of these rhythms. Meaning we only have one day at a time to make a difference. We should live every day fully and completely for His glory. Then, one day, when the last day of the Lord dawns, we will receive a crown of victory from Jesus' hand.

# Your Death Unlocks Eternal Life

Therefore, just as through one man sin entered the world, and death through sin, and thus death spread to all men, because all sinned. Romans 5:12 NKJV

"Truly, truly, I say to you, whoever hears My word and believes Him who sent Me has eternal life. He does not come into judgment, but has passed from death to life." John 5:24 ESV

For the wages of sin is death, but the gift of God is eternal life in Christ Jesus our Lord. Romans 6:23 NIV

Whoever believes in the Son has eternal life. John 3:36 NIV

"I am the resurrection and the life. Anyone who believes in Me will live, even after dying." John 11:25 NLT

Just as it is appointed for man to die once, and after that comes judgment. Hebrews 9:27 ESV

Then death and the grave were thrown into the lake of fire. This lake of fire is the second death. Revelation 20:14 NLT

"For God so loved the world that He gave His one and only Son, that whoever believes in Him shall not perish but have eternal life." John 3:16 NIV

Death is a reality. We're going to live until we die. We are going to breathe our last breath someday. But death is not the last straw. Christ removed death's sting. He walked through the gates of death and came out alive on the other side. On the third day He was resurrected from the grave.

# Debt-Free Living

She came and told the man of God, and he said, "Go, sell the oil and pay your debts, and you and your sons can live on the rest."
**2 Kings 4:7 ESV**

"But neither of them could repay him, so he kindly forgave them both, canceling their debts. Who do you suppose loved him more after that?" Simon answered, "I suppose the one for whom he canceled the larger debt." "That's right," Jesus said.
**Luke 7:42-43 NLT**

"And forgive us our debts, as we also have forgiven our debtors."
**Mark 6:12 NIV**

Owe no one anything except to love one another, for he who loves another has fulfilled the law. For the commandments, "You shall not commit adultery," "You shall not murder," "You shall not steal," "You shall not bear false witness," "You shall not covet," and if there is any other commandment, are all summed up in this saying, namely, "You shall love your neighbor as yourself."
**Romans 13:8-9 NKJV**

I, Paul, am writing this with my own hand. I will pay it back – not to mention that you owe me your very self.
**Philemon 19 NIV**

Make sure you owe no one anything, except more love. It's timeless, but difficult words. Usually we owe others everything else besides this one. We don't love people enough to lift them up and to turn over a new leaf for them. Let's get our priorities straight. Let's pay our debt of love to each other. Only then will we be truly debt free! He lives. We who believe in Him are not afraid of death. Christ holds the keys of death and Hades in His hands. He unlocks eternal life for us.

# Letting Go of Lies

Youths oppress my people, women rule over them. My people, your guides lead you astray; they turn you from the path.
Isaiah 3:12 NIV

For false christs and false prophets will arise and perform signs and wonders, to lead astray, if possible, the elect. Mark 13:22 ESV

An honest witness tells the truth, but a false witness tells lies.
Proverbs 12:17 NIV

A lying tongue hates those it hurts, and a flattering mouth works ruin.
Proverbs 26:28 NIV

We should no longer be children, tossed to and fro and carried about with every wind of doctrine, by the trickery of men, in the cunning craftiness of deceitful plotting. Ephesians 4:14 NKJV

I am telling you this so no one will deceive you with well-crafted arguments.
Colossians 2:4 NLT

No one who practices deceit shall dwell in my house; no one who utters lies shall continue before my eyes.
Psalm 101:7 ESV

Deliver me, O LORD, from lying lips, from a deceitful tongue. Psalm 120:2 ESV

You mislead and deceive people when you exchange the truth for lies, and believe them. The truth gets twisted. Half-truths are all that are left. But it is far from the truth. The Lord's spirit only guides us in the full truth. He unlocks the Bible for us. Therefore, we trust Him and surround ourselves with faithful followers of the Lord. We also test our own opinions constantly against Scripture.

# Dedicated to God

She made a vow, saying, "Lord Almighty, if You will only look on Your servant's misery and remember me, and not forget Your servant but give her a son, then I will give him to the Lord for all the days of his life, and no razor will ever be used."
1 Samuel 1:11 NIV

God has called us to live holy lives, not impure lives.
1 Thessalonians 4:7 NLT

Some of the spoils won in battles they dedicated to maintain the house of the Lord.
1 Chronicles 26:27 NKJV

Therefore, I urge you, brothers and sisters, in view of God's mercy, to offer your bodies as a living sacrifice, holy and pleasing to God – this is your true and proper worship. Romans 12:1 NIV

May He work in us what is pleasing to Him, through Jesus Christ, to whom be glory for ever and ever. Amen.
Hebrews 13:21 NIV

Therefore I have lent him to the Lord. As long as he lives, he is lent to the Lord. And he worshiped the Lord there.
1 Samuel 1:28 ESV

To dedicate something or someone to the Lord, is to separate them exclusively for His service. In the Old Testament, certain prophets, judges and kings were separated for His work. Today each of us is dedicated to the Lord. All of us belong to Him exclusively. Our whole lives are dedicated to His service. We are living offerings to the Lord, glorifying Him in everything.

# Obstacles to Deliverance

The righteousness of God has been manifested apart from the law, although the Law and the Prophets bear witness to it – the righteousness of God through faith in Jesus Christ for all who believe. For there is no distinction: for all have sinned and fall short of the glory of God, and are justified by His grace as a gift, through the redemption that is in Christ Jesus. **Romans 3:21-24 ESV**

I know that through your prayers and God's provision of the Spirit of Jesus Christ what has happened to me will turn out for my deliverance. **Philippians 1:19 NIV**

For the Kingdom of God is not a matter of what we eat or drink, but of living a life of goodness and peace and joy in the Holy Spirit. **Romans 14:17 NLT**

The righteous cry out, and the LORD hears them; He delivers them from all their troubles. **Psalm 34:17 NIV**

Then they cried out to the LORD in their trouble, and He delivered them out of their distresses. **Psalm 107:6 NKJV**

To stand in front of God's throne is the most revealing moment of your life. It is to appear in the fullness of the glory of the Almighty God without being able to hide a single thing. The good news is Jesus takes His place next to you. He covers you with righteousness. And He covers you with His blessings. That is what deliverance is about. For this reason you can look God in the eye, and live your life dedicated to Him.

# Into the Depths of God

I am convinced that neither death nor life, neither angels nor demons, neither the present nor the future, nor any powers, neither height nor depth, nor anything else in all creation, will be able to separate us from the love of God that is in Christ Jesus our Lord. Romans 8:38-39 NIV

Who says to the deep, "Be dry; I will dry up your rivers." Isaiah 44:27 ESV

The Lord says, "I will bring them from Bashan; I will bring them from the depths of the sea."
Psalm 68:22 NIV

Oh, the depth of the riches both of the wisdom and knowledge of God! How unsearchable are His judgments and His ways past finding out!
Romans 11:33 NKJV

For the LORD is a great God, a great King above all gods. He holds in His hands the depths of the earth and the mightiest mountains. The sea belongs to Him, for He made it. His hands formed the dry land, too.
Psalm 95:3-5 NLT

Parents teach their children that the shallow end of a swimming pool is the safe end. Deep water is dangerous. You can drown. Yet there is one safe depth. It's on God's end. He is the deepest depth there is. God is unsearchable. He is the Almighty God who is greater, more holy and endlessly stronger than we can ever imagine. Therefore our earthly depths are not a problem for Him. Nothing can ever separate us from His love.

# Yearning after God

You shall not covet your neighbor's house; you shall not covet your neighbor's wife, or his male servant, or his female servant, or his ox, or his donkey, or anything that is your neighbor's.
**Exodus 20:17 ESV**

O God, You are my God; early will I seek You; my soul thirsts for You; my flesh longs for You. In a dry and thirsty land where there is no water.
**Psalm 63:1 NKJV**

My soul yearns, even faints, for the courts of the LORD; my heart and my flesh cry out for the living God.
**Psalm 84:2 NIV**

You want what you don't have, so you scheme and kill to get it. You are jealous of what others have, but you can't get it, so you fight and wage war to take it away from them. Yet you don't have what you want because you don't ask God for it. **James 4:2 NLT**

May He grant you your heart's desire and fulfill all your plans! **Psalm 20:4 ESV**

And let the one who hears say, "Come." And let the one who is thirsty come; let the one who desires take the water of life without price.
**Revelation 22:17 ESV**

Desires are seen in a positive and negative way in the Bible. Sinful desires are born from and urge to always want what others have. God hates such envious desires after other people's possessions, bodies and lifestyles. But the Bible also tells of healthy and good desires of yearning after God. It is a deeper hunger and thirst after God's presence that is established in us through the Spirit. This deep longing is always accompanied by greater commitment to Him.

# Tolerate All People

For He has not despised nor abhorred the affliction of the afflicted; nor has He hidden His face from Him; but when He cried to Him, He heard. **Psalm 22:24 NKJV**

"No one can serve two masters; for either he will hate the one and love the other, or else he will be loyal to the one and despise the other. You cannot serve God and mammon."
**Matthew 6:24 NKJV**

Let no one despise you for your youth, but set the believers an example in speech, in conduct, in love, in faith, in purity. **1 Timothy 4:12 ESV**

"'Love the Lord your God with all your heart and with all your soul and with all your mind.' This is the first and greatest commandment. And the second is like it: 'Love your neighbor as yourself.'"
**Matthew 22:37-39 NIV**

What do You gain by oppressing me? Why do You reject me, the work of Your own hands, while smiling on the schemes of the wicked? **Job 10:3 NLT**

I hate, I despise your religious festivals; your assemblies are a stench to me. **Amos 5:21 NIV**

The word *despise* is a strong emotional term. It says so much more than merely "I don't like someone or something". To despise someone is literally to think nothing of them, and even to hate them. The Bible says we must feel that way about sin, not people. We must detest sin to such an extent that it disgusts and nauseates us. Avoid it at all cost. Then you're living for God's glory.

# Serving God in a Messy World

And the Pharisees and the scribes asked Him, "Why do Your disciples not walk according to the tradition of the elders, but eat with defiled hands?" And He said to them, "Well did Isaiah prophesy of you hypocrites, as it is written, This people honors Me with their lips, but their heart is far from Me; in vain do they worship Me, teaching as doctrines the commandments of men."
**Mark 7:5-7 ESV**

Jesus answered, "It is written: 'Worship the Lord your God and serve Him only.'"
**Luke 4:8 NIV**

If anyone serves, they should do so with the strength God provides, so that in all things God may be praised through Jesus Christ.
**1 Peter 4:11 NIV**

"But the words you speak come from the heart – that's what defiles you. For from the heart come evil thoughts, murder, adultery, all sexual immorality, theft, lying, and slander. These are what defile you. Eating with unwashed hands will never defile you."
**Matthew 15:18-20 NLT**

And He said, "What comes out of a man, that defiles a man." **Mark 7:20 NKJV**

Uncleanliness was a Jewish tradition. When people didn't comply with the purity laws, for example to wash their hands correctly before a meal, they were regarded as dirty and impure. Jesus differed from this. Uncleanliness is something that lies in the heart, not the body. That is why we must allow Him to cleanse our soul. He can wash away the right kind of dirt. He cleanses us and makes us pure in the right ways.

# When You Suffer

The Lord God arranged for a leafy plant to grow there, and soon it spread its broad leaves over Jonah's head, shading him from the sun. This eased his discomfort, and Jonah was very grate. **Jonah 4:6 NLT**

Is anyone among you suffering? Let him pray. Is anyone cheerful? Let him sing praise.
**James 5:13 ESV**

For just as we share abundantly in the sufferings of Christ, so also our comfort abounds through Christ.
**2 Corinthians 1:5 NIV**

We also glory in our sufferings, because we know that suffering produces perseverance. **Romans 5:3 NIV**

My comfort in my suffering is this: Your promise preserves my life.
**Psalm 119:50 NIV**

I have labored and toiled and have often gone without sleep; I have known hunger and thirst and have often gone without food; I have been cold and naked. Besides everything else, I face daily the pressure of my concern for all the churches.
**2 Corinthians 11:27-28 NIV**

Discomfort is not enjoyable. Yet sometimes it goes hand in hand with the gospel. Ask Paul. The mission field was never just moonshine and roses. In fact, he endured many days and nights of suffering and lack of bread. But this is how God's Kingdom takes shape. When men of God are willing to put others before themselves and endure discomfort, then God's light shines through them brighter than ever before.

# Resign from the Complaints Commission

Moses said, "When the LORD gives you in the evening meat to eat and in the morning bread to the full, because the LORD has heard your grumbling that you grumble against Him – what are we? Your grumbling is not against us but against the LORD."
Exodus 16:8 ESV

How long must I put up with this wicked community and its complaints about me? Yes, I have heard the complaints the Israelites are making against me.
Numbers 14:27 NLT

Evening, morning and noon I cry out in distress, and He hears my voice. Psalm 55:17 NIV

When Jesus knew in Himself that His disciples complained about this, He said to them, "Does this offend you?" John 6:61 NKJV

"I will feast the soul of the priests with abundance, and My people shall be satisfied with My goodness," declares the LORD."
Jeremiah 31:14 ESV

Because I am righteous, I will see you. When I awake, I will see you face to face and be satisfied. Psalm 17:15 NLT

Do everything without complaining and arguing.
Philippians 2:14 NLT

It seems like some religious people like to complain. They know exactly of all the things that are wrong in the church. They are "deeply" troubled by it. The pastor is never good enough. Everybody suffers under their discontented eye. Don't be like that. Resign from the complaints commission. Choose to see the good that God has placed in each one of us. Be an expert in noticing God's handiwork, big and small. Then you won't have time to be discontented or unhappy.

# Spiritual Discernment

Do not pervert justice or show partiality. Do not accept a bribe, for a bribe blinds the eyes of the wise and twists the words of the innocent. **Deuteronomy 16:19 NIV**

Therefore give to Your servant an understanding heart to judge Your people, that I may discern between good and evil. For who is able to judge this great people of Yours. **1 Kings 3:9 NKJV**

Then she fell on her face, bowing to the ground, and said to him, "Why have I found favor in your eyes, that you should take notice of me, since I am a foreigner?" **Ruth 2:10 ESV**

So I set out to learn everything from wisdom to madness and folly. But I learned firsthand that pursuing all this is like chasing the wind. **Ecclesiastes 1:17 NLT**

Do not conform to the pattern of this world, but be transformed by the renewing of your mind. Then you will be able to test and approve what God's will is – His good, pleasing and perfect will. **Romans 12:2 NIV**

But solid food is for the mature, for those who have their powers of discernment trained by constant practice to distinguish good from evil. **Hebrews 5:14 ESV**

To distinguish between right and wrong is not always that easy. As is choosing to go left or right. To be able to distinguish correctly requires a lifetime of practice in the Lord's ways of wisdom. Pray to Him every day, and plead for the special gift of wisdom in your life, so that you can distinguish clearly which road to take at the T-junctions of life. Let His Spirit guide your thoughts and your whole life.

# Written in Your Heart

Tie them to your hands and wear them on your forehead as reminders. Write them on the doorposts of your house and on your gates.
**Deuteronomy 6:8-9 NLT**

"Enter by the narrow gate; for wide is the gate and broad is the way that leads to destruction, and there are many who go in by it."
**Matthew 7:13 NKJV**

"I am the door. If anyone enters by Me, he will be saved and will go in and out and find pasture."
**John 10:9 ESV**

"I will put My law in their minds, and write it on their hearts." **Jeremiah 31:33 NIV**

To the angel of the church in Laodicea write: These are the words of the Amen, the faithful and true witness, the ruler of God's creation.
**Revelation 3:14 NIV**

"Follow Me now. Let the spiritually dead bury their own dead."
**Matthew 8:22 NLT**

So Jesus again said to them, "Truly, truly, I say to you, I am the door of the sheep."
**John 10:7 ESV**

Fix these words of mine in your hearts and minds; tie them as symbols on your hands and bind them on your foreheads.
**Deuteronomy 11:18 NIV**

God's Word belongs in real life. Therefore the biblical instruction to us is to write the commandments on the doorposts of our hearts. Meaning, it should become part of our daily household and normal life. But we must also walk through the door of life if we want to live forever. Christ is the only door giving us entry into eternal life. He is the way, and the life. When we walk through Him to God, then He walks with us on the narrow path leading to life.

# Dealing with Doubt

"Are You the Messiah we've been expecting, or should we keep looking for someone else?" Jesus told them, "Go back to John and tell him what you have heard and seen – the blind see, the lame walk, those with leprosy are cured, the deaf hear, the dead are raised to life, and the Good News is being preached to the poor." And He added, "God blesses those who do not fall away because of Me."
**Matthew 11:2-6 NLT**

Jesus immediately reached out His hand and took hold of him, saying to him, "O you of little faith, why did you doubt?"
**Matthew 14:31 ESV**

Now faith is confidence in what we hope for and assurance about what we do not see. **Hebrews 11:1 NIV**

"For assuredly, I say to you, whoever says to this mountain, 'Be removed and be cast into the sea,' and does not doubt in his heart, but believes that those things he says will be done, he will have whatever he says."
**Mark 11:23 NKJV**

But let him ask in faith, with no doubting, for the one who doubts is like a wave of the sea that is driven and tossed by the wind.
**James 1:6 ESV**

Doubt is often hostile towards faith, but sometimes it is also a normal part of faith. The greatest figures in the Bible had moments of doubt. I remember how Abraham laughed at God when he heard that his wife was going to have a child. Or how John the Baptist asked Jesus if He was really the Messiah. Remember the golden rule: take your doubts to Jesus. Talk to Him about the questions that bother you. He can handle it.

APRIL

FOR TO ME
**TO LIVE IS**
*Christ,*
AND TO DIE
**IS GAIN.**
Philippians 1:21

# Understanding Your Dreams

"I have heard what the prophets say who prophesy lies in My name. They say, 'I had a dream! I had a dream!'"
**Jeremiah 23:25 NIV**

"And it shall come to pass in the last days," says God, "that I will pour out of My Spirit on all flesh; your sons and your daughters shall prophesy, your young men shall see visions, your old men shall dream dreams."
**Acts 2:17 NKJV**

Joseph said to them, "Do not interpretations belong to God? Please tell them to me." **Genesis 40:8 ESV**

"Let the prophet who has a dream tell the dream, but let him who has My word speak My word faithfully. What has straw in common with wheat?" declares the LORD. **Jeremiah 23:28 ESV**

Much dreaming and many words are meaningless. Therefore fear God.
**Ecclesiastes 5:7 NIV**

As he considered this, an angel of the Lord appeared to him in a dream. "Joseph, son of David," the angel said, "do not be afraid to take Mary as your wife. For the child within her was conceived by the Holy Spirit."
**Matthew 1:20 NLT**

Yes, God speaks to us through our dreams, but not everyone who lays claim to it, speaks the truth. Jeremiah warned against those people who confuse their dreams with God's voice. Even worse, such false dreamers mislead others. Godly dreams will always glorify Him. It will confirm the presence of His Spirit, and build people up in their faith. Dreams always bow before the authority of Scripture. Otherwise these dreams are just nightmares!

# Get Rid of Negativity

Repay no one evil for evil. Have regard for good things in the sight of all men. If it is possible, as much as depends on you, live peaceably with all men. Beloved, do not avenge yourselves, but rather give place to wrath; for it is written, "Vengeance is Mine, I will repay," says the Lord. Therefore "If your enemy is hungry, feed him; if he is thirsty, give him a drink; for in so doing you will heap coals of fire on his head." Romans 12:17-20 NKJV

Do not let any unwholesome talk come out of your mouths, but only what is helpful for building others up. Ephesians 4:29 NIV

Since we live by the Spirit, let us keep in step with the Spirit. Galatians 5:25 NIV

That evening many demon-possessed people were brought to Jesus. He cast out the evil spirits with a simple command, and He healed all the sick. Matthew 8:16 NLT

Finally, brothers, whatever is true, whatever is honorable, whatever is just, whatever is pure, whatever is lovely, whatever is commendable, if there is any excellence, if there is anything worthy of praise, think about these things. Philippians 4:8 ESV

To banish someone or something is to chase it away. When it is about other people, driving them out is the last option on the list. We are called by the Lord to build bridges, not to burn them. We don't turn our back on others, but we live in peace with each other, as far as it depends on us. We live over hatred and anger. Then we can banish negative emotions.

# Your Christian Duty

Then the whole assembly raised their voices and answered, "Yes, you are right; we must do as you say!"
**Ezra 10:12 NLT**

"If I then, your Lord and Teacher, have washed your feet, you also ought to wash one another's feet."
**John 13:14 NKJV**

Be shepherds of God's flock that is under your care, watching over them – not because you must, but because you are willing, as God wants you to be; not pursuing dishonest gain, but eager to serve.
**1 Peter 5:2 NIV**

Therefore we ought to support people like these, that we may be fellow workers for the truth. **3 John 8 ESV**

"Who then is the faithful and wise servant, whom the master has put in charge of the servants in his household to give them their food at the proper time? It will be good for that servant whose master finds him doing so when he returns."
**Matthew 24:45-46 NIV**

And we know that for those who love God all things work together for good, for those who are called according to His purpose.
**Romans 8:28 ESV**

We all have certain duties and responsibilities in life. There are certain things we must do and tasks to carry out without even giving them a second thought. Still our hearts should be in things we do for others and for the Lord. Otherwise it turns into monotonous routines very quickly. We also need to perform our duties faithfully and loyally for the Lord. We must fulfill our responsibilities so that His name can be glorified through our dedication and faithfulness.

# Be Eager to Learn

Instruct the wise, and they will be even wiser. Teach the righteous, and they will learn even more.
**Proverbs 9:9 NLT**

Find out what pleases the Lord. **Ephesians 5:10 NIV**

My son, do not forget my teaching, but let your heart keep my commandments, for length of days and years of life and peace they will add to you.
**Proverbs 3:1-2 ESV**

God's holy people must endure persecution patiently, obeying His commands and maintaining their faith in Jesus. **Revelation 14:12 NLT**

I applied my heart to know wisdom and to know madness and folly. I perceived that this also is but a striving after wind.
**Ecclesiastes 1:17 ESV**

Then He said to them, "Therefore every scribe instructed concerning the kingdom of heaven is like a householder who brings out of his treasure things new and old."
**Matthew 13:52 NKJV**

So teach us to number our days that we may get a heart of wisdom.
**Psalm 90:12 ESV**

To learn is to grow spiritually. Being eager to learn is to constantly yearn for more knowledge and insight into God and His Word. Without such curiosity, your head and your heart stagnate. That's when you keep walking on the same boring old route over again. Then you don't discover new and old treasures from the Word anymore. But when you're eager to learn and examine the things of God, you live in His gold mines.

# Tune Your Ears to God

Lord, let Your ear be attentive to the prayer of this Your servant and to the prayer of Your servants who delight in revering Your name. Give Your servant success today by granting him favor in the presence of this man.
**Nehemiah 1:11 NIV**

"Listen to Me, you who pursue righteousness, you who seek the LORD: look to the rock from which you were hewn, and to the quarry from which you were dug."
**Isaiah 51:1 ESV**

Incline your ear, and hear the words of the wise, and apply your heart to my knowledge. **Proverbs 22:17 ESV**

That is what the Scriptures mean when they say, "No eye has seen, no ear has heard, and no mind has imagined what God has prepared for those who love Him."
**1 Corinthians 2:9 NLT**

"He who has an ear, let Him hear what the Spirit says to the churches."
**Revelation 3:6 NKJV**

That is why the Holy Spirit says, "Today when you hear His voice, don't harden your hearts as Israel did when they rebelled, when they tested Me in the wilderness."
**Hebrews 3:7-8 NLT**

Can you recall you mom ever saying little pitchers have big ears? We use our ears to listen and to hear. We should especially use our ears correctly on God's terrain. To hear His words but not to listen and keep them, is to look for trouble. Hearing is doing our part when God speaks to us.

# Our Daily Bread

Then he said to them, "Go your way. Eat the fat and drink sweet wine and send portions to anyone who has nothing ready, for this day is holy to our Lord. And do not be grieved, for the joy of the LORD is your strength."
**Nehemiah 8:10 ESV**

"Therefore I say to you, do not worry about your life, what you will eat or what you will drink; nor about your body, what you will put on. Is not life more than food and the body more than clothing?"
**Matthew 6:25 NKJV**

So whether you eat or drink or whatever you do, do it all for the glory of God.
**1 Corinthians 10:31 NIV**

And my God will meet all your needs according to the riches of His glory in Christ Jesus. **Philippians 4:19 NIV**

He would have fed them also with the finest of wheat; and with honey from the rock I would have satisfied you. **Psalm 81:16 NKJV**

As they were eating, Jesus took some bread and blessed it. Then He broke it in pieces and gave it to the disciples, saying, "Take this and eat it, for this is My body."
**Matthew 26:26 NLT**

Food is an integral part of our lives. It also plays a big role in our spiritual lives. Passover was celebrated with food, and Holy Communion was the most prominent sin of God's new covenant, accompanied by bread and wine. The New Jerusalem will also be marked by festive food. In the meantime, we must trust God for our daily bread. He cares for us like a Father cares for His children.

# Holiness Requires Effort

Do your best to present yourself to God as one approved, a worker who has no need to be ashamed, rightly handling the word of truth.
**2 Timothy 2:15 ESV**

Therefore, brethren, be even more diligent to make your call and election sure, for if you do these things you will never stumble.
**2 Peter 1:10 NKJV**

Therefore, my beloved brothers, be steadfast, immovable, always abounding in the work of the Lord, knowing that in the Lord your labor is not in vain.
**1 Corinthians 15:58 ESV**

So let us do our best to enter that rest. But if we disobey God, as the people of Israel did, we will fall.
**Hebrews 4:11 NLT**

And Jesus answered and said to her, "Martha, Martha, you are worried and troubled about many things. But one thing is needed, and Mary has chosen that good part, which will not be taken away from her."
**Luke 10:41-42 NKJV**

Since we have these promises, beloved, let us cleanse ourselves from every defilement of body and spirit, bringing holiness to completion in the fear of God.
**2 Corinthians 7:1 ESV**

Anything worthwhile requires effort. To make an effort shows that the task or action is worth the trouble. That is why the Bible calls on us to work hard and put in great effort to acquire eternal life. Yes, it's a gift of grace to us. But it doesn't exempt us from our responsibility to live in complete obedience to God. The effort that we make in trying to align our faith with God's Word, shows how passionate we are about it.

# The Father's Embrace

Why be captivated, my son, by an immoral woman, or fondle the breasts of a promiscuous woman?
**Proverbs 5:20 NLT**

A time to scatter stones and a time to gather them, a time to embrace and a time to refrain from embracing.
**Ecclesiastes 3:5 NIV**

"He found him in a desert land, and in the howling waste of the wilderness; He encircled him, He cared for him, He kept him as the apple of His eye."
**Deuteronomy 32:10 ESV**

His left hand is under my head, and his right hand embraces me!
**Song of Songs 2:6 ESV**

"And he arose and came to his father. But when he was still a great way off, his father saw him and had compassion, and ran and fell on his neck and kissed him."
**Luke 15:20 NKJV**

For these rules are only shadows of the reality yet to come. And Christ Himself is that reality.
**Colossians 2:17 NLT**

"Sanctify them by Your truth. Your word is truth."
**John 17:17 NKJV**

People who love each other often embrace one another in love. Hug your wife often. She is the Lord's gift of joy to you, and you to her. Celebrate your love for each other. Be extravagant with your love for each other. Embrace your friends often. And always remember that God also embrace and shower you with His unending love. His arms are wide open.

# Refuel Your Tank

You speak of having plans and power for war; but they are mere words. And in whom do you trust, that you rebel against me?
**2 Kings 18:20 NKJV**

"It is the same with My word. I send it out, and it always produces fruit. It will accomplish all I want it to, and it will prosper everywhere I send it."
**Isaiah 55:11 NLT**

He made Himself nothing by taking the very nature of a servant, being made in human likeness.
**Philippians 2:7 NIV**

For, speaking loud boasts of folly, they entice by sensual passions of the flesh those who are barely escaping from those who live in error.
**2 Peter 2:18 ESV**

But, dear friends, remember what the apostles of our Lord Jesus Christ foretold.
**Jude 17 NIV**

But I am sending the brothers so that our boasting about you may not prove empty in this matter, so that you may be ready, as I said you would be.
**2 Corinthians 9:3 ESV**

Empty words abound. I'm referring to all the meaningless talks going around. Don't talk like that. Learn from God whose words never return to Him empty. Learn from Jesus who emptied Himself of His own divine glory by becoming flesh, so that you may be filled with His presence. Fill your life with His love. Then your words and your deeds will not be empty or meaningless.

# One Step at a Time

For I desire mercy and not sacrifice, and the knowledge of God more than burnt offerings. **Hosea 6:6 NKJV**

For everything that was written in the past was written to teach us, so that through the endurance taught in the Scriptures and the encouragement they provide we might have hope.
**Romans 15:4 NIV**

God blesses those who patiently endure testing and temptation. Afterward they will receive the crown of life that God has promised to those who love Him.
**James 1:12 NLT**

So, my dear brothers and sisters, be strong and immovable. Always work enthusiastically for the Lord, for you know that nothing you do for the Lord is ever useless.
**1 Corinthians 15:58 NLT**

And he believed the LORD, and he counted it to Him as righteousness.
**Genesis 15:6 ESV**

For you have need of endurance, so that when you have done the will of God you may receive what is promised. **Hebrews 10:36 ESV**

Endurance and steadfastness as it's also known, is a precious Christian characteristic. Through the work of the Spirit in and through us, we are able to endure like marathon athletes. We know faith is about enduring obedience on the way of God. Therefore we can face everything, prosperity and adversity that life throws our way. We endured on the way of Christ to the end. We never give up, even if the road is uphill.

# Overcoming the Enemy

But now the LORD my God has given me peace on every side; I have no enemies, and all is well. **1 Kings 5:4 NIV**

"You have heard the law that says, 'Love your neighbor' and hate your enemy. But I say, love your enemies! Pray for those who persecute you!"
**Matthew 5:43-44 NLT**

Be sober-minded; be watchful. Your adversary the devil prowls around like a roaring lion, seeking someone to devour. **1 Peter 5:8 ESV**

"If your enemy is hungry, feed him; if he is thirsty, give him a drink; for in so doing you will heap coals of fire on his head."
**Romans 12:20 NKJV**

"You have heard that it was said, 'An eye for an eye and a tooth for a tooth.'"
**Matthew 5:38 ESV**

"But I say to you who hear, Love your enemies, do good to those who hate you."
**Luke 6:27 ESV**

Do not rejoice when your enemy falls, and let not your heart be glad when he stumbles. **Proverbs 24:17 ESV**

Enemies are not friends. Our feelings towards them confirm this basic fact. We don't feel anything for our enemies. Wait, that's not correct, we feel something for them. We feel hatred. Jesus refuses that we harbor such feelings in our hearts. He calls us to a higher road, God's road! He calls us to walk the second mile and to care for others. Who knows, your enemies might become your friends in an instant.

# Equal Yet Different

The LORD God said, "It is not good for the man to be alone. I will make a helper suitable for him."
**Genesis 2:18 NIV**

There is neither Jew nor Greek, there is neither slave nor free, there is neither male nor female; for you are all one in Christ Jesus.
**Galatians 3:28 NKJV**

For they cannot die anymore, because they are equal to angels and are sons of God, being sons of the resurrection.
**Luke 20:36 ESV**

Since you have been raised to new life with Christ, set your sights on the realities of heaven, where Christ sits in the place of honor at God's right hand.
**Colossians 3:1 NLT**

There may be no division in the body, but that the members may have the same care for one another.
**1 Corinthians 12:25 ESV**

The student is not above the teacher, but everyone who is fully trained will be like their teacher.
**Luke 6:40 NIV**

God is unlike us. He doesn't discriminate. All people are equal in His eyes. Men and women, rich or poor, black or white, matters equally to Him. We must learn to see other people who are different to us, through His eyes. Otherwise we might think we're better than certain people. God condemns it when we think we're superior to others, because we're not.

# Equipped to Serve

Now these are the gifts Christ gave to the church: the apostles, the prophets, the evangelists, and the pastors and teachers. Their responsibility is to equip God's people to do His work and build up the church, the body of Christ.
**Ephesians 4:11-12 NLT**

All Scripture is inspired by God and is useful to teach us what is true and to make us realize what is wrong in our lives. It corrects us when we are wrong and teaches us to do what is right. God uses it to prepare and equip His people to do every good work.
**2 Timothy 3:16-17 NLT**

Now may the God of peace who brought again from the dead our Lord Jesus, the great shepherd of the sheep, by the blood of the eternal covenant, equip you with everything good that you may do His will, working in us that which is pleasing in His sight, through Jesus Christ, to whom be glory forever and ever. Amen.
**Hebrews 13:20-21 ESV**

They presented these men to the apostles, who prayed and laid their hands on them. So the word of God spread. The number of disciples in Jerusalem increased rapidly, and a large number of priests became obedient to the faith. **Acts 6:6-7 NIV**

Gallup, one of the biggest research organizations in the world, found that the most successful leaders in any company's second most important question for effectivity, is: "Do I have the necessary equipment for my job?" Well, the Lord knew this all along, and that is why He is in the equipping industry. He uses people. He gives us His church to equip believers for His work of service. God's equipment is available to you. Use it correctly, and live!

# All the Days of Your Life

But You, Lord, are a compassionate and gracious God, slow to anger, abounding in love and faithfulness.
**Psalm 86:15 NIV**

"Then He will also say to those on the left hand, 'Depart from Me, you cursed, into the everlasting fire prepared for the devil and his angels." **Matthew 25:41 NKJV**

The free gift of God is eternal life in Christ Jesus our Lord. **Romans 6:23 ESV**

For in this way there will be richly provided for you an entrance into the eternal kingdom of our Lord and Savior Jesus Christ.
**2 Peter 1:11 ESV**

"And this is the way to have eternal life – to know You, the only true God, and Jesus Christ, the one You sent to earth." **John 17:3 NLT**

But our citizenship is in heaven. And we eagerly await a Savior from there, the Lord Jesus Christ, who, by the power that enables Him to bring everything under His control, will transform our lowly bodies so that they will be like His glorious body.
**Philippians 3:20-21 NIV**

Surely goodness and mercy shall follow me all the days of my life; and I will dwell in the house of the LORD forever. **Psalm 23:6 NKJV**

Eternity is forever. It is the life that God offers us. It lasts forever … *ad infinitum*. But the main reason for God's eternity, and eternal life that He gives us, is not the length, but that it happens in His presence. With Him for all eternity is an unending celebration and privilege.

# Driven by Eternity

"I will establish My covenant between Me and you and your descendants after you in their generations, for an everlasting covenant, to be God to you and your descendants after you."
**Genesis 17:7 NKJV**

"Truly, truly, I say to you, whoever hears My word and believes Him who sent Me has eternal life. He does not come into judgment, but has passed from death to life." **John 5:24 ESV**

For the wages of sin is death, but the free gift of God is eternal life through Christ Jesus our Lord.
**Romans 6:23 NLT**

For the grace of God has appeared that offers salvation to all people.
**Titus 2:11 NIV**

"For You granted Him authority over all people that He might give eternal life to all those you have given Him. Now this is eternal life: that they know you, the only true God, and Jesus Christ, whom you have sent."
**John 17:2-3 NIV**

For you have been born again, but not to a life that will quickly end. Your new life will last forever because it comes from the eternal, living word of God.
**1 Peter 1:23 NLT**

Eternity is forever. God gives eternal life to each person who believes in Christ. No wait, Christ is Eternal Life. To believe in Him is life itself. But it is also to never be separated from Him ever again. Not even death can bring an end to the life that Christ grants His children. It lasts forever. Now and forevermore, we belong to Christ. Here and beyond death we live close to Him.

# Strengthen Your Faith

Train up a child in the way he should go; even when he is old he will not depart from it. **Proverbs 22:6 ESV**

Don't you realize that in a race everyone runs, but only one person gets the prize? So run to win!
**1 Corinthians 9:24 NLT**

But reject profane and old wives' fables, and exercise yourself toward godliness. For bodily exercise profits a little, but godliness is profitable for all things, having promise of the life that now is and of that which is to come.
**1 Timothy 4:7-8 NKJV**

Therefore, since we are surrounded by such a great cloud of witnesses, let us throw off everything that hinders and the sin that so easily entangles. And let us run with perseverance the race marked out for us.
**Hebrews 12:1 NIV**

I discipline my body like an athlete, training it to do what it should. Otherwise, I fear that after preaching to others I myself might be disqualified.
**1 Corinthians 9:27 NLT**

I have fought the good fight, I have finished the race, I have kept the faith.
**2 Timothy 4:7 ESV**

Exercise is hard. If it wasn't, then it would've been called relaxation. In any case, we are also called to exercise on spiritual terrains. Exercising the correct spiritual disciplines like Bible study, prayer, deeds of compassion done to poor and the building up of fellow believers, direct our lives towards God. If we're loyal and faithful in these disciplines, then we exercise our spiritual lives in the right way to get fit in godliness and joy.

# Great Expectations

Everyone was expecting the Messiah to come soon, and they were eager to know whether John might be the Messiah. **Luke 3:15 NLT**

For I consider that the sufferings of this present time are not worth comparing with the glory that is to be revealed to us. For the creation waits with eager longing for the revealing of the sons of God.
**Romans 8:18-19 ESV**

Jesus said to him, "I am the way, and the truth, and the life. No one comes to the Father except through Me."
**John 14:6 ESV**

But our citizenship is in heaven. And we eagerly await a Savior from there, the Lord Jesus Christ.
**Philippians 3:20 NIV**

We desire that each one of you show the same diligence to the full assurance of hope until the end, that you do not become sluggish, but imitate those who through faith and patience inherit the promises.
**Hebrews 6:11-12 NKJV**

We look forward with hope to that wonderful day when the glory of our great God and Savior, Jesus Christ, will be revealed.
**Titus 2:13 NLT**

To live in expectation is the right way to live. It is to expect good things from the Lord. To wait expectantly for the Second Coming is the best expectation! Christ is coming again! We live in expectation of His prompt return. Through our words and deeds we hasten His coming. We look forward with great expectation for Him to replace our mortal bodies with a new body that will last for eternity.

# Limit Your Expenses

And being in Bethany at the house of Simon the leper, as He sat at the table, a woman came having an alabaster flask of very costly oil of spikenard. Then she broke the flask and poured it on His head.
**Mark 14:3 NKJV**

All their neighbors assisted them with articles of silver and gold, with goods and livestock, and with valuable gifts, in addition to all the freewill offerings.
**Ezra 1:6 NIV**

Be sure to give to the LORD the best portions of the gifts given to you.
**Numbers 18.29 NLT**

Now if anyone builds on the foundation with gold, silver, precious stones, wood, hay, straw – each one's work will become manifest, for the Day will disclose it, because it will be revealed by fire, and the fire will test what sort of work each one has done.
**1 Corinthians 3:12-13 ESV**

Ephraim was the most fruitful of all his brothers, but the east wind – a blast from the LORD – will arise in the desert. All their flowing springs will run dry, and all their wells will disappear. Every precious thing they own will be plundered and carried away.
**Hosea 13:15 NLT**

The Old Testament temple was built with the most durable and best building material, and decorated with the most precious objects. But the most expensive materials mean absolutely nothing when we don't build our faith on the precious, fireproof material like gold, silver and other precious stones. Meaning, we need to give our best to God. We should serve Him without any false motives or added benefits. We should exclusively dedicate our lives to His service; otherwise our earthly construction will never remain standing.

# Seeing Through God's Eyes

For this is what the LORD Almighty says: "After the Glorious One has sent Me against the nations that have plundered you – for whoever touches you touches the apple of His eye."
**Zechariah 2:8 NIV**

"The lamp of the body is the eye. If therefore your eye is good, your whole body will be full of light. But if your eye is bad, your whole body will be full of darkness. If therefore the light that is in you is darkness, how great is that darkness!"
**Matthew 6:22-23 NKJV**

"Why do you see the speck that is in your brother's eye, but do not notice the log that is in your own eye?"
**Matthew 7:3 ESV**

But my eyes are toward You, O GOD, my LORD; in You I seek refuge; leave me not defenseless!
**Psalm 141:8 ESV**

So we fix our eyes not on what is seen, but on what is unseen, since what is seen is temporary, but what is unseen is eternal.
**2 Corinthians 4:18 NIV**

"People look at the outward appearance, but the LORD looks at the heart."
**1 Samuel 16:7 NIV**

Our eyes are vitally important to us. They allow us to see. Yet our eyes are more than mere eyesight; it also represents our spiritual sight. If we use our eyes wrong, then our eyes refocus on the things that don't bring glory to God. That is why we must take note of how we look at things and what we look at. Then we'll notice God's glory more and more. Then we're using our eyes correctly.

# Turn Mistakes into Stepping Stones

Strengthen the weak hands, and make firm the feeble knees. Say to those who are fearful-hearted, "Be strong, do not fear! Behold, your God will come with vengeance, with the recompense of God; He will come and save you."
**Isaiah 35:3-4 NKJV**

But on Mount Zion will be deliverance; it will be holy, and Jacob will possess His inheritance.
**Obadiah 1:17 NIV**

I can do all things through Him who strengthens me.
**Philippians 4:13 ESV**

The LORD is good, a strong refuge when trouble comes. He is close to those who trust in Him.
**Nahum 1:7 NLT**

My flesh and my heart may fail, but God is the strength of my heart and my portion forever.
**Psalm 73:26 ESV**

I take pleasure in infirmities, in reproaches, in needs, in persecutions, in distresses, for Christ's sake. For when I am weak, then I am strong.
**2 Corinthians 12:10 NKJV**

Have you ever felt like a complete failure? Well, here is the good news: God never gives up on any human failure. Time after time, His people reached the end of their rope, and then He intervened. He still does it today. He will never allow us to drown in our sorrows and failures. He delivers us. Call out to Him, and experience His presence like never before.

# Keeping the Faith

Faith shows the reality of what we hope for; it is the evidence of things we cannot see.
**Hebrews 11:1 NLT**

I wait for the LORD, my soul waits, and in His word I do hope.
**Psalm 130:5 NKJV**

A faithful man will abound with blessings, but whoever hastens to be rich will not go unpunished.
**Proverbs 28:20 ESV**

"For God so loved the world that He gave His one and only Son, that whoever believes in Him shall not perish but have eternal life."
**John 3:16 NIV**

For we live by faith, not by sight.
**2 Corinthians 5:7 NIV**

You see then that a man is justified by works, and not by faith only.
**James 2:24 NKJV**

Have faith in the LORD your God and you will be upheld; have faith in His prophets and you will be successful.
**2 Chronicles 20:20 NIV**

Therefore, since we have been justified by faith, we have peace with God through our Lord Jesus Christ.
**Romans 5:1 ESV**

Faith is not a leap in the dark. Faith is the firm trust and confidence in God. It is to trust Jesus with our entire lives. It is to believe that He traded places with us. He paid in full with His life for everything we couldn't afford ourselves. On the cross Christ restored the way between God and us forever. That is why we now live in faith. We do what we believe.

# Falling into God's Arms

For I know that my Redeemer lives, and He shall stand at last on the earth; and after my skin is destroyed, this I know. That in my flesh I shall see God, whom I shall see for myself, and my eyes shall behold, and not another. How my heart yearns within me!
Job 19:25-27 NKJV

Don't keep looking at my sins. Remove the stain of my guilt. Psalm 51:9 NLT

Rejoice not over me, O my enemy; when I fall, I shall rise; when I sit in darkness, the LORD will be a light to me. Micah 7:8 ESV

Though the fig tree should not blossom, nor fruit be on the vines, the produce of the olive fail and the fields yield no food, the flock be cut off from the fold and there be no herd in the stalls, yet I will rejoice in the LORD; I will take joy in the God of my salvation.
Habakkuk 3:17-18 ESV

The LORD is good, a refuge in times of trouble. He cares for those who trust in Him.
Nahum 1:7 NIV

The godly may trip seven times, but they will get up again.
Proverbs 24:16 NLT

At the end of October 2012, Felix Baumgartner skydived from space 39.26 km above the earth. For about 4 minutes and 20 seconds he was free falling. Finally he was traveling faster than the speed of sound at 1342 kilometers per hour. It is astonishing what people will do to break records and chase after their dreams. Talking about falling, if you do fall, make sure you fall into God's arms. Then you'll have a soft landing.

# The Truth about Deceit

Then I will teach Your ways to rebels, and they will return to You.
**Psalm 51:13 NLT**

I will praise You with an upright heart as I learn Your righteous laws.
**Psalm 119:7 NIV**

But I am afraid that as the serpent deceived Eve by his cunning, your thoughts will be led astray from a sincere and pure devotion to Christ.
**2 Corinthians 11:3 ESV**

He who works deceit shall not dwell within my house; he who tells lies shall not continue in my presence.
**Psalm 101:7 NKJV**

For I want you to understand what really matters, so that you may live pure and blameless lives until the day of Christ's return.
**Philippians 1:10 NLT**

I will set nothing wicked before my eyes; I hate the work of those who fall away; it shall not cling to me. A perverse heart shall depart from me; I will not know wickedness.
**Psalm 101:3-4 NKJV**

Deliver me, O LORD, from lying lips, from a deceitful tongue.
**Psalm 120:2 ESV**

Falseness can sometimes be disguised very well. People will for example not know that I sing false, until I open my mouth. I can talk in tune, but I sing off key. I know I must open myself up to God's work so that my other hidden falsity can be uncovered. The Spirit doesn't tolerate falseness. He overturns the dark drawers of my life to expose what is fake. His light is my next breath.

# Family Matters

"Shout it aloud, do not hold back. Raise your voice like a trumpet. Declare to My people their rebellion and to the descendants of Jacob their sins."
**Isaiah 58:1 NIV**

Now when he had brought them into his house, he set food before them; and he rejoiced, having believed in God with all his household.
**Acts 16:34 NKJV**

Therefore, whenever we have the opportunity, we should do good to everyone – especially to those in the family of faith.
**Galatians 6:10 NLT**

For if someone does not know how to manage his own household, how will he care for God's church?
**1 Timothy 3:5 ESV**

Children's children are a crown to the aged, and parents are the pride of their children.
**Proverbs 17:6 NIV**

Love one another with brotherly affection. Outdo one another in showing honor.
**Romans 12:10 ESV**

You are citizens along with all of God's holy people. You are members of God's family.
**Ephesians 2:19 NLT**

Family is bound by blood. Therefore the Bible also calls us as believers the new family of God. We made children of the King through the blood of Christ. Yet, our earthly families also matter to God, so much so that He wants all of us to belong to Him. As fathers, grandfathers and sons, it is our calling and purpose to dedicate our families and carry them in prayer constantly, and help them direct their lives to God.

# A Hunger for God

"Is this not the fast that I have chosen: To loose the bonds of wickedness, to undo the heavy burdens, to let the oppressed go free, and that you break every yoke?" **Isaiah 58:6 NKJV**

"When you fast, do not look somber as the hypocrites do, for they disfigure their faces to show others they are fasting. Truly I tell you, they have received their reward in full."
**Matthew 6:16 NIV**

"Yet even now," declares the LORD, "return to Me with all your heart, with fasting, with weeping, and with mourning."
**Joel 2:12 ESV**

Once when John's disciples and the Pharisees were fasting, some people came to Jesus and asked, "Why don't your disciples fast like John's disciples and the Pharisees do?"
**Mark 2:18 NLT**

Jesus replied, "Do wedding guests fast while celebrating with the groom? Of course not. They can't fast while the groom is with them."
**Mark 2:19 NLT**

The people of Nineveh believed God. They called for a fast and put on sackcloth, from the greatest of them to the least of them.
**Jonah 3:5 ESV**

In Old Testament times fasting was an important way of humbling yourself before God. In the New Testament, the pendulum shifted somewhat. Jesus feels neutral about it in Matthew 6 when He says those who fast mustn't make a public spectacle of it. In Mark 2 He feels negative about it, because fasting could be a slap in the face of Him as the bridegroom who prepared the food for His church. Eat with the Lord regularly, and fast out of necessity.

# Fear vs. Faith

"Have I not commanded you? Be strong and courageous. Do not be frightened, and do not be dismayed, for the LORD your God is with you wherever you go."
Joshua 1:9 ESV

"Fear not, for I am with you; be not dismayed, for I am your God. I will strengthen you, yes, I will help you, I will uphold you with My righteous right hand."
Isaiah 41:10 NKJV

"Peace I leave with you; My peace I give you. I do not give to you as the world gives. Do not let your hearts be troubled and do not be afraid." John 14:27 NIV

As we live in God, our love grows more perfect. So we will not be afraid on the day of judgment, but we can face Him with confidence because we live like Jesus here in this world. Such love has no fear, because perfect love expels all fear. If we are afraid, it is for fear of punishment, and this shows that we have not fully experienced His perfect love.
1 John 4:17-18 NLT

He replied, "I heard You walking in the garden, so I hid. I was afraid because I was naked."
Genesis 3:10 NLT

Fear is a normal human emotion. We all know fear. In one way or another, life scares us. We are scared of criminals, illness, danger and the future … You name it, we're afraid of it. Fear paralyzes us. It strips us of our faith in God. Therefore He commands us over and over not to fear. The reason is because He is with us. We belong to Him.

# Feasting with Christ

The poor will eat and be satisfied. All who seek the LORD will praise Him. Their hearts will rejoice with everlasting joy. **Psalm 22:26 NLT**

On this mountain the LORD Almighty will prepare a feast of rich food for all peoples, a banquet of aged wine – the best of meats and the finest of wines.
**Isaiah 25:6 NIV**

Rejoice with those who rejoice, weep with those who weep. Live in harmony with one another. Do not be haughty, but associate with the lowly. Never be wise in your own sight.
**Romans 12:15-16 ESV**

Then He also said to him who invited Him, "When you give a dinner or a supper, do not ask your friends, your brothers, your relatives, nor rich neighbors, lest they also invite you back, and you be repaid. But when you give a feast, invite the poor, the maimed, the lame, the blind."
**Luke 14:12-13 NKJV**

Therefore let us keep the feast, not with old leaven, nor with the leaven of malice and wickedness, but with the unleavened bread of sincerity and truth.
**1 Corinthians 5:8 NKJV**

Feasting is synonymous with God. He is the God of joy and jubilation. To be in His presence is to have a continual feast. No wonder then that feasts are so prominent throughout the Bible. But feasting and celebrations also happen in our everyday lives. God wants us to prepare a feast for those who are not invited when there are formal feasts, like the poor, blind, outcasts and lonely ones. When we invite them, we make God's heart glad.

# A Life Together

They devoted themselves to the apostles' teaching and the fellowship, to the breaking of bread and the prayers. **Acts 2:42 ESV**

All the believers were united in heart and mind. And they felt that what they owned was not their own, so they shared everything they had. **Acts 4:32 NLT**

I pray that your partnership with us in the faith may be effective in deepening your understanding of every good thing we share for the sake of Christ. **Philemon 6 NIV**

That which we have seen and heard we declare to You, that You also may have fellowship with us; and truly our fellowship is with the Father and with His Son Jesus Christ. **1 John 1:3 NKJV**

Therefore encourage one another and build one another up, just as you are doing. **1 Thessalonians 5:11 ESV**

Let us consider how to stir up one another to love and good works. **Hebrews 10:24 ESV**

Koinonia is Christian fellowship or communion with God or, more commonly, with fellow Christians in the New Testament. It is a precious bond of faith that the Spirit has established between all God's children. From our side we need to make this bond of love visible by caring for others, and through our gatherings of love and harmony. By our mutual love and respect for each other, we mirror our faith.

# The Godly Man

Now this was the custom in former times in Israel concerning redeeming and exchanging, to confirm anything: one man took off his sandal and gave it to the other, and this was a confirmation in Israel.
**Ruth 4:7 NKJV**

Whoever belittles his neighbor lacks sense, but a man of understanding remains silent.
**Proverbs 11:12 ESV**

So stop telling lies. Let us tell our neighbors the truth, for we are all parts of the same body.
**Ephesians 4:25 NLT**

If you really keep the royal law found in Scripture, "Love your neighbor as yourself," you are doing right. **James 2:8 NIV**

"Do not spread slanderous gossip among your people. Do not stand idly by when your neighbor's life is threatened. I am the LORD. Do not nurse hatred in your heart for any of your relatives. Confront people directly so you will not be held guilty for their sin. Do not seek revenge or bear a grudge against a fellow Israelite, but love your neighbor as yourself. I am the LORD."
**Leviticus 19:16-18 NLT**

There is another neighbor on your radar. It is everyone who crosses your path today. How you treat the people you meet every day, will determine whether you are the neighbor Jesus spoke of in the parable of the Good Samaritan in Luke 10. To be someone's neighbor is to see him or her through the eyes of Jesus. It is to cross the street to meet other people, and to embrace them and shower them with God's love.

# Winning the Battle that Matters Most

"They will fight against you, but they shall not prevail against you. For I am with you," says the LORD, "to deliver you."
Jeremiah 1:19 NKJV

I have fought the good fight, I have finished the race, I have kept the faith.
2 Timothy 4:7 NIV

Fight the good fight for the true faith. Hold tightly to the eternal life to which God has called you, which you have declared so well before many witnesses.
1 Timothy 6:12 NLT

For it pleased the Father that in Him all the fullness should dwell, and by Him to reconcile all things to Himself, by Him, whether things on earth or things in heaven, having made peace through the blood of His cross.
Colossians 1:19-20 NKJV

For we do not wrestle against flesh and blood, but against the rulers, against the authorities, against the cosmic powers over this present darkness, against the spiritual forces of evil in the heavenly places.
Ephesians 6:12 ESV

We often read about wars in the Bible. In the Old Testament the people fought in battles. But by the time of the New Testament, God said enough is enough. Jesus' blood is more than enough for the whole world. The battle between heaven and earth is over. Jesus won. He is the Prince of Peace. He is our Wonderful Counselor. He allowed us to be good neighbors with God once again. Even better, we are His children.

MAY

I WILL **PRAISE** YOU, *Lord,* AMONG THE NATIONS; I WILL SING THE *praises* OF YOUR NAME.

2 Samuel 22:50

# Filled with the Spirit

And do not get drunk with wine, for that is debauchery, but be filled with the Spirit, addressing one another in psalms and hymns and spiritual songs, singing and making melody to the Lord with your heart.
**Ephesians 5:18-19 ESV**

For this reason we also, since the day we heard it, do not cease to pray for you, and to ask that you may be filled with the knowledge of His will in all wisdom and spiritual understanding.
**Colossians 1:9 NKJV**

They were all filled with the Holy Spirit, and they spoke the word of God with boldness. **Acts 4:31 NKJV**

You prepare a table before me in the presence of my enemies. You anoint my head with oil; my cup overflows. Surely Your goodness and love will follow me all the days of my life, and I will dwell in the house of the LORD forever.
**Psalm 23:5-6 NIV**

Wise words satisfy like a good meal; the right words bring satisfaction.
**Proverbs 18:20 NLT**

Do not quench the Spirit.
**1 Thessalonians 5:19 ESV**

To fill a bucket is to fill up all the empty space in a container. The fuller it is the less space is left open. In the same way the Spirit is our life's container. He fills every corner of our hearts with His holy presence. He transforms us into living temples of the Almighty God. From our side we must make sure that our container is not being polluted with our own mess.

# There Is No One Like You

Then you will tell him, "This is what the LORD says: 'Israel is My firstborn son.'"
**Exodus 4:22 NLT**

I will make him the firstborn, the highest of the kings of the earth.
**Psalm 89:27 ESV**

He is the head of the body, the church, who is the beginning, the firstborn from the dead, that in all things He may have the preeminence.
**Colossians 1:18 NKJV**

He is the image of the invisible God, the firstborn of all creation. **Colossians 1:15 ESV**

For those God foreknew He also predestined to be conformed to the image of His Son, that He might be the firstborn among many brothers and sisters.
**Romans 8:29 NIV**

God, for whom and through whom everything was made, chose to bring many children into glory. And it was only right that He should make Jesus, through His suffering, a perfect leader, fit to bring them into their salvation. **Hebrews 2:10 NLT**

He existed before anything else, and He holds all creation together.
**Colossians 1:17 NLT**

In Israel, the firstborn was always very important. They were the bearers of the family name and honor. In the New Testament Jesus is called God's Firstborn Son. It doesn't mean that He was born first of all the things in Creation, but rather that He is the most important in ranking of the whole universe. Jesus is the image of God. In Him we are blessed with all the spiritual blessings in heaven. He transforms us in the likeness and image of God.

# Giving God Our Best

The best of the firstfruits of your ground you shall bring into the house of the LORD your God. You shall not boil a young goat in its mother's milk. **Exodus 23:19 ESV**

Throughout the generations to come, you are to present a sacred offering to the LORD each year from the first of your ground flour.
**Numbers 15:21 NLT**

When you believed, you were marked in Him with a seal, the promised Holy Spirit, who is a deposit guaranteeing our inheritance until the redemption of those who are God's possession – to the praise of His glory.
**Ephesians 1:13-14 NIV**

These are the ones who were not defiled with women, for they are virgins. These are the ones who follow the Lamb wherever He goes. These were redeemed from among men, being firstfruits to God and to the Lamb.
**Revelation 14:4 NKJV**

For as in Adam all die, so also in Christ shall all be made alive. But each in his own order: Christ the firstfruits, then at His coming those who belong to Christ. **1 Corinthians 15:22-23 ESV**

Honor the LORD with the firstfruits of all your crops. **Proverbs 3:9 NIV**

In Old Testament times, the Israelites had to offer the first harvests to the Lord. By doing this they thanked the Lord for the harvest, but also confirmed that the rest of the harvest also belonged to Him. In the New Testament things switched. Now the Holy Spirit is God's first offering to us. He guarantees us that the rest of God's harvest will soon follow. We are fortunate that the Spirit is at work in us mightily, now and forever.

# Empty Words

Everyone lies to their neighbor; they flatter with their lips but harbor deception in their hearts. May the LORD silence all flattering lips and every boastful tongue – those who say, "By our tongues we will prevail; our own lips will defend us – who is lord over us?"
**Psalm 12:2-4 NIV**

These are grumblers, malcontents, following their own sinful desires; they are loud-mouthed boasters, showing favoritism to gain advantage.
**Jude 16 ESV**

The wise don't engage in empty chatter. **Job 15:3 NLT**

I won't play favorites or try to flatter anyone.
**Job 32:21 NLT**

Now I urge you, brethren, note those who cause divisions and offenses, contrary to the doctrine which you learned, and avoid them. For those who are such do not serve our Lord Jesus Christ, but their own belly, and by smooth words and flattering speech deceive the hearts of the simple.
**Romans 16:17-18 NKJV**

A man who flatters his neighbor spreads a net for his feet.
**Proverbs 29:5 ESV**

Flattery is to say nice things of others without really meaning it. To flatter someone means to exalt them in order to use them for your own benefit. God doesn't tolerate such flattery on the lips of His children. We struggle to give genuine compliments, without expecting anything in return. Our words build others up. We should never use our words to benefit ourselves alone.

# A Call to Live Like Jesus

Blessed is the man who walks not in the counsel of the ungodly, nor stands in the path of sinners, nor sits in the seat of the scornful.
**Psalm 1:1 NKJV**

"Whoever wants to be My disciple must deny themselves and take up their cross daily and follow Me."
**Luke 9:23 NIV**

"My sheep hear My voice, and I know them, and they follow Me."
**John 10:27 ESV**

Follow my example, as I follow the example of Christ.
**1 Corinthians 11:1 NIV**

For God called you to do good, even if it means suffering, just as Christ suffered for you. He is your example, and you must follow in His steps.
**1 Peter 2:21 NLT**

After these things He went out and saw a tax collector named Levi, sitting at the tax office. And He said to him, "Follow Me." So he left all, rose up, and followed Him. **Luke 5:27-28 NKJV**

Again Jesus spoke to them, saying, "I am the light of the world. Whoever follows Me will not walk in darkness, but will have the light of life." **John 8:12 ESV**

Jesus doesn't call us to obey a bunch of instructions and laws. He calls us to follow in His steps. He doesn't call us to a specific task, but to a new relationship. Our first and foremost calling is not to do something for Jesus, but to be the right person to Him, namely a disciple and follower! Our whole lives we are following Jesus, not laws, regulations and instructions. We serve Him. We live for Him.

# Foolproofing Your Life

Your eye is like a lamp that provides light for your body. When your eye is healthy, your whole body is filled with light.
**Matthew 6:22 NLT**

I said in my heart, "Come now, I will test you with mirth; therefore enjoy pleasure"; but surely, this also was vanity. I said of laughter – "Madness!"; and of mirth, "What does it accomplish?" **Ecclesiastes 2:1-2 NKJV**

It is better to trust in the LORD than to put confidence in man. **Psalm 118:8 NKJV**

But avoid foolish controversies, genealogies, dissensions, and quarrels about the law, for they are unprofitable and worthless.
**Titus 3:9 ESV**

Fear of the LORD is the foundation of true knowledge, but fools despise wisdom and discipline.
**Proverbs 1:7 NLT**

The fool says in his heart, "There is no God." They are corrupt, they do abominable deeds, there is none who does good.
**Psalm 14:1 ESV**

Foolishness is the result of a life that is not anchored. It is to float around without any fixed anchors in the Lord. Foolish people make a laughing matter of everything. Nothing is ever taken serious. Such a life of superficial pleasure leads to foolish comments and talks. Don't lapse into this kind of a life. It can be deadly. Sometimes you need to take matters serious.

# With God on Your Side

The seventh day is a sabbath to the LORD your God. On it you shall not do any work, neither you, nor your son or daughter, nor your male or female servant, nor your ox, your donkey or any of your animals, nor any foreigner residing in your towns, so that your male and female servants may rest, as you do.
**Deuteronomy 5:14 NIV**

Then David said to the young man who had brought the news, "Where are you from?" And he replied, "I am a foreigner, an Amalekite, who lives in your land."
**2 Samuel 1:13 NLT**

Circumcise your hearts, therefore, and do not be stiff-necked any longer. For the LORD your God is God of gods and Lord of lords, the great God, mighty and awesome, who shows no partiality and accepts no bribes. He defends the cause of the fatherless and the widow, and loves the foreigner residing among you, giving them food and clothing.
**Deuteronomy 10:16-18 NIV**

Do not mistreat or oppress a foreigner, for you were foreigners in Egypt.
**Exodus 22:21 NIV**

"For you will be treated as you treat others."
**Matthew 7:2 NLT**

God expected Israel to have a generous heart towards foreigners. They were the people who had no rights in their own countries. Yet the Israelites had to welcome them with open arms, just like God did with them. Xenophobia is not part of God's plan for people to treat others. We're not afraid of foreigners. We walk the way of grace and mercy with them.

# God's Perfect Forgetfulness

Be careful that you do not forget the LORD your God, failing to observe His commands, His laws and His decrees that I am giving you this day. **Deuteronomy 8:11 NIV**

Arise, O LORD; O God, lift up Your hand; forget not the afflicted. **Psalm 10:12 ESV**

"Can a woman forget her nursing child, and not have compassion on the son of her womb? Surely they may forget, yet I will not forget you." **Isaiah 49:15 NKJV**

Are Your wonders known in the darkness, or Your righteousness in the land of forgetfulness? **Psalm 88:12 ESV**

Don't forget to show hospitality to strangers, for some who have done this have entertained angels without realizing it! **Hebrews 13:2 NLT**

Now it happened on another Sabbath, also, that He entered the synagogue and taught. And a man was there whose right hand was withered. So the scribes and Pharisees watched Him closely, whether He would heal on the Sabbath, that they might find an accusation against Him. **Luke 6:6-7 NKJV**

Forgetfulness is part our lives. We forget this and that. Appointments, purchases, promises ... you name it, we forget about it. Fortunately God doesn't share in our forgetfulness. He remembers us. He hears us. He sees us. Remember from your side to remember God. Reflect on His Word every step of the way. Remember Him when you rise and when you go to sleep. Remember Him at home and on the road. Remember Him everywhere you go.

# Total Forgiveness

"If you forgive those who sin against you, your heavenly Father will forgive you."
**Matthew 6:14 NLT**

Be kind and compassionate to one another, forgiving each other, just as in Christ God forgave you.
**Ephesians 4:32 NIV**

Make allowance for each other's faults, and forgive anyone who offends you. Remember, the Lord forgave you, so you must forgive others. **Colossians 3:13 NLT**

And Jesus said, "Father, forgive them, for they know not what they do."
**Luke 23:34 ESV**

If we confess our sins, He is faithful and just to forgive us our sins and to cleanse us from all unrighteousness.
**1 John 1:9 NKJV**

Now instead, you ought to forgive and comfort him, so that he will not be overwhelmed by excessive sorrow.
**2 Corinthians 2:7 NIV**

Whenever you stand praying, forgive, if you have anything against anyone, so that your Father also who is in heaven may forgive you your trespasses.
**Mark 11:25 ESV**

Forgiveness is difficult, especially when the person who needs to be forgiven, shows no remorse. Or he or she isn't even aware of the injustice they've done to you. Well, true forgiveness doesn't mean to suffer from amnesia. No, we forgive while we remember. How? Well, we stop the cycle of bitterness and pain to circulate in our hearts over and over. And we shift our focus to the Lord. Then it's easier to forget.

# The Bond of Freedom

And so, dear brothers and sisters, we can boldly enter heaven's Most Holy Place because of the blood of Jesus. By His death, Jesus opened a new and life-giving way through the curtain into the Most Holy Place.
**Hebrews 10:19-20 NLT**

"See, I have inscribed you on the palms of My hands; your walls are continually before Me." **Isaiah 49:16 NKJV**

Keep your life free from love of money, and be content with what you have, for He has said, "I will never leave you nor forsake you."
**Hebrews 13:5 ESV**

They will walk with Me, dressed in white, for they are worthy. The one who is victorious will, like them, be dressed in white. I will never blot out the name of that person from the book of life, but will acknowledge that name before My Father and His angels.
**Revelation 3:4-5 NIV**

"Then you will know the truth, and the truth will set you free."
**John 8:32 NIV**

"Therefore if the Son makes you free, you shall be free indeed."
**John 8:36 NKJV**

The freedom of Christ is true and permanent freedom. When He touches your life, freedom is the first thing that you experience – God's eternal freedom! This kind of freedom is the deep assurance that God has touched your heart. And that you are now a beloved son of the Most High. He accepted you in Christ forever and always. His Spirit is poured out on you. Your name is written in the Book of Life. You're kept safe in the gentle hands of the Almighty God.

# Freedom in Christ

But now that you have been set free from sin and have become slaves of God, the fruit you get leads to sanctification and its end, eternal life. **Romans 6:22 ESV**

As for you also, because of the blood of my covenant with you, I will set your prisoners free from the waterless pit. **Zechariah 9:11 ESV**

"The Spirit of the LORD is upon Me, because He has anointed Me to preach the gospel to the poor; He has sent Me to heal the brokenhearted, to proclaim liberty to the captives and recovery of sight to the blind, to set at liberty those who are oppressed." **Luke 4:18 NKJV**

He will bring back many of the people of Israel to the Lord their God. **Luke 1:16 NIV**

For the law of the Spirit of life in Christ Jesus has made me free from the law of sin and death. **Romans 8:2 NKJV**

We know that our old sinful selves were crucified with Christ so that sin might lose its power in our lives. We are no longer slaves to sin. For when we died with Christ we were set free from the power of sin. **Romans 6:6-7 NLT**

"You will know the truth, and the truth will set you free." **John 8:32 NLT**

Freedom is to throw off the bonds of slavery and death. Freedom is to start over with the Lord by your side. Ask the woman in Luke 13 who was a slave to an illness for 18 years, which made her unclean in the eyes of religious people. She knew what it meant to be touched by Jesus. His mere touch equaled her freedom.

# The Company We Keep

A friend loves at all times, and a brother is born for adversity. **Proverbs 17:17 ESV**

Many will say they are loyal friends, but who can find one who is truly reliable? **Proverbs 20:6 NLT**

"Therefore if you bring your gift to the altar, and there remember that your brother has something against you, leave your gift there before the altar, and go your way. First be reconciled to your brother, and then come and offer your gift." **Matthew 5:23-24 NKJV**

Don't befriend angry people or associate with hot-tempered people. **Proverbs 22:24 NLT**

You adulterous people, don't you know that friendship with the world means enmity against God? Therefore, anyone who chooses to be a friend of the world becomes an enemy of God. **James 4:4 NIV**

As soon as he had finished speaking to Saul, the soul of Jonathan was knit to the soul of David, and Jonathan loved him as his own soul. **1 Samuel 18:1 ESV**

The most genuine form of friendship is the kind that needs nothing from each other, besides the bond of care and love that bind them together. True friendship doesn't use each other up. Real friendship is there for each other. They do life together. Jesus is our heavenly Friend. He gave up His life for us. That is why we can depend on Him all the way. He never lets His earthly friends down.

# The Fruit-Bearing Christian

But the fruit of the Spirit is love, joy, peace, patience, kindness, goodness, faithfulness, gentleness, self-control; against such things there is no law.
**Galatians 5:22-23 ESV**

"A good tree can't produce bad fruit, and a bad tree can't produce good fruit."
**Matthew 7:18 NLT**

"Every branch in Me that does not bear fruit He takes away, and every branch that does bear fruit He prunes, that it may bear more fruit."
**John 15:2 ESV**

"Every tree that does not bear good fruit is cut down."
**Matthew 7:19 NIV**

And even now the ax is laid to the root of the trees. Therefore every tree which does not bear good fruit is cut down and thrown into the fire.
**Matthew 3:10 NKJV**

The land produced vegetation: plants bearing seed according to their kinds and trees bearing fruit with seed in it according to their kinds. And God saw that it was good.
**Genesis 1:12 NIV**

"This is to My Father's glory, that you bear much fruit, showing yourselves to be My disciples."
**John 15:8 NIV**

Trees bear fruit; people too. God regards our lives as a tree. No, not any kind of tree, we are fruit trees. Jesus says He is the Vine and we are the branches. We are in Him. Our calling is to bear fruit, fruit that are sweet to God's taste and life giving to the rest of the people around us. To continuously bear good fruit we have to make sure that the Holy Spirit's living water flows through us.

# A Secure Future in God

So I perceived that nothing is better than that a man should rejoice in his own works, for that is his heritage. For who can bring him to see what will happen after him?
**Ecclesiastes 3:22 NKJV**

"For I know the plans I have for you," declares the LORD, "plans for welfare and not for evil, to give you a future and a hope."
**Jeremiah 29:11 ESV**

I consider that our present sufferings are not worth comparing with the glory that will be revealed in us.
**Romans 8:18 NIV**

But God had mercy on me so that Christ Jesus could use me as a prime example of His great patience with even the worst sinners. Then others will realize that they, too, can believe in Him and receive eternal life.
**1 Timothy 1:16 NLT**

"There is hope in your future," says the LORD, "that your children shall come back to their own border."
**Jeremiah 31:17 NKJV**

It was by faith that Isaac promised blessings for the future to his sons, Jacob and Esau.
**Hebrews 11:20 NLT**

The future belongs to God. None of us knows what is awaiting us tonight, but it's not necessary to know, because we know Someone who holds the future in His hand. His name is Jesus Christ. We follow Him. He knows the way. No, He is the way. We trust Him with our future, and with the future of our loved ones. Therefore we can live in peace because we know the future is secure in Him.

# A Cheerful Giver

But God had mercy on me so that Christ Jesus could use me as a prime example of His great patience with even the worst sinners. Then others will realize that they, too, can believe in Him and receive eternal life.
**1 Timothy 1:16 NLT**

"Give to him who asks you, and from him who wants to borrow from you do not turn away."
**Matthew 5:42 NKJV**

A man who is kind benefits himself, but a cruel man hurts himself.
**Proverbs 11:17 ESV**

You will be enriched in every way so that you can be generous on every occasion, and through us your generosity will result in thanksgiving to God. This service that you perform is not only supplying the needs of the Lord's people but is also overflowing in many expressions of thanks to God. Because of the service by which you have proved yourselves, others will praise God for the obedience that accompanies your confession of the gospel of Christ, and for your generosity in sharing with them and with everyone else.
**2 Corinthians 9:11-13 NIV**

Being generous is synonymous to our faith. Christians are generous. It is not an option. Generosity is not to give away a few pennies that you have left in your purse. Or to sometimes share with others. Generosity is the heart of the Gospel message. It is to continuously give, as Jesus gave. It is to give in every situation and within every relationship. Generosity comes from the heart; that's why it should be done abundantly. It is offerings that often empty our purses.

# The Mark of a Christian

Seek the LORD, all you humble of the land, who do His just commands; seek righteousness; seek humility; perhaps you may be hidden on the day of the anger of the LORD.
**Zephaniah 2:3 ESV**

Rejoice greatly, Daughter Zion! Shout, Daughter Jerusalem! See, your King comes to you, righteous and victorious, lowly and riding on a donkey, on a colt, the foal of a donkey.
**Zechariah 9:9 NIV**

"Blessed are the meek, for they shall inherit the earth."
**Matthew 5:5 NKJV**

"Take My yoke upon you. Let Me teach you, because I am humble and gentle at heart, and you will find rest for your souls."
**Matthew 11:29 NLT**

Be gentle, and show perfect courtesy toward all people.
**Titus 3:2 ESV**

You have given me the shield of Your salvation, and Your right hand supported me, and Your gentleness made me great.
**Psalm 18:35 ESV**

"God opposes the proud, but gives grace to the humble." **James 4:6 NLT**

The gentleness and humility of Christ also triumph in our hearts. It doesn't turn us into crybabies. Yet we are "soft" enough to care, to apologize, and to help carry others' pain and heartache. Other people's troubles always get a place on our shoulders. We help carry and listen to the heartache of others. Gentle hearts beat in our chests. Our hearts must never be hardened.

# The Gift of Life

For the wages of sin is death, but the free gift of God is eternal life through Christ Jesus our Lord.
**Romans 6:23 NLT**

Having gifts that differ according to the grace given to us, let us use them: if prophecy, in proportion to our faith. **Romans 12:6 ESV**

Therefore I remind you to stir up the gift of God which is in you through the laying on of my hands.
**2 Timothy 1:6 NKJV**

"I came that they may have life and have it abundantly."
**John 10:10 ESV**

But to each one of us grace was given according to the measure of Christ's gift.
**Ephesians 4:7 NKJV**

Every good and perfect gift is from above, coming down from the Father of the heavenly lights, who does not change like shifting shadows. **James 1:17 NIV**

Each of you should use whatever gift you have received to serve others, as faithful stewards of God's grace in its various forms.
**1 Peter 4:10 NIV**

God showers us with abundant life because of our faith in Jesus. He gives this life to us at no cost. God also gives us certain gifts through His Spirit. Some Christians can preach, others can sing, others are good with administration, or to encourage others. The truth is each of us has received at least one spiritual gift from the Lord that we should use for His glory and to build each other up. The ones you have received are not as important as to use them correctly to bring honor to His name.

# Gracious Giving

Every moving thing that lives shall be food for you. I have given you all things, even as the green herbs.
**Genesis 9:3 NKJV**

"In everything I did, I showed you that by this kind of hard work we must help the weak, remembering the words the Lord Jesus Himself said: 'It is more blessed to give than to receive.'"
**Acts 20:35 NIV**

Each one must give as he has decided in his heart, not reluctantly or under compulsion, for God loves a cheerful giver.
**2 Corinthians 9:7 ESV**

And so, dear brothers and sisters, I plead with you to give your bodies to God because of all He has done for you. Let them be a living and holy sacrifice – the kind He will find acceptable. This is truly the way to worship Him.
**Romans 12:1 NLT**

"Give, and it will be given to you. A good measure, pressed down, shaken together and running over, will be poured into your lap. For with the measure you use, it will be measured to you."
**Luke 6:38 NIV**

Every man shall give as he is able, according to the blessing of the LORD your God.
**Deuteronomy 16:17 ESV**

Giving is at the heart of God. He is the great Giver of all good things. Because Christ transplanted His heart into us, we are also givers. We know that it is better to give than to receive. We often share our hearts, our lives, our time, our wisdom, and money with other people because we know that it brings joy to God's heart. We know that to give is to receive.

# A Giving Heart

Sell your possessions and give to the poor. Provide purses for yourselves that will not wear out, a treasure in heaven that will never fail, where no thief comes near and no moth destroys. For where your treasure is, there your heart will be also."
**Luke 12:33-34 NIV**

Moreover, I will give all the wealth of the city, all its gains, all its prized belongings, and all the treasures of the kings of Judah into the hand of their enemies, who shall plunder them and seize them and carry them to Babylon.
**Jeremiah 20:5 ESV**

Give to everyone who asks of you. And from him who takes away your goods do not ask them back.
**Luke 6:30 NKJV**

If I give all I possess to the poor and give over my body to hardship that I may boast, but do not have love, I gain nothing.
**1 Corinthians 13:3 NIV**

A time to scatter stones and a time to gather stones. A time to embrace and a time to turn away. A time to search and a time to quit searching. A time to keep and a time to throw away.
**Ecclesiastes 3:5-6 NLT**

To give something away means to have less of it for your own use. Therefore, people struggle to part from their earthly things. For years, people are storing up and collecting things they'll probably not use again, just because giving away is so hard. Make sure this doesn't happen to you. Give some of your stuff away before it's too late. God granted us big hearts of giving to others. Share what you have. In God's eyes you are richer when you give.

# Never Give Up

The steps of a man are established by the LORD, when He delights in his way; though he fall, he shall not be cast headlong, for the LORD upholds his hand. I have been young, and now am old, yet I have not seen the righteous forsaken or His children begging for bread.
Psalm 37:23-25 ESV

Let us not become weary in doing good, for at the proper time we will reap a harvest if we do not give up.
Galatians 6:9 NIV

Let us run with endurance the race that is set before us. Hebrews 12:1 NKJV

Even when we are weighed down with troubles, it is for your comfort and salvation! For when we ourselves are comforted, we will certainly comfort you. Then you can patiently endure the same things we suffer. We are confident that as you share in our sufferings, you will also share in the comfort God gives us. 2 Corinthians 1:6-7 NLT

Watch, stand fast in the faith, be brave, be strong.
1 Corinthians 16:13 NKJV

Though they stumble, they will never fall, for the LORD holds them by the hand.
Psalm 37:24 NLT

To give up means to reach the end of your rope. It's to reach the point of utter despair. The good news is that God is not absent during such times. He knows when His children are about to stumble and fall face down. Therefore, He stoops down beside us to bind up our wounds, as David wrote in Psalm 37. Let this truth sink in, God bends down beside His children who want to give up hope. He encourages us every time with His special comfort and encouragement.

# Making Good Decisions

"For I have come down from heaven, not to do My own will, but the will of Him who sent Me."
**John 6:38 NKJV**

Always be joyful.
**1 Thessalonians 5:16 NLT**

For this is the will of God, that by doing good you should put to silence the ignorance of foolish people.
**1 Peter 2:15 ESV**

"I will instruct you and teach you in the way you should go; I will guide you with My eye."
**Psalm 32:8 NKJV**

Make me to know Your ways, O Lord; teach me Your paths. Lead me in Your truth and teach me, for You are the God of my salvation; for You I wait all the day long.
**Psalm 25:4-5 ESV**

For it is better, if it is God's will, to suffer for doing good than for doing evil.
**1 Peter 3:17 NIV**

Trust in the LORD with all your heart, and lean not on your own understanding; in all your ways acknowledge Him, and He shall direct your paths.
**Proverbs 3:5-6 NKJV**

God's will is not one or other mysterious plan. God's will has a name: Jesus Christ. God's only will is to save the world through His Son Jesus Christ. Therefore we follow God's will for our lives. His family rules include doing good to others in Jesus' name. And to be able to face opposition, and remain happy and cheerful. That is His will. The Bible teaches us this truth.

# The Goodness of God

Jethro was delighted when he heard about all the good things the LORD had done for Israel as He rescued them from the hand of the Egyptians.
**Exodus 18:9 NLT**

He has shown you, O mortal, what is good. And what does the LORD require of you? To act justly and to love mercy and to walk humbly with your God.
**Micah 6:8 NIV**

The LORD is good to all; He has compassion on all He has made.
**Psalm 145:9 NIV**

Or do you presume on the riches of His kindness and forbearance and patience, not knowing that God's kindness is meant to lead you to repentance?
**Romans 2:4 ESV**

The fruit of the Spirit is love, joy, peace, longsuffering, kindness, goodness, faithfulness.
**Galatians 5:22 NKJV**

So Jesus said to him, "Why do you call Me good? No one is good but One, that is, God."
**Mark 10:18 NKJV**

God's goodness has no end. His goodness and grace becomes visible through His deeds of salvation. He reveals His character when He saves people. This same goodness of the Lord is carried over into the hearts of His children. That is why we do good to others. Through our brotherly love for others, our care, help, compassion, support, prayers and assistance, we carry others and lift them up. We practice God's goodness every day in everything we think, do and say.

# Don't Gossip

"Do not spread slanderous gossip among your people. Do not stand idly by when your neighbor's life is threatened. I am the LORD."
Leviticus 19:16 NLT

A worthless man plots evil, and his speech is like a scorching fire. A dishonest man spreads strife, and a whisperer separates close friends.
Proverbs 16:27-28 ESV

Where there is no wood, the fire goes out; and where there is no talebearer, strife ceases.
Proverbs 26:20 NKJV

The one whose walk is blameless, who does what is righteous, who speaks the truth from their heart; whose tongue utters no slander, who does no wrong to a neighbor, and casts no slur on others.
Psalm 15:2-3 NIV

Let no corrupting talk come out of your mouths, but only such as is good for building up, as fits the occasion, that it may give grace to those who hear.
Ephesians 4:29 ESV

A gossip goes around telling secrets, so don't hang around with chatterers.
Proverbs 20:19 NLT

Gossip is a favorite pastime of many people on earth. My definition of gossip is to profess others weaknesses on their behalf in their absence. Well, don't! God doesn't like gossipers. If you have nothing constructive or positive to say about another person, rather keep your mouth shut. Build people up with your words, don't break them down. Have their backs with your words, don't make others a gossip target.

# What's So Amazing About Grace?

Once you were dead because of your disobedience and your many sins.
**Ephesians 2:1 NLT**

Concerning this thing I pleaded with the Lord three times that it might depart from me.
**2 Corinthians 12:8 NKJV**

As each has received a gift, use it to serve one another, as good stewards of God's varied grace.
**1 Peter 4:10 ESV**

"My grace is all you need."
**2 Corinthians 12:9 NLT**

O LORD of hosts, blessed is the one who trusts in You!
**Psalm 84:12 ESV**

For it is by grace you have been saved, through faith – and this is not from yourselves, it is the gift of God.
**Ephesians 2:8 NIV**

But by the grace of God I am what I am, and His grace toward me was not in vain; but I labored more abundantly than they all, yet not I, but the grace of God which was with me.
**1 Corinthians 15:10 NKJV**

The LORD is compassionate and gracious, slow to anger, abounding in love.
**Psalm 103:8 NIV**

Grace is in the first place not something God does. It is one of His characteristics. God is gracious. When He saves sinners, He proves it. When He makes enemies children of God, He proves His heart filled with unending love. God even loves His enemies. Therefore, Jesus laid down His life for sinner – to show us God's grace-filled heart.

# Discover Joy in Everyday Life

The trumpeters and singers performed together in unison to praise and give thanks to the LORD. Accompanied by trumpets, cymbals, and other instruments, they raised their voices and praised the LORD with these words: "He is good! His faithful love endures forever!" At that moment a thick cloud filled the Temple of the LORD.
**2 Chronicles 5:13 NLT**

I will give thanks to the LORD because of His righteousness; I will sing the praises of the name of the LORD Most High.
**Psalm 7:17 NIV**

And when you offer a sacrifice of thanksgiving to the LORD, offer it of your own free will.
**Leviticus 22:29 NKJV**

To You, O God of my fathers, I give thanks and praise, for You have given me wisdom and might, and have now made known to me what we asked of You, for You have made known to us the king's matter.
**Daniel 2:23 ESV**

Be thankful in all circumstances, for this is God's will for you who belong to Christ Jesus.
**1 Thessalonians 5:18 NLT**

Gratitude is one of the deepest expressions of our faith. To thank God over and over is to believe the right way. When we become aware of who God really is, and what He has done to save us, we can't but sing about His goodness and mercy. Then gratitude flows continuously from our lips. It happens spontaneously. It is the language of the heart that flows to our lips, hands and feet. A thankful heart is our offering to God.

# Trapped by Greed

The righteousness of the upright will deliver them, but the unfaithful will be caught by their lust.
**Proverbs 11:6 NKJV**

Then He said, "Beware! Guard against every kind of greed. Life is not measured by how much you own."
**Luke 12:15 NLT**

Put to death therefore what is earthly in you: sexual immorality, impurity, passion, evil desire, and covetousness, which is idolatry.
**Colossians 3:5 ESV**

Greed causes fighting; trusting the LORD leads to prosperity. **Proverbs 28:25 NLT**

But those who desire to be rich fall into temptation, into a snare, into many senseless and harmful desires that plunge people into ruin and destruction. For the love of money is a root of all kinds of evils. It is through this craving that some have wandered away from the faith and pierced themselves with many pangs.
**1 Timothy 6:9-10 ESV**

The increase from the land is taken by all; the king himself profits from the fields.
**Ecclesiastes 5:9 NIV**

Greed is destructive. It is to always want more and more material possessions. Greedy people never have enough. It steals your soul. It strips you of your freedom before God. It makes you a slave of an insatiable desire for more stuff. Never allow this deadly enslavement to get a grip on your heart. Trust God.

# Renewed Day by Day

Prize her highly, and she will exalt you; she will honor you if you embrace her.
**Proverbs 4:8 ESV**

But those who trust in the LORD will find new strength. They will soar high on wings like eagles. They will run and not grow weary. They will walk and not faint.
**Isaiah 40:31 NLT**

Now He who supplies seed to the sower and bread for food will also supply and increase your store of seed and will enlarge the harvest of your righteousness.
**2 Corinthians 9:10 NIV**

Speaking the truth in love, may grow up in all things into Him who is the head – Christ.
**Ephesians 4:15 NKJV**

But grow in the grace and knowledge of our Lord and Savior Jesus Christ. To Him be glory both now and forever! Amen.
**2 Peter 3:18 NIV**

We ought always to give thanks to God for you, brothers, as is right, because your faith is growing abundantly, and the love of every one of you for one another is increasing.
**2 Thessalonians 1:3 ESV**

Change requires growth. Organisms that don't grow are dead. The same principles apply on the Lord's road. We grow continuously, otherwise we stagnate. We are renewed by the Spirit every day, or else our hearts become hardened. There is no middle ground. We increase in love and righteousness, or we become all the more unforgiving, unloving and callous. To grow puts us in the hands of God's Spirit every day. He takes care of the real growth.

# Be on Your Guard

May the LORD bless you and protect you.
**Numbers 6:24 NLT**

Keep your heart with all vigilance, for from it flow the springs of life.
**Proverbs 4:23 ESV**

At that time Michael shall stand up, the great prince who stands watch over the sons of your people; and there shall be a time of trouble, such as never was since there was a nation, even to that time. And at that time your people shall be delivered, every one who is found written in the book.
**Daniel 12:1 NKJV**

Keep watch over yourselves and all the flock of which the Holy Spirit has made you overseers. Be shepherds of the church of God, which He bought with His own blood. **Acts 20:28 NIV**

The LORD is my shepherd, I lack nothing. **Psalm 23:1 NIV**

Care for the flock that God has entrusted to you. Watch over it willingly, not grudgingly – not for what you will get out of it, but because you are eager to serve God. **1 Peter 5:2 NLT**

Keep my commands and you will live; guard my teachings as the apple of your eye. **Proverbs 7:2 NIV**

People who look after something or someone are watchers or guards. You see them everywhere. Around every corner there are guards because there are so many dangerous people out there. Well, the Lord undertakes to also fulfill this role. No, it doesn't mean that we will never end up in a dangerous situation, or be assaulted or get hurt. It rather means that He will watch over us in such a way that nothing of no one will be able to snatch us from His hand.

# Moving Past Guilt

Carry each other's burdens, and in this way you will fulfill the law of Christ. If anyone thinks they are something when they are not, they deceive themselves. Each one should test their own actions. Then they can take pride in themselves alone, without comparing themselves to someone else, for each one should carry their own load.
**Galatians 6:2-5 NIV**

Therefore, since we have been made right in God's sight by faith, we have peace with God because of what Jesus Christ our Lord has done for us.
**Romans 5:1 NLT**

There is therefore now no condemnation for those who are in Christ Jesus.
**Romans 8:1 ESV**

Beloved, if our heart does not condemn us, we have confidence toward God.
**1 John 3:21 NKJV**

The creation will be set free from its bondage to corruption and obtain freedom of the glory of the Children of God.
**Romans 8:21 ESV**

For everyone has sinned; we all fall short of God's glorious standard.
**Romans 3:23 NLT**

Feelings of guilt are difficult masters. They keep you in chains and torture your soul. Make sure the guilt that you feel at the moment is valid. Don't become a lifelong prisoner of guilt. Let go, today! If people want to manipulate you with it, give it back to them immediately. God called you to be free of others' unresolved hang-ups. Only carry their burdens, not their guilty feelings.

# The Power of Habit

They said, "Turn now, each of you, from your evil ways and your evil practices, and you can stay in the land the LORD gave to you and your ancestors for ever and ever."
**Jeremiah 25:5 NIV**

And Jesus, answering, spoke to the lawyers and Pharisees, saying, "Is it lawful to heal on the Sabbath?"
**Luke 14:3 NKJV**

Now the tax collectors and sinners were all drawing near to hear Him.
**Luke 15:1 ESV**

Let us not neglect our meeting together, as some people do, but encourage one another, especially now that the day of His return is drawing near.
**Hebrews 10:25 NLT**

All Scripture is breathed out by God and profitable for teaching, for reproof, for correction, and for training in righteousness.
**2 Timothy 3:16 ESV**

Do not be deceived: "Evil company corrupts good habits." **1 Corinthians 15:33 NKJV**

Habits are formed through repetition. As soon as a habit is established, it happens automatically. That is why habits should continuously be examined under the magnifying glass. Habits can be destructive. It maintains sin. On the other hand, good habits are highly needed. To learn good rhythms, like regularly listen to God's Words, or to lift the poor and broken up, is to make God's heart glad.

# His Gracious Hand Holds You Tight

"How can I give you up, Ephraim? How can I hand you over, Israel? How can I make you like Admah? How can I set you like Zeboiim? My heart churns within Me; My sympathy is stirred. I will not execute the fierceness of My anger; I will not again destroy Ephraim. For I am God, and not man, the Holy One in your midst; and I will not come with terror."
**Hosea 11:8-9 NKJV**

"The hand of our God is for good on all who seek Him, and the power of His wrath is against all who forsake Him." So we fasted and implored our God for this, and He listened to our entreaty.
**Ezra 8:22-23 ESV**

"What do you think? If a man has a hundred sheep, and one of them has gone astray, does he not leave the ninety-nine on the mountains and go in search of the one that went astray? And if he finds it, truly, I say to you, he rejoices over it more than over the ninety-nine that never went astray. So it is not the will of My Father who is in heaven that one of these little ones should perish."
**Matthew 18:12-14 ESV**

Though he may stumble, he will not fall, for the LORD upholds him with His hand.
**Psalm 37:24 NIV**

To hand someone over, is to let go of his or her hand. God doesn't do this. Underneath the paint of sin and disobedience, His image shines brightly. He knows we are His. Therefore He never leaves us alone. Giving up and handing over don't exist in His heavenly vocabulary when He thinks about His children. He looks for us when we fall behind. Jesus is the Good Shepherd who looks for us when we get lost.

JUNE

DRAW NEAR
to
**GOD**
& He will
draw
NEAR TO YOU.

JAMES 4:8

# Happy and Blessed

"Blessed are the merciful, for they will be shown mercy. Blessed are the pure in heart, for they will see God. Blessed are the peacemakers, for they will be called children of God."
**Matthew 5:7-9 NIV**

Blessed is the man who remains steadfast under trial, for when he has stood the test he will receive the crown of life, which God has promised to those who love Him. **James 1:12 ESV**

May the righteous be glad and rejoice before God; may they be happy and joyful.
**Psalm 68:3 NIV**

What joy for those whose strength comes from the LORD.
**Psalm 84:5 NLT**

Taste and see that the LORD is good. Oh, the joys of those who take refuge in Him!
**Psalm 34:8 NLT**

Blessed is the man who walks not in the counsel of the wicked, nor stands in the way of sinners, nor sits in the seat of scoffers.
**Psalm 1:1 ESV**

A happy heart makes the face cheerful, but heartache crushes the spirit.
**Proverbs 15:13 NIV**

In the Bible being happy is linked to being in relationships. You can't be happy on your own. True joy is when God sees you as a happy and blessed person. It depends how you live. When you're gentle or you're a peacemaker, then God regards you as a happy and joyous person in His presence. Then He showers you with blessings. Talk about joy and happiness!

# How to Work Hard

So God blessed the seventh day and made it holy, because on it God rested from all His work that He had done in creation.
**Genesis 2:3 ESV**

When goods increase, they increase who eat them; so what profit have the owners except to see them with their eyes?
**Ecclesiastes 5:11 NKJV**

You yourselves know that these hands of mine have supplied my own needs and the needs of my companions.
**Acts 20:34 NIV**

Work willingly at whatever you do, as though you were working for the Lord rather than for people.
**Colossians 3:23 NLT**

Good planning and hard work lead to prosperity, but hasty shortcuts lead to poverty.
**Proverbs 21:5 NLT**

We ought always to give thanks to God for you, brothers, as is right, because your faith is growing abundantly, and the love of every one of you for one another is increasing.
**2 Thessalonians 1:3 ESV**

To work hard is an instruction from the Lord. Nothing that is worthwhile happens by chance. No, we don't have to work ourselves to the bone, but we're not scared of hard work. We work willingly for the Lord, and not for people. We serve and honor Him by doing our work to the best of our abilities. But we should also learn to rest after we've given our all. To be able to rest is also a gift from the Lord.

# Head in the Clouds

God placed all things under His feet and appointed Him to be head over everything for the church.
**Ephesians 1:22 NIV**

For the husband is head of the wife, as also Christ is head of the church; and He is the Savior of the body.
**Ephesians 5:23 NKJV**

Yet now He has reconciled you to Himself through the death of Christ in His physical body. As a result, He has brought you into His own presence, and you are holy and blameless as you stand before Him without a single fault. **Colossians 1:22 NLT**

He has showered His kindness on us, along with all wisdom and understanding. God has now revealed to us His mysterious will regarding Christ – which is to fulfill His own good plan. And this is the plan: At the right time He will bring everything together under the authority of Christ – everything in heaven and on earth.
**Ephesians 1:8-10 NLT**

But I want you to understand that the head of every man is Christ, the head of a wife is her husband, and the head of Christ is God.
**1 Corinthians 11:3 ESV**

It is not actually right to say that the husband is the head of the wife, because it implies that he is the boss. Paul used the literal meaning of the Greek word head. The head is the visible part that represents the rest of the body. Especially 1 Corinthians 11, Paul didn't use it to depict a certain hierarchy, but rather functionality. Men as well as Christ fulfill certain "head" functions, with which they serve and build others up.

# A Pure Heart

Love the LORD your God with all your heart and with all your soul and with all your strength.
**Deuteronomy 6:5 NIV**

For from within, out of the heart of men, proceed evil thoughts, adulteries, fornications, murders.
**Mark 7:21 NKJV**

Trust in the LORD with all your heart, and do not lean on your own understanding.
**Proverbs 3:5 ESV**

Guard your heart above all else, for it determines the course of your life.
**Proverbs 4:23 NLT**

Create in me a clean heart, O God, and renew a steadfast spirit within me.
**Psalm 51:10 NKJV**

If you openly declare that Jesus is Lord and believe in your heart that God raised Him from the dead, you will be saved.
**Romans 10:9 NLT**

I will give you a new heart, and a new spirit I will put within you. And I will remove the heart of stone from your flesh and give you a heart of flesh.
**Ezekiel 36:26 ESV**

"Blessed are the pure in heart, for they will see God."
**Matthew 5:8 NIV**

Our hearts are the core of our being according to the Bible. We live from our hearts. That is why we should love God first of all with our whole hearts. He should be at the center of our decisions, emotions, feelings, thoughts and habits. God should saturate our entire being. It starts in-house, or rather, in-heart and spills over to every thought, deed and word. Every day we show our love for God.

# Christle the Healer

The Spirit of the Sovereign LORD is upon me, for the LORD has anointed me to bring good news to the poor. He has sent me to comfort the brokenhearted and to proclaim that captives will be released and prisoners will be freed. **Isaiah 61:1 NLT**

Come, and let us return to the LORD; for He has torn, but He will heal us; He has stricken, but He will bind us up. **Hosea 6:1 NKJV**

Heal the sick, raise the dead, cleanse those who have leprosy, drive out demons. Freely you have received; freely give. **Matthew 10:8 NIV**

Therefore, confess your sins to one another and pray for one another, that you may be healed. The prayer of a righteous person has great power as it is working. **James 5:16 ESV**

He heals the brokenhearted and bandages their wounds. **Psalm 147:3 NLT**

"If you diligently heed the voice of the LORD your God and do what is right in His sight, give ear to His commandments and keep all His statutes, I will put none of the diseases on you which I have brought on the Egyptians. For I am the LORD who heals you." **Exodus 15:26 NKJV**

God likes to heal people. He uses doctors, medicine, prayer, operations, miracles and faith … but He doesn't do it on a continuous basis. Therefore you need to follow certain routes when disease strikes. The one never excludes the other. But also remember that God's greatest healing wonder is the healing of our souls. Only when our hearts are touched by the Triune God, can true healing take place. Pray therefore for illness, but pray more specifically for the healing of their soul and body.

# His Helping Hand

Therefore, confess your sins to one another and pray for one another, that you may be healed. The prayer of a righteous person has great power as it is working.
James 5:16 ESV

I lift up my eyes to the hills. From where does my help come?
Psalm 121:1 ESV

Keep silence before Me, O coastlands, and let the people renew their strength! Let them come near, then let them speak; let us come near together for judgment.
Isaiah 41:1 NKJV

Let us then approach God's throne of grace with confidence, so that we may receive mercy and find grace to help us in our time of need. Hebrews 4:16 NIV

"When you give to someone in need, don't do as the hypocrites do – blowing trumpets in the synagogues and streets to call attention to their acts of charity! I tell you the truth, they have received all the reward they will ever get. But when you give to someone in need, don't let your left hand know what your right hand is doing. Give your gifts in private, and your Father, who sees everything, will reward you." Matthew 6:2-4 NLT

We don't travel through life alone. Others are with us on this journey. Sometimes we need their help because we can't manage on our own. Other times they need our help because they're going through a difficult time. We should be there for each other. That's what the Lord asks of us. Our greatest Helper is the Lord. From Him comes all our help and strength. He is the Rock on which we build our lives, and where our salvation comes from.

# A Heavenly Helper

The LORD had seen how bitterly everyone in Israel, whether slave or free, was suffering; there was no one to help them.
**2 Kings 14:26 NIV**

Because I delivered the poor who cried out, the fatherless and the one who had no helper.
**Job 29:12 NKJV**

The name of the LORD is a strong fortress; the godly run to Him and are safe.
**Proverbs 18:10 NLT**

Hear, O LORD, and be merciful to me! O LORD, be my helper!
**Psalm 30:10 ESV**

God is our refuge and strength, always ready to help in times of trouble.
**Psalm 46:1 NLT**

My lovingkindness and my fortress, my high tower and my deliverer, my shield and the One in whom I take refuge, who subdues my people under me.
**Psalm 144:2 NKJV**

"But the Helper, the Holy Spirit, whom the Father will send in My name, He will teach you all things and bring to your remembrance all that I have said to you."
**John 14:26 ESV**

God is our heavenly Helper. He is Lord, and is ever near to us. He is our Protector. He is our Strength. He is the one who never falters or falls. Always and everywhere, He is ready to save, be gracious and extend a helping hand. If we discover this about God's heart, then we learn to also help others. Then the poor, voiceless, downtrodden, and lonely ones can take refuge with us. Then we can stand in the gap for us.

# Glory to God Alone

"Honor your father and your mother, so that you may live long in the land the LORD your God is giving you." Exodus 20:12 NIV

"I am the LORD; that is My name! I will not give My glory to anyone else, nor share My praise with carved idols." Isaiah 42:8 NLT

Therefore, having these promises, beloved, let us cleanse ourselves from all filthiness of the flesh and spirit, perfecting holiness in the fear of God.
2 Corinthians 7:1 NKJV

For the Scriptures say, "You must be holy because I am holy." And remember that the heavenly Father to whom you pray has no favorites. He will judge or reward you according to what you do. So you must live in reverent fear of Him during your time here as "temporary residents." 1 Peter 1:16-17 NLT

"You are worthy, our Lord and God, to receive glory and honor and power, for you created all things, and by Your will they were created and have their being." Revelation 4:11 NIV

Honor the LORD with your wealth and with the first-fruits of all your produce. Proverbs 3:9 ESV

God is holy. He doesn't share His glory and honor with any person or god. His name should be honored by everyone who knows Him as Lord. How? Well, through worship and holy reverence for His name. God is glorified when His children serve Him with their possessions and their whole lives. God's children always pay the necessary respect to Him. The safest place in His presence is bowed down at His feet.

# The Great House of God

Then the LORD said to Noah, "Come into the ark, you and all your household, because I have seen that you are righteous before Me in this generation." **Genesis 7:1 NKJV**

Consequently, you are no longer foreigners and strangers, but fellow citizens with God's people and also members of His household.
**Ephesians 2:19 NIV**

You shall teach them diligently to your children, and shall talk of them when you sit in your house, and when you walk by the way, and when you lie down, and when you rise. **Deuteronomy 6:7 ESV**

For if a man cannot manage his own household, how can he take care of God's church? **1 Timothy 3:5 NLT**

But if anyone does not provide for his relatives, and especially for members of his household, he has denied the faith and is worse than an unbeliever. **1 Timothy 5:8 ESV**

"And if it seems evil to you to serve the LORD, choose for yourselves this day whom you will serve, whether the gods which your fathers served that were on the other side of the River, or the gods of the Amorites, in whose land you dwell. But as for me and my house, we will serve the LORD." **Joshua 24:15 NKJV**

God's house is all about people. He is not in a building, but in the lives of people. His church is His earthly home. Believers, individually and in unison, make up the household of the Most High. Our earthly homes should also reflect God's presence. Therefore, we as husbands and men need to take the lead in our homes, and guide our families in wisdom. We need to take care of their earthly needs, as well as provide in their spiritual needs for His glory.

# God's Cure for Pride

Foreigners will be your servants. They will feed your flocks and plow your fields and tend your vineyards.
Isaiah 61:5 NLT

Rejoice greatly, Daughter Zion! Shout, Daughter Jerusalem! See, your King comes to you, righteous and victorious, lowly and riding on a donkey, on a colt, the foal of a donkey. Zechariah 9:9 NIV

Finally, all of you, be like-minded, be sympathetic, love one another, be compassionate and humble.
1 Peter 3:8 NIV

Blessed are the meek, for they shall inherit the earth. Matthew 5:5 NKJV

Likewise, you who are younger, be subject to the elders. Clothe yourselves, all of you, with humility toward one another, for "God opposes the proud but gives grace to the humble."
1 Peter 5:5 ESV

So get rid of all the filth and evil in your lives, and humbly accept the word God has planted in your hearts, for it has the power to save your souls. James 1:21 NLT

Humility is a relationship term. It becomes evident in the way you live before God and how you behave among other people. True humility is to be empty of those selfish human desires for recognition, glory and honor. It is to be filled with God. Then you're ready to be used by Him. Then you're free because you don't remember your own achievements and position anymore.

# Learning to Slow Down

Better one handful with tranquility than two handfuls with toil and chasing after the wind.
**Ecclesiastes 4:6 NIV**

This is the case of a man who is all alone, without a child or a brother, yet who works hard to gain as much wealth as he can. But then he asks himself, "Who am I working for? Why am I giving up so much pleasure now?" It is all so meaningless and depressing.
**Ecclesiastes 4:8 NLT**

The fruit of that righteousness will be peace; its effect will be quietness and confidence forever. **Isaiah 32:17 NIV**

When I applied my heart to know wisdom, and to see the business that is done on earth, how neither day nor night do one's eyes see sleep.
**Ecclesiastes 8:16 ESV**

And further, my son, be admonished by these. Of making many books there is no end, and much study is wearisome to the flesh.
**Ecclesiastes 12:12 NKJV**

"In repentance and rest is your salvation, in quietness and trust is your strength."
**Isaiah 30:15 NIV**

A hurried life is a busy life. It is to run around like a headless chicken. Yet people, who are always in a hurry and chasing after all sorts of things, get little done. They are busy. They never have time for anything or anyone. But no mountains ever move in their surroundings. Don't live that way. Be urgent, but not hurried. Do what you need to do for the Lord every day. Then you're doing enough.

# Crisis of Faith

That is why the Lord takes no pleasure in the young men and shows no mercy even to the widows and orphans. For they are all wicked hypocrites, and they all speak foolishness. But even then the LORD's anger will not be satisfied. His fist is still poised to strike.
**Isaiah 9:17 NLT**

The Lord answered him, "You hypocrites! Doesn't each of you on the Sabbath untie your ox or donkey from the stall and lead it out to give it water?"
**Luke 13:15 NIV**

"Hypocrite! First remove the plank from your own eye, and then you will see clearly to remove the speck from your brother's eye."
**Matthew 7:5 NKJV**

Slaves, obey your earthly masters with deep respect and fear. Serve them sincerely as you would serve Christ. Try to please them all the time, not just when they are watching you. As slaves of Christ, do the will of God with all your heart.
**Ephesians 6:5-6 NLT**

With his mouth the godless man would destroy his neighbor, but by knowledge the righteous are delivered.
**Proverbs 11:9 ESV**

Hypocrisy is false holiness. It is to pretend to serve God but you're actually serving yourself. It is to put on a pious face in the company of religious people, but elsewhere you're a completely different person. God seeks holiness. He wants men with strong character to be consistent as they walk on His way, and everywhere else they go. Be a man who makes God proud. Be genuinely holy.

# You Must Avoid Idleness

Talk no more so very proudly, let not arrogance come from your mouth; for the LORD is a God of knowledge, and by Him actions are weighed.
**1 Samuel 2:3 ESV**

Not so with you. Instead, whoever wants to become great among you must be your servant.
**Mark 10:43 NIV**

But He gives more grace. Therefore He says: "God resists the proud, but gives grace to the humble."
**James 4:6 NKJV**

For we hear that some among you walk in idleness, not busy at work, but busybodies.
**2 Thessalonians 3:11 ESV**

Besides that, they learn to be idlers, going about from house to house, and not only idlers, but also gossips and busybodies, saying what they should not.
**1 Timothy 5:13 ESV**

Pride goes before destruction, and haughtiness before a fall.
**Proverbs 16:18 NLT**

One who is slack in his work is brother to one who destroys.
**Proverbs 18:9 NIV**

Idleness doesn't impress God. He can't stand arrogant people. They're so full of themselves that there is no place for God in their lives. Pride comes to ruin. Idle people's egos stand in the way of God. He wants His people to have humble hearts. He asks of us to fall in the back of the line, and to be the least. Then, at the right time, God will exalt you.

# Trust the Great Physician

But now even more the report about Him went abroad, and great crowds gathered to hear Him and to be healed of their infirmities.
Luke 5:15 ESV

He was pierced for our transgressions, He was crushed for our iniquities ... by His wounds we are healed.
Isaiah 53:5 NIV

Are any of you sick? You should call for the elders of the church to come and pray over you, anointing you with oil in the name of the Lord. Such a prayer offered in faith will heal the sick, and the Lord will make you well.
James 5:14-15 NLT

Bless the LORD, O my soul, and forget not all His benefits: who forgives all your iniquities, who heals all your diseases, who redeems your life from destruction, who crowns you with lovingkindness and tender mercies.
Psalm 103:2-4 NKJV

He went down with them and stood on a level place. A large crowd of His disciples was there and a great number of people from all over Judea, from Jerusalem, and from the coastal region around Tyre and Sidon, who had come to hear Him and to be healed of their diseases.
Luke 6:17-18 NIV

God encourages us to call out to Him when we're sick. No, He doesn't make every disease disappear. Because we live in the reality of sin, some Christians will still die of serious diseases. But still we can call on His name in such times, and trust Him for healing. We must also make sure we get the necessary medical treatment, because God doesn't rule out medical doctors. Whichever way He chooses to heal us – we honor His name for each act of wonder!

# Under God's Influence

"It would be better for him if a millstone were hung around his neck, and he were thrown into the sea, than that he should offend one of these little ones."
**Luke 17:2 NKJV**

Jesus called them to Him and said to them, "You know that those who are considered rulers of the Gentiles lord it over them, and their great ones exercise authority over them. But it shall not be so among you. But whoever would be great among you must be your servant."
**Mark 10:42-43 NKJV**

Brothers and sisters, think of what you were when you were called. Not many of you were wise by human standards; not many were influential; not many were of noble birth.
**1 Corinthians 1:26 NIV**

For if you live according to the flesh, you will die; but if by the Spirit you put to death the misdeeds of the body, you will live.
**Romans 8:13 NIV**

Show yourself in all respects to be a model of good works, and in your teaching show integrity, dignity.
**Titus 2:7 ESV**

Influence is power. The more you have of the one, the more you have of the other. Influence can be good or bad. If it is used to acquire naked power over someone, and to play the boss of others, influence is negative. When it is used to carry the burdens of others, and to draw them closer to God, then influence is good. Use your influence for the good, be it little or much.

# Insight for Life

I know that there is nothing better for people than to be happy and to do good while they live.
**Ecclesiastes 3:12 NIV**

I will give you shepherds according to My heart, who will feed you with knowledge and understanding.
**Jeremiah 3:15 NKJV**

It is my prayer that your love may abound more and more, with knowledge and all discernment.
**Philippians 1:9 ESV**

Trust in the LORD with all your heart; do not depend on your own understanding.
**Proverbs 3:5 NLT**

If any of you lacks wisdom, let him ask God, who gives generously to all without reproach, and it will be given him.
**James 1:5 ESV**

Wisdom belongs to the aged, and understanding to the old. "But true wisdom and power are found in God; counsel and understanding are His."
**Job 12:12-13 NLT**

Counsel and sound judgment are mine; I have insight, I have power.
**Proverbs 8:14 NIV**

Insight is more than understanding. Insight is an "Aha!" moment leading to the point of seeing someone or something in a complete new light. Insight is the moment of complete illumination where you understand something as for the first time. Only when such insight is established in you regarding the things of God, that's when you really change and grow. Then your head as well as your heart are touched deeply. Then you can never live the same way again. Let's pray for such new insights into God's Word.

# God's Commands for Us

He said, "If you will listen carefully to the voice of the LORD your God and do what is right in His sight, obeying His commands and keeping all His decrees, then I will not make you suffer any of the diseases I sent on the Egyptians; for I am the LORD who heals you." **Exodus 15:26 NLT**

And they were left, that He might test Israel by them, to know whether they would obey the commandments of the LORD, which He had commanded their fathers by the hand of Moses.
**Judges 3:4 NKJV**

All His laws are before me; I have not turned away from His decrees. **2 Samuel 22:23 NIV**

"If you keep My commandments, you will abide in My love, just as I have kept My Father's commandments and abide in His love."
**John 15:10 NIV**

Listen to advice and accept instruction, that you may gain wisdom in the future.
**Proverbs 19:20 ESV**

"I will instruct you and teach you in the way you should go; I will counsel you with My eye upon you."
**Psalm 32:8 ESV**

Love the LORD your God and keep His requirements, His decrees, His laws and His commands always.
**Deuteronomy 11:1 NIV**

God's prescriptions are concise summaries of His will. To do His will is to obey His commands and instructions. The most important of all is love. We follow His instructions as we find it in the Bible. But His commands are not clinical laws. As children we obey our Heavenly Father's prescriptions. We walk in His way. We obey Him because it is the way to eternal life.

# Drawing Near to God

The secret of the LORD is with those who fear Him, and He will show them His covenant.
**Psalm 25:14 NKJV**

Today I fulfilled my vows, and I have food from my fellowship offering at home.
**Proverbs 7:14 NIV**

A troublemaker plants seeds of strife; gossip separates the best of friends.
**Proverbs 16:28 NLT**

All my intimate friends abhor me, and those whom I loved have turned against me.
**Job 19:19 ESV**

In Him lie hidden all the treasures of wisdom and knowledge.
**Colossians 2:3 NLT**

Commit your works to the LORD, and your thoughts will be established.
**Proverbs 16:3 NKJV**

Draw near to God, and He will draw near to you. Cleanse your hands, you sinners, and purify your hearts, you double-minded.
**James 4:8 ESV**

Whoever dwells in the shelter of the Most High will rest in the shadow of the Almighty.
**Psalm 91:1 NIV**

Intimacy means bare knowledge; that is why this image is sometimes used for sexuality in the Bible. But intimacy is also used for friendship that is very sincere, as well as for godly wisdom. Whoever discovers wisdom gets to know His heart in a very personal way. That is why we should pursue wisdom with our whole beings. It makes us understand how to live in the Lord's presence with respect and discernment.

# An Invitation from Above

"But when the king came in to see the guests, he noticed a man there who was not wearing wedding clothes. He asked, 'How did you get in here without wedding clothes, friend?' The man was speechless. Then the king told the attendants, 'Tie him hand and foot, and throw him outside, into the darkness, where there will be weeping and gnashing of teeth.'" Matthew 22:11-13 NIV

"All who are victorious will inherit all these blessings, and I will be their God, and they will be My children." Revelation 21:7 NLT

Then one of the elders addressed me, saying, "Who are these, clothed in white robes, and from where have they come?" I said to him, "Sir, you know." And he said to me, "These are the ones coming out of the great tribulation. They have washed their robes and made them white in the blood of the Lamb." Revelation 7:13-14 ESV

For He who is called in the Lord while a slave is the Lord's freedman. Likewise He who is called while free is Christ's slave. You were bought at a price; do not become slaves of men.
1 Corinthians 7:22-23 NKJV

To be invited to a special celebration, is a great honor. Well, the King of the universe invited all of us to His Banquet. The dress code? White clothes, washed by the blood of the Lamb. These clothes are free for all. You just need to get it at Jesus' feet. The occasion: a celebration of Jesus' victory. Time: For eternity. There is still space available. Don't waste your chance on eternity!

# A Jealous God

Now when Rachel saw that she bore Jacob no children, Rachel envied her sister, and said to Jacob, "Give me children, or else I die!"
**Genesis 30:1 NKJV**

The LORD is a jealous and avenging God; the LORD takes vengeance and is filled with wrath. The LORD takes vengeance on His foes and vents His wrath against His enemies.
**Nahum 1:2 NIV**

Love is patient and kind; love does not envy or boast; it is not arrogant.
**1 Corinthians 13:4 ESV**

"For I am jealous for you with the jealousy of God Himself. I promised you as a pure bride to one husband – Christ."
**2 Corinthians 11:2 NLT**

Transgression speaks to the wicked deep in his heart; there is no fear of God before his eyes. For he flatters himself in his own eyes that his iniquity cannot be found out and hated.
**Psalm 36:1-2 ESV**

For wherever there is jealousy and selfish ambition, there you will find disorder and evil of every kind.
**James 3:16 NLT**

Jealousy is used in a positive light in the Bible with regards to God, and it's always negative where people are concerned. God's jealousy means His burning love for His people; therefore He doesn't share us with any idols. He refuses that we walk away from Him, and run after sin. We in turn should never yield to jealousy where we start coveting others' material possessions. Jealousy leads to us not allowing others good things.

# A Joy-Driven Life

For the kingdom of God is not a matter of eating and drinking but of righteousness and peace and joy in the Holy Spirit.
**Romans 14:17 ESV**

May the God of hope fill you with all joy and peace as you trust in Him, so that you may overflow with hope by the power of the Holy Spirit.
**Romans 15:13 NIV**

Always be joyful.
**1 Thessalonians 5:16 NLT**

Therefore my heart is glad, and my glory rejoices; my flesh also will rest in hope.
**Psalm 16:9 NKJV**

The hope of the righteous brings joy.
**Proverbs 10:28 ESV**

You will show me the path of life; in Your presence is fullness of joy; at Your right hand are pleasures forevermore.
**Psalm 16:11 NKJV**

But be glad and rejoice forever in what I will create, for I will create Jerusalem to be a delight and its people a joy.
**Isaiah 65:18 NIV**

The life of the godly is full of light and joy, but the light of the wicked will be snuffed out.
**Proverbs 13:9 NLT**

God's will for us is to find joy and happiness. It's what the Bible teaches us. Joy is not a fleeting emotion or a passing feeling. Joy is the deep-rooted rest we find in the Lord. This joy can never be bottled up; it flows freely and constantly from our hearts in the direction of God and other people. Joy forms an integral part of our identity in Christ; therefore it characterizes our words and deeds.

# Let Your Life Radiate Joy

They worshiped together at the Temple each day, met in homes for the Lord's Supper, and shared their meals with great joy and generosity. **Acts 2:46 NLT**

Let us be glad and rejoice and give Him glory, for the marriage of the Lamb has come, and His wife has made herself ready.
**Revelation 19:7 NKJV**

Rejoice greatly, Daughter Zion! Shout, Daughter Jerusalem! See, your King comes to you, righteous and victorious, lowly and riding on a donkey, on a colt, the foal of a donkey.
**Zechariah 9:9 NIV**

Rejoice always.
**1 Thessalonians 5:16 ESV**

This is the day that the LORD has made; let us rejoice and be glad in it.
**Psalm 118:24 ESV**

You will show me the way of life, granting me the joy of Your presence and the pleasures of living with You forever.
**Psalm 16:11 NLT**

Our mouths were filled with laughter, our tongues with songs of joy.
**Psalm 126:2 NIV**

Joy is always tangible and visible. One can't keep it in. The Lord's presence is filled with joy. This joy overflows from our soul. It spill over in our words and deeds. The closer we live to Christ, the deeper and more permanent this heavenly joy become in our lives. It is a fountain of life that always bubbles up in us. Live close to Him, and you'll always know this kind of joy.

# The Judgment Seat of Christ

Since you judge others for doing these things, why do you think you can avoid God's judgment when you do the same things?
Romans 2:3 NLT

Therefore do not pronounce judgment before the time, before the Lord comes, who will bring to light the things now hidden in darkness and will disclose the purposes of the heart. Then each one will receive his commendation from God.
1 Corinthians 4:5 ESV

For He is coming to judge the earth. With righteousness He shall judge the world, and the peoples with equity. Psalm 98:9 NKJV

Then I saw heaven opened, and a white horse was standing there. Its rider was named Faithful and True, for He judges fairly and wages a righteous war.
Revelation 19:11 NLT

"He who believes in Him is not condemned; but he who does not believe is condemned already, because he has not believed in the name of the only begotten Son of God. And this is the condemnation, that the light has come into the world, and men loved darkness rather than light, because their deeds were evil."
John 3:18-19 NKJV

Judgment is for God alone. On the Last Day He will pass judgment on every person. Yet Jesus teaches us that judgment has been done already. Every person who doesn't' believe in Him is already condemned. They are judged by their own choice. But everyone who believes in Him can be certain of the Lord's deliverance and salvation. God's unending glory awaits us. What wonderful news!

# The Kingdom of God

"Again, the kingdom of heaven is like a merchant seeking beautiful pearls, who, when he had found one pearl of great price, went and sold all that he had and bought it."
**Matthew 13:45-46 NKJV**

"The time has come," He said. "The kingdom of God has come near. Repent and believe the good news!"
**Mark 1:15 NIV**

Your kingdom is an everlasting kingdom, and Your dominion endures throughout all generations.
**Psalm 145:13 NKJV**

And He said, "With what can we compare the kingdom of God, or what parable shall we use for it? It is like a grain of mustard seed, which, when sown on the ground, is the smallest of all the seeds on earth."
**Mark 4:30-31 ESV**

He replied, "You are permitted to understand the secret of the Kingdom of God. But I use parables for everything I say to outsiders." **Mark 4:11 NLT**

Seek the Kingdom of God above all else, and live righteously, and He will give you everything you need.
**Matthew 6:33 NLT**

The kingdom of God is the heartbeat of Jesus' ministry. He didn't establish the church in the first place, but the kingdom. The kingdom is God's new world that has dawned here on earth. Little by little it infiltrates our current reality, and pushes all other empires to the background. No, it's not a centralized government with military service, currency and the likes. The kingdom consists of ordinary people who live lives in honor of God throughout the whole world.

# Knowledge Is Power

The fear of the LORD is the beginning of knowledge, but fools despise wisdom and instruction.
**Proverbs 1:7 NKJV**

My people are destroyed for lack of knowledge; because you have rejected knowledge, I reject you from being a priest to me. And since you have forgotten the law of your God, I also will forget your children.
**Hosea 4:6 ESV**

"But I will send you the Advocate – the Spirit of truth. He will come to you from the Father and will testify all about Me."
**John 15:26 NLT**

Whoever does not love does not know God, because God is love. **1 John 4:8 NIV**

To the person who pleases Him, God gives wisdom, knowledge and happiness, but to the sinner He gives the task of gathering and storing up wealth to hand it over to the one who pleases God. This too is meaningless, a chasing after the wind.
**Ecclesiastes 2:26 NIV**

For the LORD gives wisdom; from His mouth come knowledge and understanding; He stores up sound wisdom for the upright; He is a shield to those who walk uprightly.
**Proverbs 2:6-7 NKJV**

Knowledge is power. Without the right information, we are stuck. The same goes for God. Without the correct knowledge about Him you're going to live your whole life on spiritual crutches. Where do you get the right knowledge? Well, in His Word. Moreover, the Spirit is your Master to instruct and teach you in the complete truth about Christ. With Him you get knowledge of life.

# Give to Those in Desperate Need

The sons of Kohath were Amram, Izhar, Hebron and Uzziel. Kohath lived 133 years. Exodus 6:18 NIV

"The time is surely coming," says the Sovereign LORD, "when I will send a famine on the land – not a famine of bread or water but of hearing the words of the LORD."
Amos 8:11 NLT

For I do not mean that others should be eased and you burdened; but by an equality, that now at this time your abundance may supply their lack, that their abundance also may supply your lack – that there may be equality.
2 Corinthians 8:13-14 NKJV

Now the full number of those who believed were of one heart and soul, and no one said that any of the things that belonged to him was his own, but they had everything in common. Acts 4:32 ESV

"For I was hungry, and you fed Me. I was thirsty, and you gave Me a drink. I was a stranger, and you invited Me into your home."
Matthew 25:35 NLT

Sell what you have and give alms; provide yourselves money bags which do not grow old, a treasure in the heavens that does not fail, where no thief approaches nor moth destroys.
Luke 12:33 NKJV

To suffer from hunger is the worst thing ever. It is terrible not to be able to provide for the needs of your family. God's Word teaches to make sure our fellow believers never end up in this position. We must help when they don't have enough to eat. God's love urges us not to only open our hearts, but also our hands and pockets to each other.

# The Language of God

Get rid of all bitterness, rage and anger, brawling and slander, along with every form of malice.

**Ephesians 4:31 NIV**

Let your speech always be gracious, seasoned with salt, so that you may know how you ought to answer each person.

**Colossians 4:6 ESV**

"You are worthy to take the scroll, and to open its seals; for You were slain, and have redeemed us to God by Your blood out of every tribe and tongue and people and nation, and have made us kings and priests to our God; and we shall reign on the earth.

**Revelation 5:9-10 NKJV**

Never once did we try to win you with flattery, as you well know. And God is our witness that we were not pretending to be your friends just to get your money!

**1 Thessalonians 2:5 NLT**

Let the words of my mouth and the meditation of my heart be acceptable in Your sight, O Lord, my strength and my Redeemer.

**Psalm 19:14 NKJV**

Whatever you do or say, do it as a representative of the Lord Jesus, giving thanks through Him to God the Father.

**Colossians 3:17 NLT**

The language that we speak is windows to our souls. That is why we should choose and use our words with wisdom and insight. Constructive and uplifting words should continuously flow from our lips; the kind that will draw others closer to God. In the same way we put salt on our food to season it, we need to season our words with hope and strength and convey it to others. The words that we speak must continually bring glory to God. Then we're using our words wisely.

# Fortunate to Be Last

Jesus called them to Him and said to them, "You know that those who are considered rulers of the Gentiles lord it over them, and their great ones exercise authority over them. But it shall not be so among you. But whoever would be great among you must be your servant, and whoever would be first among you must be slave of all. For even the Son of Man came not to be served but to serve, and to give His life as a ransom for many."
**Mark 10:42-45 ESV**

"So those who are last now will be first then, and those who are first will be last."
**Matthew 20:16 NLT**

"If I then, your Lord and Teacher, have washed your feet, you also ought to wash one another's feet. For I have given you an example, that you should do as I have done to you. If you know these things, blessed are you if you do them."
**John 13:14-15,17 NKJV**

"Some who seem least important now will be the greatest then, and some who are the greatest now will be least important then."
**Luke 13:30 NLT**

Humble yourselves before the Lord, and He will lift you up. **James 4:10 NIV**

They say it's not about winning or losing, but how you've competed. But honestly, who likes to be last? It's not the favorite place to hang out on earth. But I know Someone for whom it was a good place. His name is Jesus. To be last doesn't scare Him. In fact, most of His friends look for Him at that position. First place doesn't matter to Jesus. He often picks up losers, and carries them in His arms. Therefore, there is also a place for me with Him.

# Living in the Last Days

"In the last days," God says, "I will pour out My Spirit on all people. Your sons and daughters will prophesy, your young men will see visions, your old men will dream dreams."
**Acts 2:16-17 NIV**

God, who at various times and in various ways spoke in time past to the fathers by the prophets, has in these last days spoken to us by His Son, whom He has appointed heir of all things, through whom also He made the worlds.
**Hebrews 1:1-2 NKJV**

"You also must be ready, for the Son of Man is coming at an hour you do not expect."
**Matthew 24:44 ESV**

Children, it is the last hour, and as you have heard that antichrist is coming, so now many antichrists have come. Therefore we know that it is the last hour.
**1 John 2:18 ESV**

"The Good News about the Kingdom will be preached throughout the whole world, so that all nations will hear it; and then the end will come."
**Matthew 24:14 NLT**

Thinking about the end times make believers a bit anxious. They are always speculating about when exactly it will come. If they make an effort to read their Bibles, they would know that it has happened a long time ago already. The Last Days, or end times according to the New Testament, is the time between Jesus' first and Second Coming. It is the era of the antichrist, but specifically the time when God's Spirit is poured out on His children.

# Laughing Matters

Then the LORD said to Abraham, "Why did Sarah laugh? Why did she say, 'Can an old woman like me have a baby?'"
**Genesis 18:13 NLT**

And Sarah said, "God has made laughter for me; everyone who hears will laugh over me."
**Genesis 21:6 ESV**

But You, O LORD, laugh at them; You hold all the nations in derision.
**Psalm 59:8 ESV**

He will once again fill your mouth with laughter and your lips with shouts of joy.
**Job 8:21 NLT**

I in turn will laugh when disaster strikes you; I will mock when calamity overtakes you.
**Proverbs 1:26 NIV**

The wicked plots against the righteous and gnashes his teeth at him, but the Lord laughs at the wicked, for He sees that his day is coming.
**Psalm 37:12-13 ESV**

A time to weep, and a time to laugh; a time to mourn, and a time to dance.
**Ecclesiastes 3:4 NKJV**

Happy is the man who finds wisdom, and the man who gains understanding.
**Proverbs 3:13 NKJV**

To laugh is part of living. You need to laugh for the right reasons. Sarah laughed sarcastically when God told her she was going to have a baby. God didn't like it. God Himself laughed mockingly at the wicked who challenged His authority. Together with Him you can only shake your head in amazement at their foolishness. But with God, true happiness, joy and laughter are found.

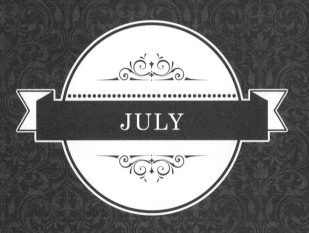

JULY

YOU CROWN the year with a BOUNTIFUL HARVEST; even the hard PATHWAYS *overflow* with ABUNDANCE.

Psalm 65:11

# You Must Avoid Laziness

Take a lesson from the ants, you lazybones. Learn from their ways and become wise!
**Proverbs 6:6 NLT**

He who has a slack hand becomes poor, but the hand of the diligent makes rich.
**Proverbs 10:4 NKJV**

The sluggard buries his hand in the dish and will not even bring it back to his mouth.
**Proverbs 19:24 ESV**

Sluggards do not plow in season; so at harvest time they look but find nothing.
**Proverbs 20:4 NIV**

As vinegar to the teeth and smoke to the eyes, so is the lazy man to those who send him.
**Proverbs 10:26 NKJV**

Work hard and become a leader; be lazy and become a slave.
**Proverbs 12:24 NLT**

A lazy person is as bad as someone who destroys things. **Proverbs 18:9 NLT**

The way of the lazy man is like a hedge of thorns, but the way of the upright is a highway.
**Proverbs 15:19 NKJV**

The book of Proverbs often speaks about idleness. Lazy people become poor. They don't move a muscle to do something for themselves. They hang around lazily, and are surprised when bad things happen to them. Idleness is not a virtue, rather diligence. God expects His children to be hardworking. No, we are not workaholics, but we definitely don't sit around all day doing nothing.

# Leadership Is a Gift from God

"Come," they said, "be our commander, so we can fight the Ammonites."
**Judges 11:6 NIV**

"Now, therefore, thus you shall say to My servant David, 'Thus says the LORD of hosts, I took you from the pasture, from following the sheep, that you should be prince over My people Israel."
**2 Samuel 7:8 ESV**

"But not so among you; on the contrary, he who is greatest among you, let him be as the younger, and he who governs as he who serves."
**Luke 22:26 NKJV**

In His grace, God has given us different gifts for doing certain things well. So if God has given you the ability to prophesy, speak out with as much faith as God has given you.
**Romans 12:6 NLT**

"But among you it will be different. Whoever wants to be a leader among you must be your servant, and whoever wants to be first among you must be the slave of everyone else. For even the Son of Man came not to be served but to serve others and to give His life as a ransom for many."
**Mark 10:43-45 NLT**

Leadership is a gift and quality from the Lord that needs to be developed all the time. No, it's not a position, title or some or other formal appointment. Biblical leaders use their leadership abilities to guide and influence others to the glory of God, and to extend His Kingdom on earth. Such leaders never try to be in the spotlight themselves, but they want the focus to be on the Lord, as it should be.

# Don't Be Left Behind

Therefore a man shall leave his father and mother and be joined to his wife, and they shall become one flesh.
**Genesis 2:24 NKJV**

The LORD had said to Abram, "Go from your country, your people and your father's household to the land I will show you."
**Genesis 12:1 NIV**

If you are honest men, let one of your brothers remain confined where you are in custody, and let the rest go and carry grain for the famine of your households.
**Genesis 42:19 ESV**

"I am leaving you with a gift – peace of mind and heart. And the peace I give is a gift the world cannot give. So don't be troubled or afraid."
**John 14:27 NLT**

"Have I not commanded you? Be strong and courageous. Do not be frightened, and do not be dismayed, for the LORD your God is with you wherever you go."
**Joshua 1:9 ESV**

By faith he left Egypt, not fearing the king's anger; he persevered because he saw Him who is invisible.
**Hebrews 11:27 NIV**

Many Bible figures had to leave behind everything that was dear and precious to them, when God called them. Abraham had to leave his land and family to walk into the unknown and after God's calling. Joseph had to call his whole family to find God's favor in a far-off country. You often need to leave something behind when God calls you closer. But it's also a time to be found – by God.

# Spiritual Liberation

"The Spirit of the LORD is upon Me, because He has anointed Me to preach the gospel to the poor; He has sent Me to heal the broken-hearted, to proclaim liberty to the captives and recovery of sight to the blind, to set at liberty those who are oppressed."
Luke 4:18 NKJV

"Do not judge others, and you will not be judged. Do not condemn others, or it will all come back against you. Forgive others, and you will be forgiven."
Luke 6:37 NLT

"If the Son sets you free, you are truly free."
John 8:36 NLT

For we know that our old self was crucified with Him so that the body ruled by sin might be done away with, that we should no longer be slaves to sin – because anyone who has died has been set free from sin.
Romans 6:6-7 NIV

Whoever looks intently into the perfect law that gives freedom, and continues in it – not forgetting what they have heard, but doing it – they will be blessed in what they do. James 1:25 NIV

For freedom Christ has set us free; stand firm therefore, and do not submit again to a yoke of slavery.
Galatians 5:1 ESV

To be free is to truly live. That is exactly what Christ came to do for us. He came to lift the burden of death and sin from our shoulders. Jesus also came to take the burden of the suffering. He sees the need of the poor, the sick and the outcasts. He let them live in His grace. We should follow His example, and care for them.

# Let Go of Lies

You destroy those who speak lies; the LORD abhors the bloodthirsty and deceitful man.
**Psalm 5:6 ESV**

I have heard what the prophets say who prophesy lies in My name. They say, "I had a dream! I had a dream!"
**Jeremiah 23:25 NIV**

"For three transgressions of Judah, and for four, I will not turn away its punishment, because they have despised the law of the LORD, and have not kept His commandments. Their lies lead them astray, lies which their fathers followed."
**Amos 2:4 NKJV**

For you are the children of your father the devil, and you love to do the evil things he does. He was a murderer from the beginning. He has always hated the truth, because there is no truth in him. When he lies, it is consistent with his character; for he is a liar and the father of lies.
**John 8:44 NLT**

Truthful lips endure forever, but a lying tongue is but for a moment. **Proverbs 12:19 ESV**

Therefore each of you must put off falsehood and speak truthfully to your neighbor, for we are all members of one body. **Ephesians 4:25 NIV**

To twist the truth to fit with your own selfish needs and desires are not on. It is like playing in the opposition's hand. Satan is not called the father of lies for nothing. Don't speak his language. Don't deal with the truth lightly. Speak the truth. Live the truth; God's truth! Otherwise you jeopardize your own integrity as a believer.

# Learn to Listen

"Now if you obey Me fully and keep My covenant, then out of all nations you will be My treasured possession. Although the whole earth is Mine."
**Exodus 19:5 NIV**

Listen, O Israel! The LORD is our God, the LORD alone.
**Deuteronomy 6:4 NLT**

"My sheep hear My voice, and I know them, and they follow Me."
**John 10:27 ESV**

So then, my beloved brethren, let every man be swift to hear, slow to speak, slow to wrath.
**James 1:19 NKJV**

The way of a fool is right in his own eyes, but a wise man listens to advice.
**Proverbs 12:15 ESV**

"Anyone who listens to My teaching and follows it is wise, like a person who builds a house on solid rock."
**Matthew 7:24 NLT**

Faith comes from hearing, that is, hearing the Good News about Christ.
**Romans 10:17 NLT**

Do not merely listen to the word, and so deceive yourselves. Do what it says.
**James 1:22 NIV**

To listen and obey the Lord is a lifelong command and calling. To really listen and not only hear. To hear and then to do something, that's what it's all about. Ears that are opened to the voice of the Lord are equal to a responsive and impressionable life. To listen like this is to make God's heart glad, because it always leads to a life lived for His glory. Listen and do the right thing today.

# Living the Christian Life

"Honor your father and mother. Then you will live a long, full life in the land the LORD your God is giving you."
**Exodus 20:12 NLT**

He has shown you, O man, what is good; and what does the LORD require of you but to do justly, to love mercy, and to walk humbly with your God? **Micah 6:8 NKJV**

I have been crucified with Christ. It is no longer I who live, but Christ who lives in me. And the life I now live in the flesh I live by faith in the Son of God, who loved me and gave Himself for me.
**Galatians 2:20 ESV**

So I say, walk by the Spirit, and you will not gratify the desires of the flesh.
**Galatians 5:16 NIV**

Everyone who goes on ahead and does not abide in the teaching of Christ, does not have God. Whoever abides in the teaching has both the Father and the Son.
**2 John 9 ESV**

Hold fast the pattern of sound words which you have heard from me, in faith and love which are in Christ Jesus.
**2 Timothy 1:13 NKJV**

The right way to live in God's presence is to know and keep His Word. Obedience to Him equals life. To allow God to shape and transform us through His Spirit, is to truly live. To know that our identity lies in the crucified and resurrected Christ is to know true life. If we lose our lives in Him, we find it for all eternity!

# Live Upwards!

"You are the salt of the earth; but if the salt loses its flavor, how shall it be seasoned? It is then good for nothing but to be thrown out and trampled underfoot by men. You are the light of the world. A city that is set on a hill cannot be hidden. Nor do they light a lamp and put it under a basket, but on a lampstand, and it gives light to all who are in the house. Let your light so shine before men, that they may see your good works and glorify your Father in heaven."
**Matthew 5:13-16 NKJV**

Then the LORD God formed the man of dust from the ground and breathed into his nostrils the breath of life, and the man became a living creature.
**Genesis 2:7 ESV**

So get rid of all evil behavior. Be done with all deceit, hypocrisy, jealousy, and all unkind speech. Like newborn babies, you must crave pure spiritual milk so that you will grow into a full experience of salvation.
**1 Peter 2:1-2 NLT**

Grow in the grace and knowledge of our Lord and Savior Jesus Christ. To Him be glory both now and forever! **2 Peter 3:18 NIV**

The church is about the building up, growth and development of our faith. Yes, first off it is about glorifying God's name and faith in God. But faith is about how we magnetically live out and share our relationship with Christ with others. Growth and development are linked to witnessing about Jesus, and doing the right things in brotherly love in His name. Faith is always lived upwards, otherwise it dies.

# Losing Faith

"Anyone who loves their father or mother more than Me is not worthy of Me; anyone who loves their son or daughter more than Me is not worthy of Me. Whoever does not take up their cross and follow Me is not worthy of Me. Whoever finds their life will lose it, and whoever loses their life for My sake will find it. Anyone who welcomes you welcomes, and anyone who welcomes Me welcomes the one who sent Me." Matthew 10:37-40 NIV

For the one who sows to his own flesh will from the flesh reap corruption, but the one who sows to the Spirit will from the Spirit reap eternal life. Galatians 6:8 ESV

When He had called the people to Himself, with His disciples also, He said to them, "Whoever desires to come after Me, let him deny himself, and take up his cross, and follow Me. For whoever desires to save his life will lose it, but whoever loses his life for My sake and the gospel's will save it." Mark 8:34-35 NKJV

"Stop doubting and believe." John 20:27 NIV

Then Jesus told him, "You believe because you have seen Me. Blessed are those who believe without seeing Me." John 20:29 NLT

To lose is … well to lose! Everyone knows the feeling. That is why winning is so important. Everyone wants to be in the front of the line. Yet, you can't win before you've lost a few times. You need to lose yourself in order to find yourself. That is what Jesus said. Whoever loses his life for the sake of God, gain in it. If you do not feel up to it, you'll lose, even though you're winning!

# Love Has a Name: Jesus!

Love never gives up, never loses faith, is always hopeful, and endures through every circumstance.

1 Corinthians 13:7 NLT

Beloved, let us love one another, for love is of God; and everyone who loves is born of God and knows God. He who does not love does not know God, for God is love. In this the love of God was manifested toward us, that God has sent His only begotten Son into the world, that we might live through Him. In this is love, not that we loved God, but that He loved us and sent His Son to be the propitiation for our sins.

1 John 4:7-10 NKJV

By this we know love, that He laid down His life for us, and we ought to lay down our lives for the brothers.

1 John 3:16 ESV

Whoever believes that Jesus is the Christ is born of God, and everyone who loves Him who begot also loves him who is begotten of Him.

1 John 5:1 NKJV

The Word became human and made His home among us. He was full of unfailing love and faithfulness. And we have seen His glory, the glory of the Father's one and only Son.

John 1:14 NLT

God is love. It is a concise and very powerful way of presenting Himself to us. He defined what love is all about. God's love is unselfish and sacrificial. His love has a Name: Jesus Christ. Jesus showed us what godly love looks like when He gave up His life as a ransom for many. God invites us to emulate this same love where we gave ourselves as living sacrifices in His service.

# Every Man's Battle

"But I say to you that everyone who looks at a woman with lustful intent has already committed adultery with her in his heart."
**Matthew 5:28 ESV**

Put to death, therefore, whatever belongs to your earthly nature: sexual immorality, impurity, lust, evil desires and greed, which is idolatry.
**Colossians 3:5 NIV**

Dear friends, I warn you as "temporary residents and foreigners" to keep away from worldly desires that wage war against your very souls.
**1 Peter 2:11 NLT**

For all that is in the world – the lust of the flesh, the lust of the eyes, and the pride of life – is not of the Father but is of the world.
**1 John 2:16 NKJV**

For lust is a shameful sin, a crime that should be punished. **Job 31:11 NLT**

He said, "What comes out of a person is what defiles him. For from within, out of the heart of man, come evil thoughts, sexual immorality, theft, murder, adultery, coveting, wickedness, deceit, sensuality, envy, slander, pride, foolishness. All these evil things come from within, and they defile a person."
**Mark 7:20-23 ESV**

Stay away from improper sexual desires. Don't fall prey to pornography. Avoid those office parties or nightclubs where lust is the order of the day. Let God guard your heart from these sinful desires. Allow Him to shift your focus to where it is supposed to be at, on Him, and ask Him to make you holy. Love your wife and bypass those sinful desires of the flesh. Then your life will be pure and holy, as God requires of us.

# The Meaning of Marriage

"And if she divorces her husband and marries another man, she commits adultery."
**Mark 10:12 NIV**

The wife gives authority over her body to her husband, and the husband gives authority over his body to his wife.
**1 Corinthians 7:4 NLT**

However, let each one of you love his wife as himself, and let the wife see that she respects her husband.
**Ephesians 5:33 ESV**

Love each other with genuine affection, and take delight in honoring each other.
**Romans 12:10 NLT**

For He who said, "Do not commit adultery," also said, "Do not murder." Now if you do not commit adultery, but you do murder, you have become a transgressor of the law. **James 2:11 NKJV**

Now to the married I command, yet not I but the Lord: A wife is not to depart from her husband. But even if she does depart, let her remain unmarried or be reconciled to her husband. And a husband is not to divorce his wife. **1 Corinthians 7:10-11 NKJV**

A wife of noble character is her husband's crown.
**Proverbs 12:4 NIV**

God is the Author of marriage. It was His invention. To choose marriage is to choose God's way. In marriage, as God intended it, there is only space for each other. Husband and wife love each other unconditionally. They give themselves to each other. Men love their wives deeply, and women act with a heart of servitude in marriage. Third parties have no place there.

# For the Love of Money

But his sons did not follow his ways. They turned aside after dishonest gain and accepted bribes and perverted justice. 1 Samuel 8:3 NIV

For the iniquity of his covetousness I was angry and struck him; I hid and was angry, and he went on backsliding in the way of his heart. Isaiah 57:17 NKJV

Do not love the world or the things in the world. If anyone loves the world, the love of the Father is not in him. For all that is in the world – the desires of the flesh and the desires of the eyes and pride of life – is not from the Father but is from the world. 1 John 2:15-16 ESV

Yet true godliness with contentment is itself great wealth. After all, we brought nothing with us when we came into the world, and we can't take anything with us when we leave it.
1 Timothy 6:6-7 NLT

If someone has enough money to live well and sees a brother or sister in need but shows no compassion – how can God's love be in that person? 1 John 3:17 NLT

The love of money is a root of all kinds of evils. It is through this craving that some have wandered away from the faith and pierced themselves with many pangs.
1 Timothy 6:10 ESV

Materialism and greed go hand in hand. To always want more and more stuff, is to fall into the trap of a sinful attitude towards life. Materialism pulls your attention away from the Lord and focuses on earthly possessions. Then it happens that you are never satisfied with what you have. There is always something else that you want or need. Don't become a slave of a material world. It robs you of your freedom in Christ.

# Make Every Meal a Festive One

"Imagine it! You set before them as a sacrifice the choice flour, olive oil, and honey I had given you," says the Sovereign LORD.
**Ezekiel 16:19 NLT**

Then he said to them, "Go your way. Eat the fat and drink sweet wine and send portions to anyone who has nothing ready, for this day is holy to our Lord. And do not be grieved, for the joy of the LORD is your strength."
**Nehemiah 8:10 ESV**

They worshiped together at the Temple each day, met in homes for the Lord's Supper, and shared their meals with great joy and generosity. **Acts 2:46 NLT**

Be silent before the Sovereign LORD, for the day of the LORD is near. The LORD has prepared a sacrifice; He has consecrated those He has invited.
**Zephaniah 1:7 NIV**

Now when he had brought them into his house, he set food before them; and he rejoiced, having believed in God with all his household.
**Acts 16:34 NKJV**

"Behold, I stand at the door and knock. If anyone hears My voice and opens the door, I will come in to him and eat with him, and he with Me."
**Revelation 3:20 ESV**

God is involved in all our meals too. He wants to eat and feast with us every day. He is the Guest of Honor at every meal. He also wants to break bread with us, as the Lord of the feast. He longs to be invited in, so that the true Feast can commence. He wants the honorary seat at each table, so that the Bread of Life can also be shared. Receive Him as the Lord at every meal.

# The Measure of a Man

A ten-acre vineyard will produce only a bath of wine; a homer of seed will yield only an ephah of grain.
**Isaiah 5:10 NIV**

Give, and you will receive. Your gift will return to you in full – pressed down, shaken together to make room for more, running over, and poured into your lap. The amount you give will determine the amount you get back.
**Luke 6:38 NLT**

And of His fullness we have all received, and grace for grace.
**John 1:16 NKJV**

He saved us, not because of works done by us in righteousness, but according to His own mercy, by the washing of regeneration and renewal of the Holy Spirit, whom He poured out on us richly through Jesus Christ our Savior.
**Titus 3:5-6 ESV**

Praise the LORD! Oh, give thanks to the LORD, for He is good! For His mercy endures forever. Who can utter the mighty acts of the LORD? Who can declare all His praise?
**Psalm 106:1-2 NKJV**

Measuring plays a big role in our lives. We buy items in measured metered units. Milk, soft drinks, gas, and water are bought in gallons, and meat is sold per gram. God's grace is often described as immeasurable. It is so great and overwhelming that no earthly metric unit can be used to measure it. It overflows unto us. God's goodness for us is unending; it can never be used up.

# The God of Second Chances

The LORD passed before him and proclaimed, "The LORD, the LORD God, merciful and gracious, longsuffering, and abounding in goodness and truth."

Exodus 34:6 NKJV

Have mercy on me, O God, according to Your steadfast love; according to Your abundant mercy blot out my transgressions.

Psalm 51:1 ESV

Hear the word of the LORD, O people of Israel! The LORD has brought charges against you, saying: "There is no faithfulness, no kindness, no knowledge of God in your land."

Hosea 4:1 NLT

Therefore, as God's chosen people, holy and dearly loved, clothe yourselves with compassion, kindness, humility, gentleness and patience.

Colossians 3:12 NIV

The steadfast love of the LORD never ceases; His mercies never come to an end; they are new every morning; great is Your faithfulness.

Lamentations 3:22-23 ESV

The Mighty One has done great things for me – holy is His name. His mercy extends to those who fear Him, from generation to generation.

Luke 1:49-50 NIV

To have mercy on someone concerns matters of the heart. God's heart is filled with compassion for us. He cares. He feels sorry for us. He starts fresh and He starts over with each one whom He cares for. We walk in His steps. That is why we also give second chances. We have mercy on people who suffer and endure hardships. Our hearts are not hardened and our hands are open to serve. We don't allow our hearts to calcify with bitterness and unlovingness.

# Ministering Like a Master

"The Spirit of the Lord is upon me, because He has anointed me to proclaim good news to the poor. He has sent me to proclaim liberty to the captives and recovering of sight to the blind, to set at liberty those who are oppressed."
**Luke 4:18 ESV**

As was his custom, Paul went into the synagogue, and on three Sabbath days he reasoned with them from the Scriptures, explaining and proving that the Messiah had to suffer and rise from the dead. "This Jesus I am proclaiming to you is the Messiah," he said.
**Acts 17:2-3 NIV**

And how shall they preach unless they are sent? As it is written: "How beautiful are the feet of those who preach the gospel of peace, who bring glad tidings of good things!"
**Romans 10:15 NKJV**

Since God in His wisdom saw to it that the world would never know Him through human wisdom, He has used our foolish preaching to save those who believe.
**1 Corinthians 1:21 NLT**

Of this gospel I was made a minister according to the gift of God's grace.
**Ephesians 3:7 ESV**

Christianity is about constant growth and learning. The gospel is revealed through talking and preaching. Ministering is to practically set out God's Word for the people. Through sermons, faith works in our hearts, as Paul wrote. Our faith is also deepened in this way. That is why it is important to often visit places where God's Word is preached. Hear the Word, hide it in your heart, and then go out and apply it practically. Then ministering is bearing good fruits.

# The Christian Mind

Jesus replied: "Love the Lord your God with all your heart and with all your soul and with all your mind."
**Matthew 22:37 NIV**

Is there any encouragement from belonging to Christ? Any comfort from His love? Any fellowship together in the Spirit? Are your hearts tender and compassionate?
**Philippians 2:1 NLT**

Therefore, preparing your minds for action, and being sober-minded, set your hope fully on the grace that will be brought to you at the revelation of Jesus Christ.
**1 Peter 1:13 ESV**

Be sober, be vigilant; because your adversary the devil walks about like a roaring lion, seeking whom he may devour.
**1 Peter 5:8 NKJV**

Then you will experience God's peace, which exceeds anything we can understand. His peace will guard your hearts and minds as you live in Christ Jesus. And now, dear brothers and sisters, one final thing. Fix your thoughts on what is true, and honorable, and right, and pure, and lovely, and admirable. Think about things that are excellent and worthy of praise.
**Philippians 4:7-8 NLT**

Our thoughts matter to the Lord. He wants us to serve Him with our mind. He asks us to have an open mind. We must think, and think correctly so that the things of God take precedence in our minds. It means we have to purposefully will our wandering thoughts back to God and refocus on God. We must love Him with our thoughts, not only our emotions.

# Follow His Instructions

Two things I ask of You, LORD; do not refuse me before I die: keep falsehood and lies far from me; give me neither poverty nor riches, but give me only my daily bread.
**Proverbs 30:7-8 NIV**

For the land is full of adulterers; for because of a curse the land mourns. The pleasant places of the wilderness are dried up. Their course of life is evil, and their might is not right.
**Jeremiah 23:10 NKJV**

Bless those who curse you. Pray for those who hurt you.
**Luke 6:28 NLT**

Let us purify ourselves from everything that contaminates body and spirit, perfecting holiness out of reverence for God.
**2 Corinthians 7:1 NIV**

In your hearts revere Christ as Lord. Always be prepared to give an answer to everyone who asks you to give the reason for the hope that you have. But do this with gentleness and respect.
**1 Peter 3:15 NIV**

You shall not take the name of the LORD your God in vain, for the LORD will not hold him guiltless who takes His name in vain.
**Exodus 20:7 ESV**

New appliances come with instructions. You need to read and do what it says. Otherwise, your new appliance is going to be used wrong. In the same way we must make sure to follow God's instructions. His Name is on our lips. We need to know His will, so that we don't misuse Him for our benefit. God is holy, and we need to live with great reverence and caution in His presence.

# The Potter's Hands

The earth was formless and empty, and darkness covered the deep waters. And the Spirit of God was hovering over the surface of the waters.
**Genesis 1:2 NLT**

Therefore watch yourselves very carefully. Since you saw no form on the day that the LORD spoke to you at Horeb out of the midst of the fire, beware lest you act corruptly by making a carved image for yourselves, in the form of any figure, the likeness of male or female.
**Deuteronomy 4:15-16 ESV**

"O my dove, in the clefts of the rock, in the secret places of the cliff, let me see your face, let me hear your voice; for your voice is sweet, and your face is lovely."
**Song of Songs 2:14 NKJV**

I looked, and I saw the likeness of a throne of lapis lazuli above the vault that was over the heads of the cherubim.
**Ezekiel 10:1 NIV**

You, LORD, are our Father. We are the clay, You are the potter; we are all the work of Your hand.
**Isaiah 64:8 NIV**

Shapelessness is lifelessness. God gives shape to everything. He changed a shapeless eternity into Creation. He shaped everything through His mighty words. Yet God's shape can't be captured in human forms or shapes. We are created in God's image. We reflect His image when we live and act in honor of His name.

# Manage Your Money Well

He who loves money will not be satisfied with money, nor he who loves wealth with his income; this also is vanity. **Ecclesiastes 5:10 ESV**

Come, all you who are thirsty, come to the waters; and you who have no money, come, buy and eat! Come, buy wine and milk without money and without cost. **Isaiah 55:1 NIV**

"No servant can serve two masters; for either he will hate the one and love the other, or else he will be loyal to the one and despise the other. You cannot serve God and mammon." **Luke 16:13 NKJV**

Don't love money; be satisfied with what you have. For God has said, "I will never fail you. I will never abandon you." **Hebrews 13:5 NLT**

Command those who are rich in this present world not to be arrogant nor to put their hope in wealth, which is so uncertain, but to put their hope in God, who richly provides us with everything for our enjoyment. Command them to do good, to be rich in good deeds, and to be generous and willing to share. **1 Timothy 6:17-18 NIV**

Money can be either good or bad. It depends in whose hands it is. Or should I rather say, in whose heart! When money is your master, you're the slave. But when you use money to serve God and others, then you are free. Then at a certain point, enough becomes enough. And you are free to share your money with others. Then you're not always trying to save every penny while you choke in your greediness.

# A Messy Matter of Motives

Examine me, O LORD, and prove me; try my mind and my heart. **Psalm 26:2 NKJV**

All a person's ways seem pure to them, but motives are weighed by the LORD. **Proverbs 16:2 NIV**

So don't make judgments about anyone ahead of time – before the Lord returns. For He will bring our darkest secrets to light and will reveal our private motives. Then God will give to each one whatever praise is due. **1 Corinthians 4:5 NLT**

"I, the LORD, search all hearts and examine secret motives." **Jeremiah 17:10 NLT**

For our boast is this, the testimony of our conscience, that we behaved in the world with simplicity and godly sincerity, not by earthly wisdom but by the grace of God, and supremely so toward you. **2 Corinthians 1:12 ESV**

For the appeal we make does not spring from error or impure motives, nor are we trying to trick you. On the contrary, we speak as those approved by God to be entrusted with the gospel. We are not trying to please people but God, who tests our hearts. **1 Thessalonians 2:3-4 NIV**

Our motives are those deep inner motivations or reasons behind our behaviors, as well as our emotions and words. Impure motives cause us to act differently to our inner convictions. Therefore, we must pray that God test the motives of our hearts and purify them. We need to plead with God to keep our hearts and thoughts pure and clean. Then our actions will automatically follow suit. Then our motives are purified by God.

# Dealing with Grief

As soon as I heard these words I sat down and wept and mourned for days, and I continued fasting and praying before the God of heaven.
**Nehemiah 1:4 ESV**

A time to weep, and a time to laugh; a time to mourn, and a time to dance.
**Ecclesiastes 3:4 NKJV**

"The LORD roars from Zion and thunders from Jerusalem; the pastures of the shepherds dry up, and the top of Carmel withers."
**Amos 1:2 NIV**

God blesses those who mourn, for they will be comforted.
**Matthew 5:4 NLT**

And I heard a loud voice from the throne saying, "Behold, the dwelling place of God is with man. He will dwell with them, and they will be His people, and God Himself will be with them as their God. He will wipe away every tear from their eyes, and death shall be no more, neither shall there be mourning, nor crying, nor pain anymore, for the former things have passed away." **Revelation 21:3-4 ESV**

I love the LORD, because He has heard my voice and my supplications. Because He has inclined His ear to me, therefore I will call upon Him as long as I live.
**Psalm 116:1-2 NKJV**

Do you know grief that throws you completely off balance? Death, serious illness of a loved one; a broken relationship, or sadness about how your life turned out before God? Mourning is necessary. We can't laugh while our hearts cry. We don't have to. We don't need to be strong all the time. Men are allowed to cry. We can share our grief with God. He will understand.

# Make Music for God

Then Miriam the prophet, Aaron's sister, took a timbrel in her hand, and all the women followed her, with timbrels and dancing.
**Exodus 15:20 NIV**

And whenever the tormenting spirit from God troubled Saul, David would play the harp. Then Saul would feel better, and the tormenting spirit would go away.
**1 Samuel 16:23 NLT**

Come, let us sing for joy to the LORD; let us shout aloud to the Rock of our salvation. Let us come before Him with thanksgiving and extol Him with music and song.
**Psalm 95:1-2 NIV**

Now these are the men whom David appointed over the service of song in the house of the LORD, after the ark came to rest. They were ministering with music before the dwelling place of the tabernacle of meeting, until Solomon had built the house of the LORD in Jerusalem, and they served in their office according to their order. **1 Chronicles 6:31-32 NKJV**

Sing joyfully to the LORD, you righteous; it is fitting for the upright to praise Him. Praise the LORD with the harp; make music to Him on the ten-stringed lyre. Sing to Him a new song; play skillfully, and shout for joy.
**Psalm 33:1-3 NIV**

Without music life is dull. Music gives meaning to our existence. Therefore music also forms an integral part of our faith. To sing and make music with a sincere heart in God's presence make Him glad. That is why we need to be joyful before Him. Our voices and our instruments lift His name on high. We glorify Him as we sing, dance and rejoice! That's what the Bible asks of us, and that's what we must enjoy doing.

# Covering Up Your Sinful Nature

And they were both naked, the man and his wife, and were not ashamed.
**Genesis 2:25 NKJV**

And he said, "Naked I came from my mother's womb, and naked shall I return. The LORD gave, and the LORD has taken away; blessed be the name of the LORD."
**Job 1:21 ESV**

Nothing in all creation is hidden from God. Everything is naked and exposed before His eyes, and He is the one to whom we are accountable.
**Hebrews 4:13 NLT**

"You say, 'I am rich; I have acquired wealth and do not need a thing.' But you do not realize that you are wretched, pitiful, poor, blind and naked."
**Revelation 3:17 NIV**

I acknowledged my sin to You, and I did not cover my iniquity; I said, "I will confess my transgressions to the LORD," and You forgave the iniquity of my sin.
**Psalm 32:5 ESV**

"You shall not go up by steps to My altar, that your nakedness be not exposed to it."
**Exodus 20:26 ESV**

Nudity is covered up. We know that since Adam and Eve's time. Sometimes people also cover their sinful lives with piety. Newsflash! God sees right through their disguises. He sees people as they really are. Therefore we shouldn't even try living hypocritical lives. We should confess our nakedness before God and allow Him to cover us with His forgiveness and grace.

# Lay Your Needs Before Him

But He said to me, "My grace is sufficient for you, for My power is made perfect in weakness." Therefore I will boast all the more gladly about my weaknesses, so that Christ's power may rest on me.

2 Corinthians 12:9 NIV

My God will supply every need of yours according to His riches in glory in Christ Jesus.

Philippians 4:19 ESV

So let us come boldly to the throne of our gracious God. There we will receive His mercy, and we will find grace to help us when we need it most.

Hebrews 4:16 NLT

Grace and peace be multiplied to you in the knowledge of God and of Jesus our Lord, as His divine power has given to us all things that pertain to life and godliness, through the knowledge of Him who called us by glory and virtue.

2 Peter 1:2-3 NKJV

For the Gentiles seek after all these things, and your heavenly Father knows that you need them all. But seek first the kingdom of God and His righteousness, and all these things will be added to you.

Matthew 6:32-33 ESV

We all experience times of crises at some point. During such times, God is our refuge. He invites us to know and acknowledge Him in our difficult times. We don't ask others to pray for us when we do nothing ourselves. No we call out to God first of all. We lay our deepest needs before His feet in faith. Then we can expect heavenly grace in abundance.

# Love Your Neighbor

"You shall not covet your neighbor's house; you shall not covet your neighbor's wife, nor his male servant, nor his female servant, nor his ox, nor his donkey, nor anything that is your neighbor's." **Exodus 20:17 NKJV**

Do not say to your neighbor, "Go, and come again, tomorrow I will give it" – when you have it with you. Do not plan evil against your neighbor, who dwells trustingly beside you. **Proverbs 3:28-29 ESV**

For the whole law can be summed up in this one command: "Love your neighbor as yourself." **Galatians 5:14 NLT**

"Do not seek revenge or bear a grudge against anyone among your people, but love your neighbor as yourself. I am the LORD." **Leviticus 19:18 NIV**

"The second is this: 'You shall love your neighbor as yourself.' There is no other commandment greater than these." **Mark 12:31 ESV**

Don't just pretend to love others. Really love them. Hate what is wrong. Hold tightly to what is good. Love each other with genuine affection, and take delight in honoring each other. **Romans 12:9-10 NLT**

We don't go through life alone. We are constantly surrounded by other people. The Bible calls on us to be people-oriented. We must notice them. Moreover, we need to love them. It is the center of God's Law as Jesus explained to us. When we don't love others, then we lie to ourselves when we say that we love God. Brotherly love becomes visible when we show respect by providing in the physical needs of the destitute.

# God Renews Us Day by Day

"Behold, the days are coming," says the LORD, "when I will make a new covenant with the house of Israel and with the house of Judah."
**Jeremiah 31:31 NKJV**

"I will give you a new heart and put a new spirit in you; I will remove from you your heart of stone and give you a heart of flesh."
**Ezekiel 36:26 NIV**

That is why we never give up. Though our bodies are dying, our spirits are being renewed every day.
**2 Corinthians 4:16 NLT**

Therefore, if anyone is in Christ, he is a new creation. The old has passed away; behold, the new has come.
**2 Corinthians 5:17 ESV**

Don't lie to each other, for you have stripped off your old sinful nature and all its wicked deeds. Put on your new nature, and be renewed as you learn to know your Creator and become like Him. In this new life, it doesn't matter if you are a Jew or a Gentile, circumcised or uncircumcised, barbaric, uncivilized, slave, or free. Christ is all that matters, and He lives in all of us. **Colossians 3:9-11 NLT**

Everything has an expiry date here on earth. Nothing lasts forever. Wait, that's not completely true. God specializes in making people new. In His new Covenant He gives a new heart to every person who believes in Him. He renews and transforms His children every day through the mighty indwelling of His Holy Spirit. He starts over and He starts again. While everything around us gets older and perishes, we are being made new day after day.

# A Good Night's Rest

This Book of the Law shall not depart from your mouth, but you shall meditate in it day and night, that you may observe to do according to all that is written in it. For then you will make your way prosperous, and then you will have good success.
**Joshua 1:8 NKJV**

He will cover you with His feathers. He will shelter you with His wings. His faithful promises are your armor and protection. Do not be afraid of the terrors of the night, nor the arrow that flies in the day. Do not dread the disease that stalks in darkness, nor the disaster that strikes at midday.
**Psalm 91:4-6 NLT**

But the day of the Lord will come as unexpectedly as a thief. Then the heavens will pass away with a terrible noise, and the very elements themselves will disappear in fire, and the earth and everything on it will be found to deserve judgment.
**2 Peter 3:10 NLT**

"In my vision at night I looked, and there before me was one like a Son of Man, coming with the clouds of heaven. He approached the Ancient of Days and was led into His presence. **Daniel 7:13 NIV**

In peace I will lie down and sleep, for You alone, LORD, make me dwell in safety.
**Psalm 4:8 NIV**

Nighttime is sleep time. Trust God to give you a good night's rest. Go to sleep in peace in His arms. Also dedicate all your loved ones to His care, and sleep peacefully. Sometimes you will lie awake at night. Don't use the time to worry and fret about problems and troubles. Use the night as time to meditate on God. Fill your thoughts with the Lord during your sleepless hours.

# The Greatest Offering

Has the LORD as great delight in burnt offerings and sacrifices, as in obeying the voice of the LORD? Behold, to obey is better than sacrifice, and to heed than the fat of rams.
**1 Samuel 15:22 NKJV**

Don't copy the behavior and customs of this world, but let God transform you into a new person by changing the way you think. Then you will learn to know God's will for you, which is good and pleasing and perfect.
**Romans 12:2 NLT**

He is the atoning sacrifice for our sins, and not only for ours but also for the sins of the whole world. **1 John 2:2 NIV**

In this is love, not that we have loved God but that He loved us and sent His Son to be the propitiation for our sins.
**1 John 4:10 ESV**

Each one must give as he has decided in his heart, not reluctantly or under compulsion, for God loves a cheerful giver.
**2 Corinthians 9:7 ESV**

For what the law was powerless to do because it was weakened by the flesh, God did by sending His own Son in the likeness of sinful flesh to be a sin offering.
**Romans 8:3 NIV**

An offering is synonymous to a substitute taking the place of something or someone else. In the Bible, the greatest sacrifice was Christ Himself. He carried the burden of God's wrath in full on our behalf. On the cross, He took everything on Himself. His blood brought complete reconciliation between heaven and earth. The punishment has been taken away for everyone who puts their hope in Christ as their only Savior.

# An Older and Wiser You

When Abram was ninety-nine years old the LORD appeared to Abram and said to him, "I am God Almighty; walk before Me, and be blameless."
**Genesis 17:1 ESV**

Train up a child in the way he should go, and when he is old he will not depart from it. **Proverbs 22:6 NKJV**

The glory of the young is their strength; the gray hair of experience is the splendor of the old.
**Proverbs 20:29 NLT**

Do not cast me off in the time of old age; forsake me not when my strength is spent. **Psalm 71:9 ESV**

I am writing to you, fathers, because you know Him who is from the beginning. I am writing to you, young men, because you have overcome the evil one. I write to you, dear children, because you know the Father. I write to you, fathers, because you know Him who is from the beginning. I write to you, young men, because you are strong, and the word of God lives in you, and you have overcome the evil one.
**1 John 2:13-14 NIV**

Wisdom belongs to the aged, and understanding to the old. **Job 12:12 NLT**

To grow old means to become wiser according to Proverbs. Don't let age alone overpower you. Live wisely. How? Well, follow the instruction in 1 John 2 carefully. Believe your sins are forgiven, but also believe that your strength is found in God. You can and will remain standing as an example to the younger generation of how to live with peace, joy and wisdom. Let your godly character be the greatest legacy that you leave to your family one day!

AUGUST

*Delight*

**YOURSELF**

in the

**LORD,**

**& HE WILL**

give you the

**DESIRES**

of your

*heart.*

PSALM 37:4

# An Open Book

"I will deliver you from the Jewish people, as well as from the Gentiles, to whom I now send you, to open their eyes, in order to turn them from darkness to light, and from the power of Satan to God, that they may receive forgiveness of sins and an inheritance among those who are sanctified by faith in Me."

**Acts 26:17-18 NKJV**

Now a certain woman named Lydia heard us. She was a seller of purple from the city of Thyatira, who worshiped God. The Lord opened her heart to heed the things spoken by Paul.

**Acts 16:14 NKJV**

I saw the dead, both great and small, standing before God's throne. And the books were opened, including the Book of Life. And the dead were judged according to what they had done, as recorded in the books.

**Revelation 20:12 NLT**

"Worthy are you to take the scroll and to open its seals, for You were slain, and by Your blood You ransomed people for God from every tribe and language and people and nation, and You have made them a kingdom and priests to our God, and they shall reign on the earth."

**Revelation 5:9-10 ESV**

When a book is opened, the information contained in it is revealed. When God opens books then we know the day of Reckonings is here. Then He will give report on our lives. Well, John tells in Revelation 20:11-15 of books being opened, and people's deeds that have been recorded in them. The dead were judged according to what they had done, and the result is eternal death. There is another book called the Book of Life where all believers' names are recorded. They will inherit eternal life.

# Use Every Opportunity

For sin, taking occasion by the commandment, deceived me, and by it killed me.
**Romans 7:11 NKJV**

You, my brothers and sisters, were called to be free. But do not use your freedom to indulge the flesh; rather, serve one another humbly in love. **Galatians 5:13 NIV**

Therefore, whenever we have the opportunity, we should do good to everyone – especially to those in the family of faith.
**Galatians 6:10 NLT**

Walk in wisdom toward outsiders, making the best use of the time.
**Colossians 4:5 ESV**

Let each of you look not only to his own interests, but also to the interests of others.
**Philippians 2:4 ESV**

Bear one another's burdens, and so fulfill the law of Christ.
**Galatians 6:2 NKJV**

For where you have envy and selfish ambition, there you find disorder and every evil practice.
**James 3:16 NIV**

Chancers and opportunists are everywhere. They stand ready to exploit a situation to benefit themselves. Paul says that is exactly what sin did with God's Law. It creeped up unannounced and gave names to sin before the Law could prevent it. But now we live in Christ's dispensation. Now we are the ones taking chances. We grab hold of every opportunity to live lives that glorify Christ.

# Responding to Opposition

When Korah had gathered all his followers in opposition to them at the entrance to the tent of meeting, the glory of the LORD appeared to the entire assembly.
**Numbers 16:19 NIV**

For I delight in the law of God, in my inner being, but I see in my members another law waging war against the law of my mind and making me captive to the law of sin that dwells in my members.
**Romans 7:22-23 ESV**

God will hear, and afflict them, even He who abides from of old. Selah Because they do not change, therefore they do not fear God.
**Psalm 55:19 NKJV**

For the flesh lusts against the Spirit, and the Spirit against the flesh; and these are contrary to one another, so that you do not do the things that you wish.
**Galatians 5:17 NKJV**

Think of all the hostility He endured from sinful people; then you won't become weary and give up.
**Hebrews 12:3 NLT**

I do not understand what I do. For what I want to do I do not do, but what I hate I do.
**Romans 7:15 NIV**

We will always experience opposition in some or other area on earth. Sports teams, businesses, schools, universities, politics and many more follow the way of opposition. They make the saying "may the best man win" true in their lives. Believers will experience opposition, because the gospel is never neutral. That is why so many people oppose the Good News of God. There is also always a constant battle in us between our sinful desires and the Spirit. Make sure that you hide in the Spirit during such times.

# He Cares for the Widows and Orphans

He administers justice for the fatherless and the widow, and loves the stranger, giving him food and clothing. **Deuteronomy 10:18 NKJV**

But you do see, for you note mischief and vexation, that you may take it into your hands; to you the helpless commits himself; you have been the helper of the fatherless.
**Psalm 10:14 ESV**

Do not oppress the widow or the fatherless, the foreigner or the poor. Do not plot evil against each other.
**Zechariah 7:10 NIV**

Pure and genuine religion in the sight of God the Father means caring for orphans and widows in their distress and refusing to let the world corrupt you.
**James 1:27 NLT**

Don't cheat your neighbor by moving the ancient boundary markers; don't take the land of defenseless orphans. For their Redeemer is strong; He Himself will bring their charges against you.
**Proverbs 23:10-11 NLT**

"I will not leave you as orphans; I will come to you."
**John 14:18 ESV**

Widows and orphans are always on God's radar in the Bible. They were especially vulnerable in those days because they didn't have a husband or parents to care for them. But God cares for such people. He expects of us to do the same. His heart breaks for poor defenseless people like orphans. Let's do the same and have mercy and compassion for at least one orphaned child. Get involved at a children's home. There are many ways to help out.

# Stand Strong

But Caleb quieted the people before Moses and said, "Let us go up at once and occupy it, for we are well able to overcome it."
**Numbers 13:30 ESV**

"And I tell you that you are Peter, and on this rock I will build My church, and the gates of Hades will not overcome it."
**Matthew 16:18 NIV**

No, despite all these things, overwhelming victory is ours through Christ, who loved us.
**Romans 8:37 NLT**

The LORD is my rock and my fortress and my deliverer ... my shield, my stronghold.
**Psalm 18:2 ESV**

These will make war with the Lamb, and the Lamb will overcome them, for He is Lord of lords and King of kings; and those who are with Him are called, chosen, and faithful."
**Revelation 17:14 NKJV**

And they have conquered him by the blood of the Lamb and by the word of their testimony, for they loved not their lives even unto death.
**Revelation 12:11 ESV**

The LORD will conquer your enemies when they attack you. They will attack you from one direction, but they will scatter from you in seven! **Deuteronomy 28:7 NLT**

To occupy or take over a city is to know that victory has been gained. Newsflash! God won. It has been sealed and guaranteed. Not even the gates of Hades could stand in the way of Christ or anyone who confesses that He is Lord. For that reason we can take over fortresses and overcome strongholds in His name. We can gain the victory. We are more than conquerors in Christ, now and forevermore!

# Walking with God Through Pain

"I will make your pains in childbearing very severe; with painful labor you will give birth to children. Your desire will be for your husband, and he will rule over you."
**Genesis 3:16 NIV**

Surely He has borne our griefs and carried our sorrows; yet we esteemed Him stricken, smitten by God, and afflicted.
**Isaiah 53:4 NKJV**

Such love has no fear, because perfect love expels all fear. If we are afraid, it is for fear of punishment, and this shows that we have not fully experienced His perfect love. **1 John 4:18 NLT**

He will wipe away every tear from their eyes, and death shall be no more, neither shall there be mourning, nor crying, nor pain anymore, for the former things have passed away."
**Revelation 21:4 ESV**

He was the one who prayed to the God of Israel, "Oh, that You would bless me and expand my territory! Please be with me in all that I do, and keep me from all trouble and pain!" And God granted him his request.
**1 Chronicles 4:10 NLT**

But I am afflicted and in pain; let Your salvation, O God, set me on high!
**Psalm 69:29 ESV**

Pain is something we all have to endure at some point. Physical, emotional and psychological pain is part life this side of heaven. Yet there is ointment to put on every wound and every hurt. God Himself guarantees His presence to each person caught in pain and suffering. Pray to Him for relief and a way out of your pain. God is the great Physician. Trust Him with this.

# Made for Paradise

Your shoots are an orchard of pomegranates with all choicest fruits, henna with nard.
**Song of Songs 4:13 ESV**

They gave Him a piece of broiled fish, and He took it and ate it in their presence.
**Luke 24:43 NIV**

Yes, only God knows whether I was in my body or outside my body. But I do know that I was caught up to paradise and heard things so astounding that they cannot be expressed in words, things no human is allowed to tell.
**2 Corinthians 12:3-4 NLT**

"He who has an ear, let him hear what the Spirit says to the churches. To him who overcomes I will give to eat from the tree of life, which is in the midst of the Paradise of God."
**Revelation 2:7 NKJV**

"Blessed are the peacemakers, for they shall be called sons of God. Blessed are those who are persecuted for righteousness' sake, for theirs is the kingdom of heaven."
**Matthew 5:9-10 NKJV**

"Truly, I say to you, today you will be with Me in Paradise."
**Luke 23:43 ESV**

Paradise is synonymous with heaven. It is God's eternal address. It is also His final address. God prepares a place for us in His eternal dwelling place. Here on earth we are only passing through. We should not pitch our tents and get too comfortable here. We are travelers underway to paradise. Our God's eternal Garden awaits us. There we will walk and live forever in His presence.

# The Stories Jesus Told

Then He spoke many things to them in parables.
**Matthew 13:3 NKJV**

He taught them many things by parables. **Mark 4:2 NIV**

The man wanted to justify his actions, so he asked Jesus, "And who is my neighbor?" Jesus replied with a story: "A Jewish man was traveling from Jerusalem down to Jericho, and he was attacked by bandits. They stripped him of his clothes, beat him up, and left him half dead beside the road."
**Luke 10:29-30 NLT**

Because of His words many more became believers.
**John 4:41 NIV**

He also told this parable to some who trusted in themselves that they were righteous, and treated others with contempt.
**Luke 18:9 ESV**

"This is why I speak to them in parables, because seeing they do not see, and hearing they do not hear, nor do they understand."
**Matthew 13:13 ESV**

All Scripture is God-breathed and is useful for teaching, rebuking, correcting and training in righteousness.
**2 Timothy 3:16 NIV**

They believed the Scripture and the words that Jesus had spoken. **John 2:22 NIV**

Jesus is a master storyteller. His stories, or parables, as we know them, open up new windows to God's Kingdom. Through His stories He gives us a glimpse to how God's Kingdom works, which principles and standards apply and how we become partakers. Don't take Jesus' words lightly. They are life changing. Read His words with the expectation to meet with God every time, then you'll understand what I mean.

# Dare to Discipline

Impress them on your children. Talk about them when you sit at home and when you walk along the road, when you lie down and when you get up.
**Deuteronomy 6:7 NIV**

Think about it: Just as a parent disciplines a child, the LORD your God disciplines you for your own good.
**Deuteronomy 8:5 NLT**

My son, hear the instruction of your father, and do not forsake the law of your mother. **Proverbs 1:8 NKJV**

Correct your son, and he will give you rest; yes, he will give delight to your soul.
**Proverbs 29:17 NKJV**

Fathers, do not provoke your children to anger, but bring them up in the discipline and instruction of the Lord.
**Ephesians 6:4 ESV**

Fathers, do not aggravate your children, or they will become discouraged.
**Colossians 3:21 NLT**

Do not withhold discipline from a child; if you strike him with a rod, he will not die.
**Proverbs 23:13 ESV**

Children are a gift from the LORD; they are a reward from Him.
**Psalm 127:3 NLT**

Parenting is not child's play. It requires bucketfuls of mercy and wisdom. Yet the most important thing we can ever teach our children is to serve God with their whole lives. We are raising children for the Lord. We pray day and night for them. We love them. We discipline and teach them. We forgive them over and over. We carry their pain in our hearts, and we delight ourselves in their joys. We are also there for them.

# The Power of Patience

Rejoice in hope, be patient in tribulation, be constant in prayer.
**Romans 12:12 ESV**

He who is slow to anger is better than the mighty, and he who rules his spirit than he who takes a city.
**Proverbs 16:32 NKJV**

Love is patient and kind. Love is not jealous or boastful or proud or rude. It does not demand its own way. It is not irritable, and it keeps no record of being wronged.
**1 Corinthians 13:4-5 NLT**

The Holy Spirit produces this kind of fruit in our lives: love, joy, peace, patience, kindness, goodness, faithfulness, gentleness, and self-control.
**Galatians 5:22-23 NLT**

Then Isaiah said, "Hear now, you house of David! Is it not enough to try the patience of humans? Will you try the patience of my God also?"
**Isaiah 7:13 NIV**

Teach the older men to exercise self-control, to be worthy of respect, and to live wisely. They must have sound faith and be filled with love and patience.
**Titus 2:2 NLT**

Patience is a rare characteristic. Patience grows in relationships. When we learn to see others with the same love that Christ looks at us, then He enables us to treat and accept others with kindness. Then we open our hearts to them and become blind to their shortcomings, mistakes and flaws. Because God is patient with us, we can also treat others with the necessary patience.

# Pursuing Peace

But He was wounded for our transgressions, He was bruised for our iniquities; the chastisement for our peace was upon Him, and by His stripes we are healed.
**Isaiah 53:5 NKJV**

"Don't imagine that I came to bring peace to the earth! I came not to bring peace, but a sword." **Matthew 10:34 NLT**

Grace and peace to you from God our Father and the Lord Jesus Christ.
**2 Corinthians 1:2 NIV**

Work at living in peace with everyone, and work at living a holy life, for those who are not holy will not see the Lord. **Hebrews 12:14 NLT**

Now the fruit of righteousness is sown in peace by those who make peace.
**James 3:18 NKJV**

"Glory to God in highest heaven, and peace on earth to those with whom God is pleased."
**Luke 2:14 NLT**

Now may the Lord of peace Himself give you peace at all times in every way. The Lord be with you all.
**2 Thessalonians 3:16 ESV**

They must turn from evil and do good; they must seek peace and pursue it.
**1 Peter 3:11 NIV**

Shalom and Eirene … these are the Hebrew and Greek words for peace. God's peace is the all-encompassing peace of the heart and mind. God establishes this peace with us. Jesus is the peace offering on our behalf. Jesus built the bridge between God and us. He is our peace. The war is over. The fighting is done. Now we live passionately from God's grace and goodness. His ceasefire is the Source of our life.

# Persecuted Because of Your Faith

"Blessed are those who are persecuted for righteousness' sake, for theirs is the kingdom of heaven."
**Matthew 5:10 NKJV**

"Then they will deliver you up to tribulation and put you to death, and you will be hated by all nations for My name's sake."
**Matthew 24:9 ESV**

On that day a great persecution broke out against the church in Jerusalem, and all except the apostles were scattered throughout Judea and Samaria.
**Acts 8:1 NIV**

Rejoice in our confident hope. Be patient in trouble, and keep on praying.
**Romans 12:12 NLT**

Attend to my cry, for I am brought very low; deliver me from my persecutors, for they are stronger than I. Bring my soul out of prison, that I may praise Your name; the righteous shall surround me, for You shall deal bountifully with me.
**Psalm 142:6-8 NKJV**

Indeed, all who desire to live a godly life in Christ Jesus will be persecuted.
**2 Timothy 3:12 ESV**

Persecution is sometimes what awaits God's children. We're not always the flavor of the week or month. When we live against the stream, then others might get annoyed or upset. And sometimes people can get insulting, and in many places on earth it can result in physical persecution. Christ, however, will never forsake His disciples. During such times, He is still with His church.

# The Practice of Piety

But select from all the people some capable, honest men who fear God and hate bribes. Appoint them as leaders over groups of one thousand, one hundred, fifty, and ten.
**Exodus 18:21 NLT**

There was a man in the land of Uz, whose name was Job; and that man was blameless and upright, and one who feared God and shunned evil. **Job 1:1 NKJV**

Now there was a man in Jerusalem called Simeon, who was righteous and devout. He was waiting for the consolation of Israel, and the Holy Spirit was on him.
**Luke 2:25 NIV**

One who heard us was a woman named Lydia, from the city of Thyatira, a seller of purple goods, who was a worshiper of God. The Lord opened her heart to pay attention to what was said by Paul. **Acts 16:14 ESV**

"Not everyone who says to Me, 'Lord, Lord,' will enter the kingdom of heaven, but the one who does the will of My Father who is in heaven."
**Matthew 7:21 ESV**

Love the LORD your God with all your heart and with all your soul and with all your strength.
**Deuteronomy 6:5 NIV**

Godly people are people with a holy fear of God. They serve the Lord with all their heart. Their lives are proof that they know Him. Holiness is not mere talk in their lives; it is a way of living. They put the Lord first in their eating, sleeping, working, and relationships … They walk their talk! Make sure that you live holy and pious before God. Then you will get noticed in the right Place.

# A Pillar of Strength

Lot's wife looked back as she was following behind him, and she turned into a pillar of salt. Genesis 19:26 NLT

By day You led them with a pillar of cloud, and by night with a pillar of fire to give them light on the way they were to take. Nehemiah 9:12 NIV

Behold, I make you this day a fortified city, an iron pillar, and bronze walls, against the whole land, against the kings of Judah, its officials, its priests, and the people of the land. Jeremiah 1:18 ESV

"On these two commandments depend all the Law and the Prophets."
Matthew 22:40 ESV

He who overcomes, I will make him a pillar in the temple of My God, and he shall go out no more. I will write on him the name of My God and the name of the city of My God, the New Jerusalem, which comes down out of heaven from My God. And I will write on him My new name.
Revelation 3:12 NKJV

If I am delayed, you will know how people ought to conduct themselves in God's household, which is the church of the living God, the pillar and foundation of the truth.
1 Timothy 3:15 NIV

A pillar is strong and steadfast. Heavy weight is resting on it. Pillars keep large buildings from collapsing. But you don't only find pillars in big buildings or temples; people can also be pillars of strength. Those who build their lives on God Almighty, are like pillars. They stand firm. Storms can come, but they won't falter. Suffering doesn't get them down. The Lord is their rock. Therefore they stand like pillars for God until the very end. They will continue to do so in eternity.

# God's Master Plan

The heart of man plans his way, but the LORD establishes his step.
**Proverbs 16:9 ESV**

I have a plan for the whole earth, a hand of judgment upon all the nations. The LORD of Heaven's Armies has spoken – who can change His plans? When His hand is raised, who can stop Him?"
**Isaiah 14:26-27 NLT**

This man was handed over to you by God's deliberate plan and foreknowledge; and you, with the help of wicked men, put Him to death by nailing Him to the cross.
**Acts 2:23 NIV**

For I have not shunned to declare to you the whole counsel of God.
**Acts 20:27 NKJV**

Now all glory to God, who is able to make you strong, just as my Good News says. This message about Jesus Christ has revealed His plan for you Gentiles, a plan kept secret from the beginning of time.
**Romans 16:25 NLT**

They spoke about His departure, which He was about to bring to fulfillment at Jerusalem.
**Luke 9:31 NIV**

God's plan is to save the entire universe. His plan is not a secret. In Scripture He reveals His plans. No, God's plans are not to work out a little detailed life plan for each person on earth. His plan is that every human on earth will join in His plan of salvation. In other words, it's not about God's plan for our lives, but about His Master Plan and how we will join in with our lives!

# Cry Out to Him

"Therefore I bring charges against you again," declares the LORD. "And I will bring charges against your children's children."
**Jeremiah 2:9 NIV**

I will bear the indignation of the LORD, because I have sinned against Him, until He pleads my case and executes justice for me. He will bring me forth to the light; I will see His righteousness.
**Micah 7:9 NKJV**

Then Peter continued preaching for a long time, strongly urging all his listeners, "Save yourselves from this crooked generation!"
**Acts 2:40 NLT**

Therefore, we are ambassadors for Christ, God making His appeal through us. We implore you on behalf of Christ, be reconciled to God.
**2 Corinthians 5:20 ESV**

Evening, morning and noon I cry out in distress, and He hears my voice.
**Psalm 55:17 NIV**

Though I were innocent, I could not answer Him; I could only plead with my Judge for mercy.
**Job 9:15 NIV**

For we hold that one is justified by faith apart from works of the law.
**Romans 3:28 ESV**

To plead is to seek grace with your entire being. When you bow down low before God like this, then you're desperate for a way out. Then you put your whole life on the line. He is not deaf or blind. He hears when we're down and out before Him. With this same determination we should plead with others to give their lives to God. Our hearts should cry out to a lost world.

# Pleading and Praying

"So do not pray for this people, or lift up a cry or prayer for them; for I will not hear them in the time that they cry out to Me because of their trouble."
**Jeremiah 11:14 NKJV**

LORD, You always give me justice when I bring a case before You. So let me bring you this complaint: Why are the wicked so prosperous? Why are evil people so happy?
**Jeremiah 12:1 NLT**

With many other words he warned them; and he pleaded with them, "Save yourselves from this corrupt generation."
**Acts 2:40 NIV**

"And now entreat the favor of God, that He may be gracious to us. With such a gift from your hand, will He show favor to any of you?" says the LORD of hosts.
**Malachi 1:9 ESV**

Do not be anxious about anything, but in everything by prayer and supplication with thanksgiving let your requests be made known to God.
**Philippians 4:6 ESV**

Pray in the Spirit at all times and on every occasion. Stay alert and be persistent in your prayers.
**Ephesians 6:18 NLT**

Prayer includes pleading. To plead is to lay yourself bare before God. It's to become nothing in His hand. It is to surrender yourself completely to His embrace, and plead earnestly that He will regard you in His grace and hear your prayers. Plead with God often for His will to be done in your life, and in the lives of the people you're pleading for with Him. Pray that the heavens will open above you.

# Overflowing Joy and Pleasures

Take delight in the LORD, and He will give you your heart's desires.
Psalm 37:4 NLT

"Behold! My Servant whom I uphold, My Elect One in whom My soul delights! I have put My Spirit upon Him; He will bring forth justice to the Gentiles."
Isaiah 42:1 NKJV

"Do not be afraid, little flock, for your Father has been pleased to give you the kingdom."
Luke 12:32 NIV

For it is God who works in you, both to will and to work for His good pleasure.
Philippians 2:13 ESV

"What woman, having ten silver coins, if she loses one coin, does not light a lamp, sweep the house, and search carefully until she finds it? And when she has found it, she calls her friends and neighbors together, saying, 'Rejoice with me, for I have found the piece which I lost!' Likewise, I say to you, there is joy in the presence of the angels of God over one sinner who repents."
Luke 15:8-10 NKJV

May the God of hope fill you with all joy and peace in believing, so that by the power of the Holy Spirit you may abound in hope.
Romans 15:13 ESV

It brings the Lord much pleasure and joy to save people. God's heart overflows with joy when one sinner turns to Him. It is a heavenly celebration when one lost sheep returns home, or when one coin that was lost is found. Are you contributing to God's joy and delight? Are you part of God's search party looking for lost souls? Then you will understand the joy it brings when one lost child returns to the feet of the Father.

# Seek Popularity in Heaven

"I will make of you a great nation, and I will bless you and make your name great, so that you will be a blessing."
**Genesis 12:2 ESV**

"For what profit is it to a man if he gains the whole world, and is himself destroyed or lost?"
**Luke 9:25 NKJV**

The women said to Naomi: "Praise be to the LORD, who this day has not left you without a guardian-redeemer. May He become famous throughout Israel!"
**Ruth 4:14 NIV**

Pride ends in humiliation, while humility brings honor.
**Proverbs 29:23 NLT**

"Now, therefore, thus you shall say to my servant David, 'Thus says the LORD of hosts, I took you from the pasture, from following the sheep that you should be prince over My people Israel. And I have been with you wherever you went and have cut off all your enemies from before you. And I will make for you a great name, like the name of the great ones of the earth.'"
**2 Samuel 7:8-9 ESV**

To be popular is vitally important to some people. Their self-image depends on it. As long as popularity is a people-driven need, it is a deadly temptation. It lets those who crave popularity lose their own souls. Don't do that. When it pleases God, He will grant you popularity to extend His Kingdom on earth. But remember, it's always about Him; never about yourself. Do not steal His honor.

# Your Position to Prosper

"Do not show partiality in judging; hear both small and great alike. Do not be afraid of anyone, for judgment belongs to God. Bring me any case too hard for you, and I will hear it."
**Deuteronomy 1:17 NIV**

If you keep quiet at a time like this, deliverance and relief for the Jews will arise from some other place, but you and your relatives will die. Who knows if perhaps you were made queen for just such a time as this?
**Esther 4:14 NLT**

Let each one remain in the same calling in which he was called.
**1 Corinthians 7:20 NKJV**

But Jesus called them to Him and said, "You know that the rulers of the Gentiles lord it over them, and their great ones exercise authority over them."
**Matthew 20:25 ESV**

"But among you it will be different. Whoever wants to be a leader among you must be your servant, and whoever wants to be first among you must be the slave of everyone else."
**Mark 10:43-44 NLT**

For you were bought with a price. So glorify God in your body.
**1 Corinthians 6:20 ESV**

Position counts. The more prominent your position on earth, the more it counts. But don't view your position in the same way. Rather use it as a platform to launch God's goodness in the direction of the people around you. Be an influencer. Make a tangible difference and impact, then you will be using your position the right way. Then you're really making the difference God asks from you.

# Speaking without Words

This is the account of Noah and his family. Noah was a righteous man, the only blameless person living on earth at the time, and he walked in close fellowship with God.
**Genesis 6:9 NLT**

At the time of the sacrifice, I stood up from where I had sat in mourning with my clothes torn. I fell to my knees and lifted my hands to the LORD my God.
**Ezra 9:5 NLT**

For the LORD God is a sun and shield; the LORD will give grace and glory; no good thing will He withhold from those who walk uprightly. **Psalm 84:11 NKJV**

The highway of the upright avoids evil; those who guard their ways preserve their lives.
**Proverbs 16:17 NIV**

And if I hold my head high, you hunt me like a lion and display your awesome power against me. **Job 10:16 NLT**

"I am the LORD your God, who brought you out of Egypt so that you would no longer be slaves to the Egyptians; I broke the bars of your yoke and enabled you to walk with heads held high." **Leviticus 26:13 NIV**

Submit to one another out of reverence for Christ.
**Ephesians 5:21 ESV**

Our posture relates to our appearance and body language. We instinctively know how to read each other's body language. Shoulders slouched forward are a sign of discouragement. Standing upright is evidence of being in control. Our body posture often reveals what is going on in your heart. Pay attention to your body language. Let your going in and your going out indeed be to the glory of God.

# The Power of God

Jesus came and told His disciples, "I have been given all authority in heaven and on earth."
**Matthew 28:18 NLT**

To all who did receive Him, who believed in His name, He gave the right to become children of God.
**John 1:12 ESV**

"You will receive power when the Holy Spirit comes on you; and you will be My witnesses in Jerusalem, and in all Judea and Samaria, and to the ends of the earth."
**Acts 1:8 NIV**

For the kingdom of God is not a matter of talk but of power. **1 Corinthians 4:20 NIV**

Jesus said, "I AM. And you will see the Son of Man seated in the place of power at God's right hand."
**Mark 14:62 NLT**

Therefore I remind you to stir up the gift of God which is in you through the laying on of my hands.
**2 Timothy 1:6 NKJV**

For God gave us a spirit not of fear but of power and love and self-control.
**2 Timothy 1:7 ESV**

"Behold, I have given you authority to tread on serpents and scorpions, and over all the power of the enemy, and nothing shall hurt you." **Luke 10:19 ESV**

People are impressed by power. See how people start to cheer excitedly when a strong forward player starts running with a rugby ball. Or to tackle each other as heavyweights in the boxing ring. Speaking of power, all power and might belong to God. The entire universe belongs to Him. We are children of the omnipotent Lord who arms us with strength and power to be witnesses for Him. We do this through the Spirit. We are live wires of the Lord.

# Becoming More in Christ

"I also say to you that you are Peter, and on this rock I will build My church, and the gates of Hades shall not prevail against it."
**Matthew 16:18 NKJV**

For in Him all things were created: things in heaven and on earth, visible and invisible, whether thrones or powers or rulers or authorities; all things have been created through Him and for Him. **Colossians 1:16 NIV**

In this way, He disarmed the spiritual rulers and authorities. He shamed them publicly by His victory over them on the cross.
**Colossians 2:15 NLT**

Now Christ has gone to heaven. He is seated in the place of honor next to God, and all the angels and authorities and powers accept His authority. **1 Peter 3:22 NLT**

Yours, LORD, is the greatness and the power and the glory and the majesty and the splendor, for everything in heaven and earth is Yours. Yours, LORD, is the kingdom; You are exalted as head over all. Wealth and honor come from You; You are the ruler of all things. In Your hands are strength and power to exalt and give strength to all. Now, our God, we give You thanks, and praise Your glorious name.
**1 Chronicles 29:11-13 NIV**

All power and strength in the universe are subject to Christ. He holds everything that can be seen and that which are unseen in His hands. No opposing force is strong enough or dangerous enough to threaten the power of God. Every knee will one day bow before His sovereignty. You and I are already doing it. The King of the universe is also our Father. He cares for us and has mercy and compassion.

# He Will Give His Power

Brothers and sisters, we urge you to warn those who are lazy. Encourage those who are timid. Take tender care of those who are weak. Be patient with everyone.
**1 Thessalonians 5:14 NLT**

Lift up your eyes and look to the heavens: Who created all these? He who brings out the starry host one by one and calls forth each of them by name. Because of His great power and mighty strength, not one of them is missing.
**Isaiah 40:26 NIV**

"O my lord, by reason of the vision pains have come upon me, and I retain no strength."
**Daniel 10:16 ESV**

They pant after the dust of the earth which is on the head of the poor, and pervert the way of the humble. A man and his father go in to the same girl, to defile My holy name.
**Amos 2:7 NKJV**

"For I have satiated the weary soul, and I have replenished every sorrowful soul."
**Jeremiah 31:25 NKJV**

This year you will eat only what grows up by itself, and next year you will eat what springs up from that. But in the third year you will plant crops and harvest them; you will tend vineyards and eat their fruit.
**2 Kings 19:29 NLT**

To be powerless or helpless is a terrifying feeling. It strips you of your dignity when you look for a job and find nothing. Or when you're supposed to protect your family, but you're powerless against the attackers. God sees the helpless. He can't stand seeing how the mighty exploit and take advantage of poor defenseless people. He will call every person to account for such deeds before His heavenly judiciary. He will have compassion on the plight of the weak and powerless.

# Powerful Praises

My heart exults in the LORD; my horn is exalted in the LORD. My mouth derides my enemies, because I rejoice in Your salvation. There is none holy like the LORD: for there is none besides You; there is no rock like our God.
**1 Samuel 2:1-2 ESV**

Therefore I will give thanks to You, O LORD, among the Gentiles, and sing praises to Your name.
**2 Samuel 22:50 NKJV**

Let us offer through Jesus a continual sacrifice of praise to God, proclaiming our allegiance to His name.
**Hebrews 13:15 NLT**

LORD, God of Israel, there is no God like You, in heaven above or on earth beneath, keeping covenant and showing steadfast love to Your servants who walk before You with all their heart.
**1 Kings 8:23 ESV**

You must fear the LORD your God and worship Him and cling to Him. Your oaths must be in His name alone. He alone is your God, the only one who is worthy of your praise, the one who has done these mighty miracles that you have seen with your own eyes.
**Deuteronomy 10:20-21 NLT**

Praise is to boast about God to God. It is to tell Him how good and wonderful His deeds are while singing and rejoicing. Praise is voiced through our songs and prayers. Praise moves the focus and attention away from us to God. Praise is to know that everything is about the Lord. He alone deserves all the glory, worship and praises from our hearts.

# Connecting with God

Now it came to pass, as He was praying in a certain place, when He ceased, that one of His disciples said to Him, "Lord, teach us to pray, as John also taught his disciples." Luke 11:1 NKJV

"Then if My people who are called by My name will humble themselves and pray and seek My face and turn from their wicked ways, I will hear from heaven and will forgive their sins and restore their land." 2 Chronicles 7:14 NLT

Do not be anxious about anything, but in every situation, by prayer and petition, with thanksgiving, present your requests to God. Philippians 4:6 NIV

"But I tell you, love your enemies and pray for those who persecute you." Matthew 5:44 NIV

Give thanks in all circumstances; for this is the will of God in Christ Jesus for you. 1 Thessalonians 5:18 ESV

Continue steadfastly in prayer, being watchful in it with thanksgiving. Colossians 4:2 ESV

"But when you pray, go away by yourself, shut the door behind you, and pray to your Father in private. Then your Father, who sees everything, will reward you." Matthew 6:6 NLT

To pray is a heavenly command. God knows what we need, but still He instructs us to pray. He wants us to call out to Him in prayer day and night. Prayer, at its core, is all about God. To pray is to praise and worship His name, and to glorify Him. Prayer is to seek God's face, and to plead that His Kingdom come on earth. We pray that His will be done in us, and in everyone else's life we pray for. Prayer is to submit ourselves constantly to God, and to trust Him for our daily bread and eternal salvation.

# A Life of Prayer

"Call to Me and I will answer you, and will tell you great and hidden things that you have not known."
**Jeremiah 33:3 ESV**

"I tell you, you can pray for anything, and if you believe that you've received it, it will be yours." **Mark 11:24 NLT**

They devoted themselves to the apostles' teaching and to fellowship, to the breaking of bread and to prayer.
**Acts 2:42 NIV**

Be anxious for nothing, but in everything by prayer and supplication, with thanksgiving, let your requests be made known to God.
**Philippians 4:6 NKJV**

But you, beloved, building yourselves up on your most holy faith, praying in the Holy Spirit.
**Jude 20 NKJV**

Never stop praying.
**1 Thessalonians 5:17 NLT**

Praying at all times in the Spirit, with all prayer and supplication. To that end keep alert with all perseverance.
**Ephesians 6:18 ESV**

I want the men everywhere to pray, lifting up holy hands without anger or disputing.
**1 Timothy 2:8 NIV**

Prayer is our life support. It is the direct connection between God and us. In the Name of Jesus we always have direct access to the throne room of the Almighty God. He hears our every prayer. That is why we need to pray. We must seek His will through our prayer and believe that He hears when we pray. When we know our place before God, at His feet, then we are praying the right kind of prayers.

# Precious in His Sight

Then one poor widow came and threw in two mites, which make a quadrans. So He called His disciples to Himself and said to them, "Assuredly, I say to you that this poor widow has put in more than all those who have given to the treasury." **Mark 12:42-43 NKJV**

Indeed, I count everything as loss because of the surpassing worth of knowing Christ Jesus my Lord. For His sake I have suffered the loss of all things and count them as rubbish, in order that I may gain Christ. **Philippians 3:8 ESV**

After a period of glory, the LORD of Heaven's Armies sent me against the nations who plundered you. For He said, "Anyone who harms you harms my most precious possession." **Zechariah 2:8 NLT**

"Because you are precious in My eyes, and honored, and I love you, I give men in return for you, peoples in exchange for your life." **Isaiah 43:4 ESV**

"Look at the birds. They don't plant or harvest or store food in barns, for your heavenly Father feeds them. And aren't you far more valuable to Him than they are?" **Matthew 6:26 NLT**

Valuable items are kept in a safe. Yet the most precious items are people. We are so valuable and precious in His sight that Christ paid the price on our behalf in full. He also notices when we serve Him with our precious items, like the last few cents of the widow in Mark 12:41-43 which she put in the temple treasury. If we are willing to share our most precious items with God, we profess that we've already given Him the most precious item we have – our lives.

# You Are a Priest of God

I beseech you therefore, brethren, by the mercies of God, that you present your bodies a living sacrifice, holy, acceptable to God, which is your reasonable service.
**Romans 12:1 NKJV**

But you are a chosen race, a royal priesthood, a holy nation, a people for His own possession, that you may proclaim the excellencies of Him who called you ... Once you were not a people, but now you are God's people; once you had not received mercy, but now you have received mercy.
**1 Peter 2:9-10 ESV**

You have made them to be a kingdom and priests to serve our God, and they will reign on the earth.
**Revelation 5:10 NIV**

I might be a minister of Jesus Christ to the Gentiles, ministering the gospel of God, that the offering of the Gentiles might be acceptable, sanctified by the Holy Spirit.
**Romans 15:16 NKJV**

To Him who loves us and has freed us from our sins by His blood and made us a kingdom, priests to His God and Father, to Him be glory and dominion forever and ever. Amen.
**Revelation 1:5-6 ESV**

Cults often have priests. It has always been that way. Christianity is not a cult and therefore the function of priests has been carried over to all believers. We are all kings and priests. Take note, the New Testament doesn't teach that only men can be priests. All of us, men and women, children and elderly people, are the Lord's priests. We dedicate our lives to His service. We pray and intercede for the world before God.

# Prioritizing Your Day

Then He said to them, "You like to appear righteous in public, but God knows your hearts. What this world honors is detestable in the sight of God." **Luke 16:15 NLT**

He must increase, but I must decrease. **John 3:30 NKJV**

One person considers one day more sacred than another; another considers every day alike. Each of them should be fully convinced in their own mind. **Romans 14:5 NIV**

Do nothing from selfish ambition or conceit, but in humility count others more significant than yourselves. **Philippians 2:3 ESV**

Peter and the other apostles replied: "We must obey God rather than human beings!" **Acts 5:29 NIV**

"For where your treasure is, there your heart will be also." **Luke 12:34 NIV**

Seek first the kingdom of God and His righteousness. **Matthew 6:33 NKJV**

First of all, then, I urge that supplications, prayers, intercessions, and thanksgivings be made for all people. **1 Timothy 2:1 ESV**

Priorities have to do with an order of precedence. To have your priorities straight means to put first things first and important relationships first. And to follow through the exact sequence and complete the tasks. Without priorities our lives easily turn into a mess. Then we run around after less important matters. Put God first, then your family and friends. But don't neglect yourself. Live healthily and in the right way.

# He Paid the Highest Price

"For even the Son of Man came not to be served but to serve others and to give His life as a ransom for many."
**Matthew 20:28 NLT**

Though they stumble, they will never fall, for the LORD holds them by the hand.
**Psalm 37:24 NLT**

"So likewise, whoever of you does not forsake all that he has cannot be My disciple."
**Luke 14:33 NKJV**

He gave His life to free us from every kind of sin, to cleanse us, and to make us His very own people, totally committed to doing good deeds. **Titus 2:14 NLT**

He was pierced for our transgressions; He was crushed for our iniquities; upon Him was the chastisement that brought us peace, and with His wounds we are healed.
**Isaiah 53:5 ESV**

For you know that it was not with perishable things such as silver or gold that you were redeemed from the empty way of life handed down to you from your ancestors.
**1 Peter 1:18 NIV**

For you were bought at a price; therefore glorify God in your body and in your spirit, which are God's.
**1 Corinthians 6:20 NKJV**

The ransom for our lives has been paid. While we were still slaves to sin and death, Jesus died in our place. By His blood, we were set free from slavery. He paid the price in full. Therefore, we are set free for eternity. No, we can't do as we please. Jesus bought us at a price to belong to Him. We are His. For that reason, we can't live how we want.

SEPTEMBER

YOU ARE THE FOUNTAIN OF LIFE, THE LIGHT BY WHICH WE SEE. PSALM 36:9

# Pride: Defeating Your Worst Enemy

Pride goes before destruction, and haughtiness before a fall.
**Proverbs 16:18 NLT**

"Let not the wise man glory in his wisdom, let not the mighty man glory in his might, nor let the rich man glory in his riches."
**Jeremiah 9:23 NKJV**

Now concerning food offered to idols: we know that "all of us possess knowledge." This "knowledge" puffs up, but love builds up.
**1 Corinthians 8:1 ESV**

When pride comes, then comes disgrace, but with the humble is wisdom.
**Proverbs 11:2 ESV**

For everything in the world – the lust of the flesh, the lust of the eyes, and the pride of life – comes not from the Father but from the world.
**1 John 2:16 NIV**

LORD, my heart is not haughty, nor my eyes lofty. Neither do I concern myself with great matters, nor with things too profound for me. Surely I have calmed and quieted my soul like a weaned child with his mother; like a weaned child is my soul within me.
**Psalm 131:1-2 NKJV**

To be proud, means to be full of yourself. Then there is no space for anyone else in your life. You fill the whole gap. God can't stand such pride. He hates it. Arrogant people are too great in their own eyes to bow down before Him. Learn to be humble. Then you shrink to the right size before God. Then He looks at you through the lens of His graciousness.

# The Profit of God

"For from the least to the greatest of them, everyone is greedy for unjust gain; and from prophet to priest, everyone deals falsely."
**Jeremiah 6:13 ESV**

"What good is it for someone to gain the whole world, yet forfeit their soul?"
**Mark 8:36 NIV**

For to me, to live is Christ, and to die is gain.
**Philippians 1:21 NKJV**

He gave His life to purchase freedom for everyone. This is the message God gave to the world at just the right time.
**1 Timothy 2:6 NLT**

Everything else is worthless when compared with the infinite value of knowing Christ Jesus my Lord. For His sake I have discarded everything else, counting it all as garbage, so that I could gain Christ.
**Philippians 3:8 NLT**

Then Jesus told His disciples, "If anyone would come after Me, let him deny himself and take up his cross and follow Me. For whoever would save his life will lose it, but whoever loses his life for My sake will find it."
**Matthew 16:24-25 ESV**

Everyone wants to get as much as possible out of life for themselves," someone said. Paul doesn't agree with this at all. He said he sacrificed his personal gain in order to get Christ as only gain. To him, Christ was all that mattered. Christ was his life, and death was his gain. What a great example to model! Do you also know this kind of freedom? Do you know this surpassing worth of knowing Jesus?

# A Lasting Promise

Rather, it was simply that the LORD loves you, and He was keeping the oath He had sworn to your ancestors. That is why the LORD rescued you with such a strong hand from your slavery.
**Deuteronomy 7:8 NLT**

God is not human, that He should lie, not a human being, that He should change His mind. Does He speak and then not act? Does He promise and not fulfill?
**Numbers 23:19 NIV**

For all the promises of God in Him are Yes, and in Him Amen, to the glory of God through us.
**2 Corinthians 1:20 NKJV**

"Behold, the days are coming," declares the LORD, "when I will raise up for David a righteous Branch, and he shall reign as king and deal wisely."
**Jeremiah 23:5 ESV**

Being assembled together with them, He commanded them not to depart from Jerusalem, but to wait for the Promise of the Father, "which," He said, "you have heard from Me."
**Acts 1:4 NKJV**

Patient endurance is what you need now, so that you will continue to do God's will. Then you will receive all that He has promised.
**Hebrews 10:36 NLT**

God keeps His word. When He makes a promise, He is faithful. Unlike many people who don't necessarily keep their word, God is faithful to all His promises. God's greatest and most impressive promise in the Old Testament is that of a new Covenant and a new intervention in history. It became a powerful reality with the outpouring of the Holy Spirit at Pentecost. The best news of all – we are currently living in this new era.

# Test Prophecies Against the Word

"But any prophet who falsely claims to speak in My name or who speaks in the name of another god must die. But you may wonder, 'How will we know whether or not a prophecy is from the LORD?' If the prophet speaks in the LORD's name but his prediction does not happen or come true, you will know that the LORD did not give that message. That prophet has spoken without My authority and need not be feared."
**Deuteronomy 18:20-22 NLT**

Do not despise prophecies.
**1 Thessalonians 5:20 NKJV**

"Therefore thus says the LORD concerning the prophets who prophesy in My name although I did not send them, and who say, 'Sword and famine shall not come upon this land': by sword and famine those prophets shall be consumed." **Jeremiah 14:15 ESV**

Dear friends, do not believe every spirit, but test the spirits to see whether they are from God, because many false prophets have gone out into the world. This is how you can recognize the Spirit of God: Every spirit that acknowledges that Jesus Christ has come in the flesh is from God.
**1 John 4:1-2 NIV**

Biblical prophets are not fortunetellers. They make known the will of God. They stand on the bridge between God and people and reveal His plan for mankind. They also indicate the future implications for all the recipients of their prophecies. Because there are so many false prophets, the Bible urges us to always test prophesies. God doesn't tolerate false prophets. Don't lend your eyes to just anybody.

# Good News for God's People

And all the people who were at the gate, and the elders, said, "We are witnesses. The LORD make the woman who is coming to your house like Rachel and Leah, the two who built the house of Israel; and may you prosper in Ephrathah and be famous in Bethlehem."
**Ruth 4:11 NKJV**

Whoever conceals his transgressions will not prosper, but he who confesses and forsakes them will obtain mercy. **Proverbs 28:13 ESV**

See, my servant will act wisely he will be raised and lifted up and highly exalted.
**Isaiah 52:13 NIV**

But now, O Jacob, listen to the LORD who created you. O Israel, the One who formed you says, "Do not be afraid, for I have ransomed you. I have called you by name; you are Mine."
**Isaiah 43:1 NLT**

God, our own God, shall bless us. God shall bless us, and all the ends of the earth shall fear Him.
**Psalm 67:6-7 NKJV**

God will supply every need of yours according to His riches in glory in Christ Jesus.
**Philippians 4:19 ESV**

Prosperity speaks of favor on the lives of people experiencing it. When God grants it, then the recipients are blessed. Their cups of blessings run over, but then their prosperity should become a means to serve others. Then they start to use God's blessings for the benefit of others. Prosperity should always be shared, and not used up selfishly. Because that goes against all the reasons why God bless people.

# Safe in His Arms

But now, this is what the LORD says, He who created you, Jacob, He who formed you, Israel: "Do not fear, for I have redeemed you; I have summoned you by name; you are Mine."
**Isaiah 43:1 NIV**

The angel of the LORD encamps around those who fear Him, and delivers them.
**Psalm 34:7 ESV**

But the Lord is faithful, who will establish you and guard you from the evil one.
**2 Thessalonians 3:3 NKJV**

"I the LORD do not change. So you, the descendants of Jacob, are not destroyed."
**Malachi 3:6 NIV**

In peace I will lie down and sleep, for You alone, LORD, make me dwell in safety.
**Psalm 4:8 NIV**

You bless the godly, O LORD; You surround them with your shield of love.
**Psalm 5:12 NLT**

I lay down and slept, yet I woke up in safety, for the LORD was watching over me.
**Psalm 3:5 NLT**

The LORD bless you and keep you. **Numbers 6:24 NKJV**

I'm not asking you to take them out of the world, but to keep them safe from the evil one.
**John 17:15 NLT**

God keeps His people safe. He does it through His Spirit. He protects us in danger and saves us from the snares of the Devil. We are often called upon to pray for God's protection over us. No, we don't ask others from the onset to pray for us in our time of need; we call out to the Lord ourselves during such times. He will be with us and deliver us. He will never let us slip from His hands.

# God's Hand of Providence

So Abraham called that place The LORD Will Provide. And to this day it is said, "On the mountain of the LORD it will be provided." **Genesis 22:14 NIV**

Weeping with joy, he embraced Benjamin, and Benjamin did the same. **Genesis 45:14 NLT**

He said to them, "Take nothing for the journey, neither staffs nor bag nor bread nor money; and do not have two tunics apiece." **Luke 9:3 NKJV**

It is my prayer that your love may abound more and more, with knowledge and all discernment. **Philippians 1:9 ESV**

He who supplies seed to the sower and bread for food will supply and multiply your seed for sowing and increase the harvest of your righteousness. **2 Corinthians 9:10 ESV**

The LORD will guide you always; He will satisfy your needs in a sun-scorched land and will strengthen your frame. You will be like a well-watered garden, like a spring whose waters never fail. **Isaiah 58:11 NIV**

The lot is cast into the lap, but its every decision is from the LORD. **Proverbs 16:33 ESV**

God provides and cares for us. In His omniscience He gives us life in abundance. Through the work of His Spirit He intervenes in our lives, and gives abundant life to everyone who confesses that He is Christ the Lord. Through His great grace He keeps us on the right track. Step by step we discover on our side how God's providence becomes a reality in our lives. We see His hand in every little detail of our lives.

# Manna when You Are out of Options

If you need anything else for your God's Temple or for any similar needs, you may take it from the royal treasury.
**Ezra 7:20 NLT**

Undoubtedly there are all sorts of languages in the world, yet none of them is without meaning.
**1 Corinthians 14:10 NIV**

He who supplies seed to the sower and bread for food will supply and multiply your seed for sowing and increase the harvest of your righteousness.
**2 Corinthians 9:10 ESV**

Now those who are such we command and exhort through our Lord Jesus Christ that they work in quietness and eat their own bread.
**2 Thessalonians 3:12 NKJV**

My God will supply every need of yours according to His riches in glory in Christ Jesus.
**Philippians 4:19 ESV**

But if anyone does not provide for his relatives, and especially for members of his household, he has denied the faith and is worse than an unbeliever.
**1 Timothy 5:8 ESV**

God provides. He gives us what we need. In fact, He gives us so much more. He showers us with grace, favor and prosperity. God is abundant in His heavenly care and provision. For that reason we should also provide in the needs of others. There is always an extra slice of bread or an extra cup of coffee that we can share with others. We never have a lack of anything. God always provides at just the right time.

# Christ Took Your Punishment

You shall not take the name of the LORD your God in vain, for the LORD will not hold him guiltless who takes His name in vain.
Exodus 20:7 ESV

Then the LORD said to Hosea, "Call him Jezreel, because I will soon punish the house of Jehu for the massacre at Jezreel, and I will put an end to the kingdom of Israel."
Hosea 1:4 NIV

"You only have I known of all the families of the earth; therefore I will punish you for all your iniquities."
Amos 3:2 NKJV

The king shouts to his officers; they stumble in their haste, rushing to the walls to set up their defenses.
Nahum 2:5 NLT

For God did not appoint us to suffer wrath but to receive salvation through our Lord Jesus Christ.
1 Thessalonians 5:9 NIV

Since we have been made right in God's sight by the blood of Christ, He will certainly save us from God's condemnation.
Romans 5:9 NLT

God's punishment is over. Well, let me put it this way, God's punishment is gone for every person who believes in Christ. He carried the punishment that we didn't deserve, in full. In the Old Testament, before Christ came to earth, God's wrath was visible and tangible. It was a one-on-one situation. That is why I'm infinitely grateful that Christ restored the way between God and us on our behalf.

# Purity Is Possible

How can a young man cleanse his way? By taking heed according to Your word.
**Psalm 119:9 NKJV**

"God blesses those whose hearts are pure, for they will see God."
**Matthew 5:8 NLT**

"Already you are clean because of the word that I have spoken to you."
**John 15:3 ESV**

But if we walk in the light, as He is in the light, we have fellowship with one another, and the blood of Jesus, His Son, purifies us from all sin.
**1 John 1:7 NIV**

Therefore if anyone cleanses himself from the latter, he will be a vessel for honor, sanctified and useful for the Master, prepared for every good work. Flee also youthful lusts; but pursue righteousness, faith, love, peace with those who call on the Lord out of a pure heart.
**2 Timothy 2:21-22 NKJV**

Pray for us, for we are sure that we have a clear conscience, desiring to act honorably in all things.
**Hebrews 13:18 ESV**

Create in me a clean heart, O God. Renew a loyal spirit within me.
**Psalm 51:10 NLT**

Purity was the basis of the religion practiced by the Pharisees. Everyone and everything had to be graded in terms of purity and impurity. To be unclean, as what happened to most sick people and outcasts, meant that you were excluded from all religious privileges. Jesus differed drastically with this way of doing things. He pushed all these codes for purity out the way to reach the hearts of people. He wants hearts that are pure. That's what matters most.

# Being Last in Line

"Everyone who has left houses or brothers or sisters or father or mother or children or lands, for My name's sake, will receive a hundredfold and will inherit eternal life. But many who are first will be last, and the last first."
**Matthew 19:29-30 ESV**

"Even the Son of Man came not to be served but to serve others and to give His life as a ransom for many."
**Mark 10:45 NLT**

"Anyone who wants to be first must be the very last, and the servant of all."
**Mark 9:35 NIV**

Be watchful, stand firm in the faith, act like men, be strong.
**1 Corinthians 16:13 ESV**

Do not put yourself forward in the king's presence or stand in the place of the great, for it is better to be told, "Come up here," than to be put lower in the presence of a noble.
**Proverbs 25:6-7 ESV**

"But many who are first will be last, and the last first."
**Mark 10:31 NKJV**

"So the last will be first, and the first will be last."
**Matthew 20:16 NIV**

To stand in a long queue can be exhausting, especially when the queue is not moving. Queuing is a waste of time for most people. But Jesus teaches us to stand at the back of the queue if we want to grow in servitude. He keeps a place for us there. From that position we can serve others without drawing the attention to our abilities or ourselves.

# Beyond the Racial Gridlock

From one man He created all the nations throughout the whole earth. He decided beforehand when they should rise and fall, and He determined their boundaries. **Acts 17:26 NLT**

There is neither Jew nor Greek, there is neither slave nor free, there is neither male nor female; for you are all one in Christ Jesus. **Galatians 3:28 NKJV**

Do we not all have one Father? Did not one God create us? Why do we profane the covenant of our ancestors by being unfaithful to one another? **Malachi 2:10 NIV**

Here there is no Gentile or Jew, circumcised or uncircumcised, barbarian, Scythian, slave or free, but Christ is all, and is in all. Therefore, as God's chosen people, holy and dearly loved, clothe yourselves with compassion, kindness, humility, gentleness and patience. **Colossians 3:11-12 NIV**

For there is no distinction between Jew and Greek; for the same Lord is Lord of all, bestowing His riches on all who call on Him. **Romans 10:12 ESV**

Racism is a word often heard nowadays. You're guilty of it when you treat people from a different race and skin color without the necessary dignity. Christians don't do this. Jesus made us colorblind and status blind. We don't measure people by their gender, origin, status, position or skin color. We accept everyone with the love of the Lord. And we condemn racists in our community who write people off who don't look like them.

# Reasoning with God

You ask, "Why?" It is because the LORD is the witness between you and the wife of your youth. You have been unfaithful to her, though she is your partner, the wife of your marriage covenant. Malachi 2:14 NIV

So we have stopped evaluating others from a human point of view. At one time we thought of Christ merely from a human point of view. How differently we know Him now!
2 Corinthians 5:16 NLT

For by the grace given to me I say to everyone among you not to think of himself more highly than he ought to think, but to think with sober judgment, each according to the measure of faith that God has assigned.
Romans 12:3 ESV

Also it is not good for a soul to be without knowledge, and he sins who hastens with his feet. The foolishness of a man twists his way, and his heart frets against the LORD.
Proverbs 19:2-3 NKJV

Therefore I have reason to glory in Christ Jesus in the things which pertain to God.
Romans 15:17 NKJV

For there is one God, and there is one mediator between God and men, the man Christ Jesus.
1 Timothy 2:5 ESV

Do you know the saying "to see reason"? Reasonableness supposes the ability to think clearly, controlled and reflective about a matter and consider all the information so that you don't blindly storm into a certain situation. Use your head before you open your mouth in tricky situations. Pray for wisdom. Speak carefully. Consider all the facts before formulating your own opinion and sharing your views. Be reasonable. Then others will get along with you easily.

# Being Logical

"Come now, let us reason together," says the LORD: "though your sins are like scarlet, they shall be as white as snow; though they are red like crimson, they shall become like wool."
Isaiah 1:18 ESV

Now someone may argue, "Some people have faith; others have good deeds." But I say, "How can you show me your faith if you don't have good deeds? I will show you my faith by my good deeds."
James 2:18 NLT

Then Paul, as his custom was, went in to them, and for three Sabbaths reasoned with them from the Scriptures. Acts 17:2 NKJV

He refuted the Jews with powerful arguments in public debate. Using the Scriptures, he explained to them that Jesus was the Messiah.
Acts 18:28 NLT

"Woe to those who quarrel with their Maker, those who are nothing but potsherds among the potsherds on the ground. Does the clay say to the potter, 'What are you making?' Does your work say, 'The potter has no hands'?" Isaiah 45:9 NIV

"Before I formed you in the womb I knew you; before you were born I sanctified you; I ordained you a prophet to the nations."
Jeremiah 1:5 NKJV

Speaking competitions and debates are prominent in school. Such competitions teach youngster the skills to formulate their thoughts logically and argue a subject matter thoroughly while interacting with other options and viewpoints. Paul didn't shy away from reasoning and arguments. He knew the gospel also had a historical and rational foundation. Therefore, he was not afraid to discuss matters concerning the clarity of the gospel message with opposition parties and other believers. Follow his example.

# Embrace the Blessing of Rebuke

And we urge you, brothers and sisters, warn those who are idle and disruptive, encourage the disheartened, help the weak, be patient with everyone. Make sure that nobody pays back wrong for wrong, but always strive to do what is good for each other and for everyone else.
**1 Thessalonians 5:14-15 NIV**

Do not rebuke an older man but encourage him as you would a father, younger men as brothers, older women as mothers, younger women as sisters, in all purity.
**1 Timothy 5:1-2 ESV**

A single rebuke does more for a person of understanding than a hundred lashes on the back of a fool.
**Proverbs 17:10 NLT**

"But he who endures to the end shall be saved."
**Matthew 24:13 NKJV**

A wise son hears his father's instruction, but a scoffer does not listen to rebuke.
**Proverbs 13:1 ESV**

Better is open rebuke than hidden love.
**Proverbs 27:5 NIV**

Do not rebuke an older man, but exhort him as a father.
**1 Timothy 5:1 NKJV**

To scold or rebuke is something that authority figures usually do to people under their rule. Parents, teachers, managers, coaches … such people have the power to rebuke and scold. Well, if you are in such a position, don't be too "loud and noisy". It doesn't help that much. If necessary correct lovingly. Never write someone off. Rebuke, but do so with compassion. Don't hurt others, build up and keep them together.

# Experience God's Abundance

"For everyone who asks receives, and the one who seeks finds, and to the one who knocks it will be opened."
**Matthew 7:8 ESV**

"If you abide in Me, and My words abide in you, you will ask what you desire, and it shall be done for you."
**John 15:7 NKJV**

His divine power has given us everything we need for a godly life through our knowledge of Him who called us by His own glory and goodness. **2 Peter 1:3 NIV**

"I have come that they may have life, and have it to the full." **John 10:10 NIV**

Peter replied, "Repent and be baptized, every one of you, in the name of Jesus Christ for the forgiveness of your sins. And you will receive the gift of the Holy Spirit."
**Acts 2:38 NIV**

Blessed is the man who remains steadfast under trial, for when he has stood the test he will receive the crown of life, which God has promised to those who love Him.
**James 1:12 ESV**

"I tell you, you can pray for anything, and if you believe that you've received it, it will be yours."
**Mark 11:24 NLT**

God loves to share gifts of grace. We must accept these gifts in faith. But we need to remain in Christ all the time, meaning we have to love Him and keep His commands. Then we remain in His love. Then we can ask whatever we want, because our prayers are in line with His will. Then we can believe that what we've prayed for is already ours. God's abundance is available to receive and experience in full!

# Rejoicing in Christ

My lips will shout for joy, when I sing praises to You; my soul also, which You have redeemed.
**Psalm 71:23 ESV**

Shout for joy to the LORD, all the earth.
**Psalm 100:1 NIV**

Rejoice, O people of Zion! Shout in triumph, O people of Jerusalem! Look, your king is coming to you. He is righteous and victorious, yet He is humble, riding on a donkey – riding on a donkey's colt.
**Zechariah 9:9 NLT**

Rejoice in the Lord always; again I will say, Rejoice.
**Philippians 4:4 ESV**

Rejoice with those who rejoice.
**Romans 12:15 ESV**

But let all those rejoice who put their trust in You; let them ever shout for joy, because You defend them; let those also who love Your name be joyful in You.
**Psalm 5:11 NKJV**

Rejoice always.
**1 Thessalonians 5:16 ESV**

"Do not rejoice that the spirits submit to you, but rejoice that your names are written in heaven."
**Luke 10:20 NIV**

When the team that you support in sports wins, you can't contain your joy. Then you sing and rejoice loudly. When God appears on the scene, His people do the same. Then celebrations are under way. People chant and sing at the top of their voices. You hear songs of joy rise up. By the way, when last did you rejoice and sing like this about God's goodness and mercy? Then it's about time. Read His Word, and rejoice!

# God Writes Your Love Story

For thus says the LORD to the house of Israel: "Seek Me and live." Amos 5:4 ESV

For the LORD your God is living among you. He is a mighty savior. He will take delight in you with gladness. With His love, He will calm all your fears. He will rejoice over you with joyful songs. Zephaniah 3:17 NLT

"For God so loved the world that He gave His one and only Son, that whoever believes in Him shall not perish but have eternal life." John 3:16 NIV

Contribute to the needs of the saints and seek to show hospitality. Romans 12:13 ESV

Do not say to your neighbor, "Go, and come back, and tomorrow I will give it," When you have it with you. Do not devise evil against your neighbor, for He dwells by you for safety's sake. Proverbs 3:28-29 NKJV

"I am the vine; you are the branches. If you remain in Me and I in you, you will bear much fruit; apart from Me you can do nothing." John 15:5 NIV

It is God who works in you both to will and to do for His good pleasure. Philippians 2:13 NKJV

Relationships are the ABC's of God. His Son came to save sinners, or those who were not on good terms with heaven. Jesus often catches up with such people with a handful of grace. And God also has new relationships in place for all His children. He is our God who loves us dearly, and enjoys our nearness day and night. In His name, we will also excel in our relationships.

# He Remembers You

And you shall remember the LORD your God, for it is He who gives you power to get wealth that He may establish His covenant which He swore to your fathers, as it is this day.
**Deuteronomy 8:18 NKJV**

"Jesus, remember me when You come into Your Kingdom."
**Luke 23:42 NLT**

"Remember the word that I said to you: 'A servant is not greater than his master.' If they persecuted Me, they will also persecute you. If they kept My word, they will also keep yours."
**John 15:20 ESV**

Remember this: Whoever sows sparingly will also reap sparingly, and whoever sows generously will also reap generously.
**2 Corinthians 9:6 NIV**

He provides food for those who fear Him; He remembers His covenant forever.
**Psalm 111:5 ESV**

Remember me, O my God, concerning this, and do not wipe out my good deeds that I have done for the house of my God, and for its services!
**Nehemiah 13:14 NKJV**

Be careful not to forget the Lord, who rescued you.
**Deuteronomy 6:12 NLT**

During my childhood years I've heard people tell each other: "The Lord always remembers." It scared me somewhat, because it sounded as if He remembers everything we ever do wrong. But then I started to study the Bible, and realized that He remembers us in grace. No, He doesn't keep record of our wrongs. Jesus paid in full for that. God remembers us as His dearly beloved children. He remembers to be gracious to us.

# The Walk of Repentance

This is what the Sovereign LORD, the Holy One of Israel, says: "Only in returning to Me and resting in Me will you be saved. In quietness and confidence is your strength. But you would have none of it."
Isaiah 30:15 NLT

They will come with weeping; they will pray as I bring them back. I will lead them beside streams of water on a level path where they will not stumble, because I am Israel's father, and Ephraim is my firstborn son.
Jeremiah 31:9 NIV

"In those days and in that time," says the LORD, "the children of Israel shall come, they and the children of Judah together; with continual weeping they shall come, and seek the LORD their God. They shall ask the way to Zion, with their faces toward it, saying, 'Come and let us join ourselves to the LORD in a perpetual covenant that will not be forgotten.'"
Jeremiah 50:4-5 NKJV

Then will You delight in right sacrifices, in burnt offerings and whole burnt offerings; then bulls will be offered on Your altar.
Psalm 51:19 ESV

True repentance because of our disobedience always leads to conversion and salvation. To be converted and saved mean to recognize and admit our sinfulness, and to surrender fully to the Triune God's grace. He is the only One to deliver us. Our repentance leaves us in shame and sorrow before Him, with the firm intent of not continuing on the path of sin. To repent is life changing, and leads to renewed obedience to God.

# You Are Irreplaceable

They said, "We will replace the broken bricks of our ruins with finished stone, and replant the felled sycamore-fig trees with cedars."
**Isaiah 9:10 NLT**

"I will give you a new heart and put a new spirit in you; I will remove from you your heart of stone and give you a heart of flesh."
**Ezekiel 36:26 NIV**

For as in one body we have many members, and the members do not all have the same function, so we, though many, are one body in Christ, and individually members one of another.
**Romans 12:4-5 ESV**

And the eye cannot say to the hand, "I have no need of you"; nor again the head to the feet, "I have no need of you." No, much rather, those members of the body which seem to be weaker are necessary. And those members of the body which we think to be less honorable, on these we bestow greater honor; and our unpresentable parts have greater modesty.
**1 Corinthians 12:21-23 NKJV**

"The Lord your God, He is the One who goes with you. He will not leave you nor forsake you."
**Deuteronomy 31:6 NKJV**

As I grew up I often heard the saying: "No one is irreplaceable." That's not completely correct. Fact is you never replace any Christian. No, no one can be replaced. Each one of us is unique. There is only one of us on this earth. That is why each one of us is so important in the body of Christ. We all have to fill our shoes in the Lord's service. If we don't, the church is going to suffer because of it.

# Loving Discipline that Works

I myself am satisfied about you, my brothers, that you yourselves are full of goodness, filled with all knowledge and able to instruct one another.
**Romans 15:14 ESV**

Therefore encourage one another and build each other up, just as in fact you are doing. **1 Thessalonians 5:11 NIV**

Those who are sinning rebuke in the presence of all, that the rest also may fear.
**1 Timothy 5:20 NKJV**

This is why I remind you to fan into flames the spiritual gift God gave you when I laid my hands on you.
**2 Timothy 1:6 NLT**

We have different gifts, according to the grace given to each of us. If your gift is prophesying, then prophesy in accordance with your faith. If it is to encourage, then give encouragement; if it is giving, then give generously; if it is to lead, do it diligently; if it is to show mercy, do it cheerfully.
**Romans 12:6,8 NIV**

Like an earring of gold and an ornament of fine gold is a wise rebuker to an obedient ear.
**Proverbs 25:12 NKJV**

The Lord disciplines those He loves, as a father the son he delights in.
**Proverbs 3:12 NIV**

It takes courage to reprimand someone. It's not always easy to instruct others of their wrongdoing. But it must be done. The Lord expects it from us. We are responsible for each other's spiritual wellbeing. We help and encourage each other to persevere on the road of the Lord. That is why we should never reprimand in a loveless and callous way, but always with godly compassion. It is to be honest and straightforward, without ripping someone to pieces.

# The Resilience Factor

Create in me a clean heart, O God, and renew a right spirit within me.
**Psalm 51:10 ESV**

Therefore, my dear brothers and sisters, stand firm. Let nothing move you. Always give yourselves fully to the work of the Lord, because you know that your labor in the Lord is not in vain.
**1 Corinthians 15:58 NIV**

"Have I not commanded you? Be strong and courageous. Do not be frightened, and do not be dismayed, for the Lord your God is with you wherever you go."
**Joshua 1:9 ESV**

Never stop praying.
**1 Thessalonians 5:17 NLT**

Resist him, steadfast in the faith, knowing that the same sufferings are experienced by your brotherhood in the world.
**1 Peter 5:9 NKJV**

Even though the fig trees have no blossoms, and there are no grapes on the vines; even though the olive crop fails, and the fields lie empty and barren; even though the flocks die in the fields, and the cattle barns are empty, yet I will rejoice in the LORD! I will be joyful in the God of my salvation!
**Habakkuk 3:17-18 NLT**

Resilience has become a scare characteristic. To persevere asks guts. It takes courage to swim upstream against popular belief, and to keep holding on to Christ through it all. It takes courage to boldly follow His way, no matter what happens. Even if we fall, we get up again, and we start walking in Christ's way once more.

# God's View on Life

Love one another with brotherly affection. Outdo one another in showing honor.
**Romans 12:10 ESV**

Live as free people, but do not use your freedom as a cover-up for evil; live as God's slaves. Show proper respect to everyone, love the family of believers, fear God, honor the emperor.
**1 Peter 2:16-17 NIV**

Sensible people control their temper; they earn respect by overlooking wrongs.
**Proverbs 19:11 NLT**

Give to everyone what you owe them: If you owe taxes, pay taxes; if revenue, then revenue; if respect, then respect; if honor, then honor.
**Romans 13:7 NIV**

Show yourself in all respects to be a model of good works, and in your teaching show integrity, dignity. **Titus 2:7 ESV**

"Do to others as you would like them to do to you."
**Luke 6:31 NLT**

Do nothing out of self ambition or vain conceit. Rather, in humility value others above yourselves.
**Philippians 2:3 NIV**

We all want to be treated with a little respect. Something as small as a quick greeting, a nod of the head, or the smile that says *I know that you exist*, make many people's lives bearable. Handle everyone with respect. Notice the sticker on their chest that was put there by God: "Fragile! Handle with Care!" Now do it. Each person is special. If you treat them with respect and dignity, God's goodness shines brightly.

# Rest and Relaxation

I will not be afraid of ten thousands of people who have set themselves against me all around.
**Psalm 3:6 NKJV**

In peace I will both lie down and sleep; for You alone, O LORD, make me dwell in safety.
**Psalm 4:8 ESV**

He will not let your foot slip – He who watches over you will not slumber; indeed He who watches over Israel will neither slumber nor sleep.
**Psalm 121:3-4 NIV**

"I will refresh the weary and satisfy the faint."
**Jeremiah 31:25 NIV**

"I have told you all this so that you may have peace in Me. Here on earth you will have many trials and sorrows. But take heart, because I have overcome the world." **John 16:33 NLT**

Truly my soul finds rest in God; my salvation comes from Him.
**Psalm 62:1 NIV**

"My presence will go with you, and I will give you rest."
**Exodus 33:14 ESV**

"Take My yoke upon you and learn from Me, for I am gentle and lowly in heart, and you will find rest for your souls."
**Matthew 11:29 NKJV**

At the end of a long day, we yearn for rest and relaxation. When you've worked yourself to the bone, and are tired of life, rest is the best medicine. God created us to rest. That's why we can lie down every night and sleep in peace, as David did. We can trust God while we sleep. He will carry us safe through the night. He never slumbers nor sleeps. Day or night doesn't influence Him.

# Vengeance Belongs to God

For true and just are His judgments. He has condemned the great prostitute who corrupted the earth by her adulteries. He has avenged on her the blood of His servants."
**Revelation 19:2 NIV**

"Do not seek revenge or bear a grudge against a fellow Israelite, but love your neighbor as yourself. I am the LORD."
**Leviticus 19:18 NLT**

Beloved, do not avenge yourselves, but rather give place to wrath; for it is written, "Vengeance is Mine, I will repay," says the Lord.
**Romans 12:19 NKJV**

As the proverb of the ancients says, 'Wickedness proceeds from the wicked.' But My hand shall not be against you.
**1 Samuel 24:13 NKJV**

They cried out with a loud voice, "O Sovereign Lord, holy and true, how long before You will judge and avenge our blood on those who dwell on the earth?" Then they were each given a white robe and told to rest a little longer, until the number of their fellow servants and their brothers should be complete, who were to be killed as they themselves had been.
**Revelation 6:10-11 ESV**

Leave the vengeance to God. That is what the Bible teaches us. We can't avenge others on the Lord's behalf and punish them left and right. God has all the facts. He will avenge the blood of His children that are spilt because of the wicked. In the meantime we can serve Him passionately, and leave the vengeance completely in His hands. He will deal with the injustices done on this earth in His own way and time.

# A Life God Rewards

"Love your enemies! Do good to them. Lend to them without expecting to be repaid. Then your reward from heaven will be very great, and you will truly be acting as children of the Most High, for He is kind to those who are unthankful and wicked." Luke 6:35 NLT

For the wages of sin is death, but the gift of God is eternal life in Christ Jesus our Lord. Romans 6:23 NIV

Watch yourselves, so that you may not lose what we have worked for, but may win a full reward.
2 John 8 ESV

"And behold, I am coming quickly, and My reward is with Me, to give to every one according to His work." Revelation 22:12 NKJV

For physical training is of some value, but godliness has value for all things, holding promise for both the present life and the life to come. This is a trustworthy saying that deserves full acceptance. That is why we labor and strive, because we have put our hope in the living God, who is the Savior of all people, and especially of those who believe.
1 Timothy 4:8-10 NIV

There are always rewards in life. A life of sin, for example, leads to eternal death. In opposition, God's reward for grace is eternal life. He grants it to all who believe in Christ as Lord at His Second Coming. That is why we work and dedicate our lives to Him so that we can receive this reward at the right time. His grace is our eternal reward.

# Your Riches in Christ

Then Jesus said to His disciples, "Truly I tell you, it is hard for someone who is rich to enter the kingdom of heaven. Again I tell you, it is easier for a camel to go through the eye of a needle than for someone who is rich to enter the kingdom of God."
**Matthew 19:23-24 NIV**

He who loves money will not be satisfied with money, nor he who loves wealth with his income; this also is vanity.
**Ecclesiastes 5:10 ESV**

Wealth gained hastily will dwindle, but whoever gathers little by little will increase it.
**Proverbs 13:11 ESV**

"For all the nations have drunk of the wine of the wrath of her fornication, the kings of the earth have committed fornication with her, and the merchants of the earth have become rich through the abundance of her luxury."
**Revelation 18:3 NKJV**

"Do not lay up for yourselves treasures on earth, where moth and rust destroy and where thieves break in and steal, but lay up for yourselves treasures in heaven, where neither moth nor rust destroys and where thieves do not break in and steal. For where your treasure is, there your heart will be also." **Matthew 6:19-21 ESV**

Wealth and riches can sometimes be a stumbling block. When our money and possessions are not used in God's Kingdom, then it is used in building our own little kingdom. If material things become our master, then we will never have enough stuff. We will always want more and more. Therefore we should never allow earthly things to become our masters. We should rather use our stuff in service to God.

# God Is Your Rock

The LORD is my rock and my fortress and my deliverer; My God, my strength, in whom I will trust; my shield and the horn of my salvation, my stronghold.
**Psalm 18:2 NKJV**

"And I tell you, you are Peter, and on this rock I will build My church, and the gates of hell shall not prevail against it." **Matthew 16:18 ESV**

The LORD is my fortress; my God is the mighty rock where I hide.
**Psalm 94:22 NLT**

Trust in the LORD always, for the LORD GOD is the eternal Rock.
**Isaiah 26:4 NLT**

He alone is my rock and my salvation, my fortress; I shall not be greatly shaken.
**Psalm 62:2 ESV**

There is none holy like the LORD: for there is none besides You; there is no rock like our God.
**1 Samuel 2:2 ESV**

May these words of my mouth and this meditation of my heart be pleasing in Your sight, LORD, my Rock and my Redeemer.
**Psalm 19:14 NIV**

"Anyone who listens to My teaching and follows it is wise, like a person who builds a house on solid rock."
**Matthew 7:24 NLT**

The Psalms and other Scripture verses often mention that God is our Rock. He is unshakable. He is solid. You can build your life on Him. No room in your life's house must be extended or rebuilt if it is not founded on the Triune God as your Rock. He is the only one to keep you firm and standing straight.

# God Is Your Guide

Gideon circled around by the caravan route east of Nobah and Jogbehah, taking the Midianite army by surprise.
**Judges 8:11 NLT**

Being warned in a dream not to return to Herod, they departed to their own country by another way.
**Matthew 2:12 ESV**

"By the way that he came he will return; he will not enter this city," declares the LORD. "I will defend this city and save it, for My sake and for the sake of David My servant."
**2 Kings 19:33-34 NIV**

He will guard the feet of His saints.
**1 Samuel 2:9 NKJV**

A wise person chooses the right road; a fool takes the wrong one.
**Ecclesiastes 10:2 NLT**

"I am the way, and the truth, and the life. No one comes to the Father except through Me."
**John 14:6 ESV**

See then that you walk circumspectly, not as fools but as wise.
**Ephesians 5:15 NKJV**

To know the route is one thing, but to walk on until you reach the end, is another thing. And yet routes are there to reach a final end. Any adventurous person likes a challenge. Think of a tough off-road course or a difficult hiking trial. Maybe you like such challenges. Remember that God always goes with you. He makes your feet like the feet of deer on the high places. He is your Guide and Host on the way.

OCTOBER

GOD ARMS ME WITH **STRENGTH.** HE MAKES ME AS SUREFOOTED AS A **DEER,** ENABLING ME TO STAND ON *mountain* HEIGHTS.

PSALM 18:32-33

# The Rhythm of Grace

When Jephthah returned home to Mizpah, his daughter came out to meet him, playing on a tambourine and dancing for joy. She was his one and only child; he had no other sons or daughters.
**Judges 11:34 NLT**

For everything there is a season, and a time for every matter under heaven: a time to be born, and a time to die; a time to plant, and a time to pluck up what is planted; a time to kill, and a time to heal; a time to break down, and a time to build up; a time to weep, and a time to laugh; a time to mourn, and a time to dance.
**Ecclesiastes 3:1-4 ESV**

They send forth their children as a flock; their little ones dance about. They sing to the music of timbrel and lyre; they make merry to the sound of the pipe.
**Job 21:11-12 NIV**

Sing to Him, sing psalms to Him; talk of all His wondrous works!
**Psalm 105:2 NKJV**

Addressing one another in psalms and hymns and spiritual songs, singing and making melody to the Lord with your heart.
**Ephesians 5:19 ESV**

Either you have rhythm or you don't. Excuses won't help you much. Yet there are also rhythms in life. There's a time for work and a time to sleep. There is a time for social interaction, and a time to mourn. God is not absent during any of these rhythms. Acknowledge Him in the daily rhythms of your life, from waking up in the morning until going to bed at night and then you'll have good rhythm. Then you will understand what I mean.

# We Can Know Him

And the word of the LORD came to me, saying, "Son of man, pose a riddle, and speak a parable to the house of Israel," and say, "Thus says the Lord GOD: 'A great eagle with large wings and long pinions, full of feathers of various colors, came to Lebanon and took from the cedar the highest branch.'"
**Ezekiel 17:1-3 NKJV**

For I am sure that neither death nor life, nor angels nor rulers, nor things present nor things to come, nor powers, nor height nor depth, nor anything else in all creation, will be able to separate us from the love of God in Christ Jesus our Lord. **Romans 8:38-39 ESV**

His disciples asked Him what this parable meant. He said, "The knowledge of the secrets of the kingdom of God has been given to you, but to others I speak in parables, so that, though seeing, they may not see; though hearing, they may not understand."
**Luke 8:9-10 NIV**

For now we see only a reflection as in a mirror; then we shall see face to face. Now I know in part; then I shall know fully, even as I am fully known.
**1 Corinthians 13:12 NIV**

God is not a riddle to be solved. Yet many people think of Him as a mystery. His will according to them is unknowable, but we will understand it some day in heaven. Or they believe there is a purpose behind everything in life, although they have no idea what it is. Well, God is not some mysterious riddle. He is our Father. We can know Him. He reveals His heart to us.

# More Love, Less Rules

So Joshua made a covenant with the people that day, and made for them a statute and an ordinance in Shechem.
**Joshua 24:25 NKJV**

For Ezra had devoted himself to the study and observance of the Law of the Lord, and to teaching its decrees and laws in Israel.
**Ezra 7:10 NIV**

We have sinned terribly by not obeying the commands, decrees, and regulations that You gave us through Your servant Moses.
**Nehemiah 1:7 NLT**

And the Lord said: "Because this people draw near with their mouth and honor Me with their lips, while their hearts are far from Me, and their fear of Me is a commandment taught by men."
**Isaiah 29:13 ESV**

"I tell you, there is one here who is even greater than the Temple! But you would not have condemned My innocent disciples if you knew the meaning of this Scripture: 'I want you to show mercy, not offer sacrifices.' For the Son of Man is Lord, even over the Sabbath!"
**Matthew 12:6-8 NLT**

At the university in the Netherlands where I work one month per year, I realized that the people love rules. Sometimes it feels like their rules are more important than building relationships with people. Rules without relationships are dead laws. Therefore Jesus often defied the religious regulations that kept the people in chains, and prevented them from reaching God. Be careful of such lifeless rules. Grow in your relationships and then you'll need less rules and laws.

# Offer Your Life to Him

"These people say they are Mine. They honor Me with their lips, but their hearts are far from Me. And their worship of Me is nothing but man-made rules learned by rote." Isaiah 29:13 NLT

"But go and learn what this means: 'I desire mercy and not sacrifice.' For I did not come to call the righteous, but sinners, to repentance." Matthew 9:13 NKJV

However, I consider my life worth nothing to me; my only aim is to finish the race and complete the task the Lord Jesus has given me – the task of testifying to the good news of God's grace. Acts 20:24 NIV

He who did not spare His own Son but gave Him up for us all, how will He not also with Him graciously give us all things? Romans 8:32 ESV

How much more shall the blood of Christ, who through the eternal Spirit offered Himself without spot to God, cleanse your conscience from dead works to serve the living God? Hebrews 9:14 NKJV

This is love: not that we loved God, but that He loved us and sent His Son as an atoning sacrifice for our sins. 1 John 4:10 NIV

Offerings without personal sacrifices don't impress God. To simply bring your offering to Him as if it is some or other business transaction, doesn't sit well with Him. He asks sacrifices. He seeks hearts dripping with love. He is looking for living sacrifices, and people who bring glory to His name. Men who live like this are "dead men walking." They've given up their lives and surrendered to Jesus. They've died to self in Him. They're living renewed lives now.

# You Are Safe in God's Hand

"Don't be afraid of the people, for I will be with you and will protect you. I, the LORD, have spoken!"
**Jeremiah 1:8 NLT**

"And lead us not into temptation, but deliver us from the evil one."
**Matthew 6:13 NIV**

"And I am no longer in the world, but they are in the world, and I am coming to you. Holy Father, keep them in Your name, which You have given Me, that they may be one, even as we are one."
**John 17:11 ESV**

Now to Him who is able to keep you from stumbling, and to present you faultless before the presence of His glory with exceeding joy.
**Jude 24 NKJV**

"My sheep hear My voice, and I know them, and they follow Me. And I give them eternal life, and they shall never perish; neither shall anyone snatch them out of My hand. My Father, who has given them to Me, is greater than all; and no one is able to snatch them out of My Father's hand."
**John 10:27-29 NKJV**

Safety is a very high priority for many people. With high levels of violence and crime, we all yearn for our own piece of safety. Well, the fact is, it will always be unsafe in the world. Life doesn't have such guarantees, but Christ has. He is our Safety. Neither death nor life can be snatched from His hand. Therefore, whether we live or die, we do it for Him.

# The Unseen Opponent

Now there was a day when the sons of God came to present themselves before the LORD, and Satan also came among them.
**Job 1:6 ESV**

The LORD said to Satan, "The LORD rebuke you, Satan! The LORD, who has chosen Jerusalem, rebuke you! Is not this man a burning stick snatched from the fire?" **Zechariah 3:2 NIV**

The sinful nature wants to do evil, which is just the opposite of what the Spirit wants. These two forces are constantly fighting each other, so you are not free to carry out your good intentions. **Galatians 5:17 NLT**

Having disarmed principalities and powers, He made a public spectacle of them, triumphing over them in it.
**Colossians 2:15 NKJV**

Stay alert! Watch out for your great enemy, the devil. He prowls around like a roaring lion, looking for someone to devour.
**1 Peter 5:8 NLT**

Therefore submit to God. Resist the devil and he will flee from you.
**James 4:7 NKJV**

The God of peace will soon crush Satan under your feet. May the grace of our Lord Jesus be with you.
**Romans 16:20 NLT**

Satan is God's invisible opponent. No, he is not a god. Jesus confirmed this fact when He Himself refused to bow before Satan. On the cross Jesus also disarmed him. All power and might belongs to Jesus. Yet, Satan is a dangerous enemy in his final days on this earth. He is determined to destroy us. Stay away from him. Hide in the shelter of the Omnipotent One.

# Sealed for Redemption

In the same way, after the supper He took the cup, saying, "This cup is the new covenant in My blood, which is poured out for you."
**Luke 22:20 NIV**

Now you Gentiles have also heard the truth, the Good News that God saves you. And when you believed in Christ, He identified you as His own by giving you the Holy Spirit, whom He promised long ago.
**Ephesians 1:13 NLT**

And do not grieve the Holy Spirit of God, by whom you were sealed for the day of redemption.
**Ephesians 4:30 ESV**

"He who has received His testimony has certified that God is true." **John 3:33 NKJV**

Unlike so many, we do not peddle the word of God for profit. On the contrary, in Christ we speak before God with sincerity, as those sent from God.
**2 Corinthians 2:17 NIV**

Then He took the cup, and gave thanks, and gave it to them, saying, "Drink from it, all of you. For this is My blood of the new covenant, which is shed for many for the remission of sins."
**Matthew 26:27-28 NKJV**

Something that is sealed has an official stamp or seal on it. The stamp of a high-ranking official guarantees the authenticity of any document. Jesus' blood is the official stamp of the New Testament, and we celebrate it during Holy Communion. Together with it, the Holy Spirit is the official stamp of God to guarantee the authenticity of His craftsmanship in our lives. We are sealed by God's mercy and grace; it's the real deal.

# The Second Coming of Christ

"But of that day and hour no one knows, not even the angels in heaven, nor the Son, but only the Father. Take heed, watch and pray; for you do not know when the time is."
**Mark 13:32-33 NKJV**

"Whatever you ask in My name, this I will do, that the Father may be glorified in the Son."
**John 14:13 ESV**

"Men of Galilee," they said, "why are you standing here staring into heaven? Jesus has been taken from you into heaven, but someday He will return from heaven in the same way you saw Him go!" **Acts 1:11 NLT**

When Christ, who is your life, appears, then you also will appear with Him in glory.
**Colossians 3:4 NIV**

Now you have every spiritual gift you need as you eagerly wait for the return of our Lord Jesus Christ.
**1 Corinthians 1:7 NLT**

But concerning that day and hour no one knows, not even the angels of heaven, nor the Son, but the Father only."
**Matthew 24:36 ESV**

"Behold, I am coming quickly! Hold fast what you have, that no one may take your crown." **Revelation 3:11 NKJV**

The Lord is coming again. He guarantees it. We don't know the date and time. But we don't have to. All that is expected of us is to be ready for His return. My grandmother used to say, "Our bags should be packed for the Lord arrives to fetch us." His Second Coming is near. We need to wait expectantly and look forward to His return. We must also invite others to share in the feast of eternity.

# Born into His Family

"And I will put enmity between you and the woman, and between your seed and her Seed; He shall bruise your head, and you shall bruise His heel."
**Genesis 3:15 NKJV**

I ask, then, has God rejected His people? By no means! For I myself am an Israelite, a descendant of Abraham, a member of the tribe of Benjamin.
**Romans 11:1 ESV**

For you have been born again, not of perishable seed, but of imperishable, through the living and enduring word of God.
**1 Peter 1:23 NIV**

Those who have been born into God's family do not make a practice of sinning, because God's life is in them. So they can't keep on sinning, because they are children of God.
**1 John 3:9 NLT**

We know that everyone who has been born of God does not keep on sinning, but he who was born of God protects him, and the evil one does not touch him.
**1 John 5:18 ESV**

He chose to give us birth through the word of truth, that we might be a kind of firstfruits of all He created.
**James 1:18 NIV**

We were born from the seeds of God. John literally writes about it in 1 John 3:9. In his turn Peter teaches us that we are born again from the seeds of God. In other words, God's DNA is in us. We take after God. His heartbeat is our heartbeat. His character is our character. No wonder John said we shouldn't sin anymore, because he knew we are God's children. That is why we also keep His commands.

# What About Me?

"'Why have we fasted, and You see it not? Why have we humbled ourselves, and You take no knowledge of it?' Behold, in the day of your fast you seek your own pleasure, and oppress all your workers."
Isaiah 58:3 ESV

Let nothing be done through selfish ambition or conceit, but in lowliness of mind let each esteem others better than himself.
Philippians 2:3 NKJV

Whoever isolates himself seeks his own desire; he breaks out against all sound judgment.
Proverbs 18:1 ESV

Then Jesus said to His disciples, "Whoever wants to be My disciple must deny themselves and take up their cross and follow Me."
Matthew 16:24 NIV

For where you have envy and selfish ambition, there you find disorder and every evil practice. But the wisdom that comes from heaven is first of all pure; then peace-loving, considerate, submissive, full of mercy and good fruit, impartial and sincere. James 3:16-17 NIV

For those who are self-seeking and who reject the truth and follow evil, there will be wrath and anger.
Romans 2:8 NIV

For selfish people only three people matter in their lives: "me, myself and I." Then your life and others' revolve around you. Selfishness brings out the worst in you, because you always fight for your own interests. You have to win no matter what. You must get all the attention. Don't let this happen. Let the Lord's selfless love flow over you today, then you'll lose all your selfish desires.

# Being Self-Controlled

But the fruit of the Spirit is love, joy, peace, patience, kindness, goodness, faithfulness, gentleness, self-control; against such things there is no law. And those who belong to Christ Jesus have crucified the flesh with its passions and desires.
**Galatians 5:22-24 ESV**

In view of all this, make every effort to respond to God's promises. Supplement your faith with a generous provision of moral excellence, and moral excellence with knowledge, and knowledge with self-control, and self-control with patient endurance, and patient endurance with godliness.
**2 Peter 1:5-6 NLT**

We all stumble in many ways. Anyone who is never at fault in what they say is perfect, able to keep their whole body in check.
**James 3:2 NIV**

For God has not given us a spirit of fear, but of power and of love and of a sound mind.
**2 Timothy 1:7 NKJV**

A man without self-control is like a city broken into and left without walls.
**Proverbs 25:28 ESV**

Teach the older men to exercise self-control, to be worthy of respect, and to live wisely. They must have sound faith. **Titus 2:2 NLT**

Self-control is self-explanatory. It is to contain your emotions. Self-controlled people don't act out in rage every so often. They are rude when they don't get their way. They also don't succumb to forbidden temptations of lust and greed. That is why self-control is one of the fruit of the Spirit.

# A Christ-Centered Self-Esteem

Do you not know that your body is the temple of the Holy Spirit who is in you, whom you have from God, and you are not your own?
**1 Corinthians 6:19 NKJV**

In the same way, husbands ought to love their wives as they love their own bodies. For a man who loves his wife actually shows love for himself. No one hates his own body but feeds and cares for it, just as Christ cares for the church.
**Ephesians 5:28-29 NLT**

So God created man in His own image; in the image of God He created him.
**Genesis 1:27 NKJV**

I eagerly expect and hope that I will in no way be ashamed, but will have sufficient courage so that now as always Christ will be exalted in my body, whether by life or by death.
**Philippians 1:20 NIV**

Have nothing to do with irreverent, silly myths. Rather train yourself for godliness; for while bodily training is of some value, godliness is of value in every way, as it holds promise for the present life and also for the life to come.
**1 Timothy 4:7-8 ESV**

A feeling of self-worth is necessary for a balanced life. Paul says that a man should love and care for his own body. Take note, he doesn't say you must be in love with yourself, only that you need to look after your body well. How? Well, you make sure your body is well groomed and looked after. You don't overeat, overwork, overstrain or drink excessively. Your body is the temple of God, and that is why you find your worth in Him who regards you as precious in His sight.

# The Highly Sensitive Person

Bow down Your ear, O LORD, hear me; for I am poor and needy.
**Psalm 86:1 NKJV**

I am overwhelmed with troubles and my life draws near to death. I am counted among those who go down to the pit; I am like one without strength. I am set apart with the dead, like the slain who lie in the grave, whom you remember no more, who are cut off from your care. You have put me in the lowest pit, in the darkest depths.
**Psalm 88:3-6 NIV**

Accept other believers who are weak in faith, and don't argue with them about what they think is right or wrong. For instance, one person believes it's all right to eat anything. But another believer with a sensitive conscience will eat only vegetables. Those who feel free to eat anything must not look down on those who don't. And those who don't eat certain foods must not condemn those who do, for God has accepted them.
**Romans 14:1-3 NLT**

Whoever heeds discipline shows the way of life, but whoever ignores correction leads others astray.
**Proverbs 10:17 NIV**

I refer to the oversensitive people who get upset so easily, as the "religious bleeders". Some church clergies get hurt so easily. Everybody is always against them. No one hears them. That is why they're bitter and bleeding. They can't add value in service to God, because they're on the bench with blood injuries all the time. Don't try to please such people. Correct them in love to stop the bleeding and to start working in His service.

# On a Mission for God

Then, after doing all those things, I will pour out My Spirit upon all people. Your sons and daughters will prophesy. Your old men will dream dreams, and your young men will see visions. **Joel 2:28 NLT**

Also I heard the voice of the Lord, saying: "Whom shall I send, and who will go for Us?" Then I said, "Here am I! Send me." **Isaiah 6:8 NKJV**

"Therefore, go and make disciples of all the nations, baptizing them in the name of the Father and the Son and the Holy Spirit." **Matthew 28:19 NLT**

The Spirit of the Lord is upon Me, because He has anointed Me to preach the gospel to the poor; He has sent Me to heal the broken-hearted, to proclaim liberty to the captives and recovery of sight to the blind, to set at liberty those who are oppressed. **Luke 4:18 NKJV**

"But the Helper, the Holy Spirit, whom the Father will send in My name, He will teach you all things and bring to your remembrance all that I have said to you." **John 14:26 ESV**

Again Jesus said, "Peace be with you! As the Father has sent Me, I am sending you." **John 20:21 NIV**

God was the first missionary. When the first people sinned, God chose to walk after them and all other broken people. As part of His mission, He sent Jesus to also look for the lost. And Jesus gave us His Spirit to equip us with power and strength. Moreover, Jesus sends us to complete His work here on earth.

# Hope for the Outcasts

But it was also called Mizpah (which means "watch-tower"), for Laban said, "May the LORD keep watch between us to make sure that we keep this covenant when we are out of each other's sight.
**Genesis 31:49 NLT**

You are severed from Christ, you who would be justified by the law; you have fallen away from grace.
**Galatians 5:4 ESV**

And you, who once were alienated and enemies in your mind by wicked works, yet now He has reconciled.
**Colossians 1:21 NKJV**

For I am sure that neither death nor life, nor angels nor rulers, nor things present nor things to come, nor powers, nor height nor depth, nor anything else in all creation, will be able to separate us from the love of God in Christ Jesus our Lord. **Romans 8:38-39 ESV**

They are darkened in their understanding and separated from the life of God because of the ignorance that is in them due to the hardening of their hearts.
**Ephesians 4:18 NIV**

If it is true that I have gone astray, my error remains my concern alone.
**Job 19:4 NIV**

God looks for the alienated and desolate people. Through Christ we are children of God. He doesn't want us to be strangers to Him. We are too precious for that. We were made to belong to Him. That is why He'll never allow us to be separated from Him. Or that our trespasses build a wall between Him and us. From our side, we should also not regard God as a stranger. He is near. He is our Father.

# Your Purpose in Life

"Behold, I send My messenger, and he will prepare the way before Me. And the Lord whom you seek will suddenly come to His temple; and the messenger of the covenant in whom you delight, behold, He is coming," says the LORD of hosts.
**Malachi 3:1 ESV**

"You are My witnesses," declares the LORD, "and My servant whom I have chosen, so that you may know and believe Me and understand that I am He. Before Me no god was formed, nor will there be one after Me."
**Isaiah 43:10 NIV**

"No one can serve two masters; for either he will hate the one and love the other, or else he will be loyal to the one and despise the other. You cannot serve God and mammon."
**Matthew 6:24 NKJV**

I now rejoice in my sufferings for you, and fill up in my flesh what is lacking in the afflictions of Christ, for the sake of His body, which is the church, of which I became a minister according to the stewardship from God which was given to me for you, to fulfill the word of God.
**Colossians 1:24-25 NKJV**

To be someone's servant is to offer your service to a person full-time. It's to be a slave. We are servants in God's service. We are on call 24/7. We live for Him, work for Him and serve Him day and night. We don't determine the conditions of how we're supposed to serve and follow. We are in the service of Christ the Lord. His wish is our command. His calling on our lives is our compass, now and forevermore.

# A Brother in Service

This letter is from Paul, a slave of God and an apostle of Jesus Christ. I have been sent to proclaim faith to those God has chosen and to teach them to know the truth that shows them how to live godly lives.
**Titus 1:1 NLT**

"No one can serve two masters. For you will hate one and love the other; you will be devoted to one and despise the other. You cannot serve God and be enslaved to money."
**Matthew 6:24 NLT**

As each has received a gift, use it to serve one another, as good stewards of God's varied grace. **1 Peter 4:10 ESV**

"For even the Son of Man came not to be served but to serve, and to give His life as a ransom for many."
**Mark 10:45 ESV**

For you, brethren, have been called to liberty; only do not use liberty as an opportunity for the flesh, but through love serve one another.
**Galatians 5:13 NKJV**

"Whoever serves Me must follow Me; and where I am, My servant also will be. My Father will honor the one who serves Me."
**John 12:26 NIV**

A friend loves at all times, and a brother is born for adversity. **Proverbs 17:17 NKJV**

To serve means to take the very nature of a slave. It is being the least, without turning into someone's doormat. Serving others is first and foremost about our humble dedication to God. We become less, and He becomes more in us. Christ is our example in this. We also serve by carrying each other's burdens. We should do it without expecting anything in return.

# Cherish Your Wife

The fig tree puts forth her green figs, and the vines with the tender grapes give a good smell. Rise up, my love, my fair one, and come away! O my dove, in the clefts of the rock in the secret places of the cliff, let me see your face, let me hear your voice; for your voice is sweet, and your face is lovely. Catch us the foxes, the little foxes that spoil the vines, for our vines have tender grapes. My beloved is mine, and I am his. He feeds his flock among the lilies. Until the day breaks and the shadows flee away, turn, my beloved, and be like a gazelle or a young stag upon the mountains of Bether.
Song of Songs 2:13-17 NKJV

"But at the beginning of creation God 'made them male and female. For this reason a man will leave his father and mother and be united to his wife, and the two will become one flesh.' So they are no longer two, but one flesh. Therefore what God has joined together, let no one separate." Mark 10:6-9 NIV

Let marriage be held in honor among all. Hebrews 13:4 ESV

He who finds a wife finds what is good and receives favor from the LORD.
Proverbs 18:22 NIV

Sexuality is often addressed in the Bible. It is a normal part of our lives, if it runs along the designated lanes set out for it. Men and women have received this precious gift in order to love each other abundantly. That is why sexuality is more than mere deeds or actions; it is love and intimacy that must be cherished between a husband and wife who also love God.

# Don't Be Covered with Shame

He answered, "I heard You in the garden, and I was afraid because I was naked; so I hid." **Genesis 3:10 NIV**

For I am not ashamed of this Good News about Christ. It is the power of God at work, saving everyone who believes – the Jew first and also the Gentile.
**Romans 1:16 NLT**

No, much rather, those members of the body which seem to be weaker are necessary. And those members of the body which we think to be less honorable, on these we bestow greater honor; and our unpresentable parts have greater modest.
**1 Corinthians 12:22-23 NKJV**

So do not be ashamed of the testimony about our Lord or of me His prisoner. Rather, join with me in suffering for the gospel, by the power of God. **2 Timothy 1:8 NIV**

It is my eager expectation and hope that I will not be at all ashamed, but that with full courage now as always Christ will be honored in my body, whether by life or by death.
**Philippians 1:20 ESV**

Those who look to Him are radiant; their faces are never covered with shame.
**Psalm 34:5 NIV**

Feeling shy or ashamed started when Adam and Eve noticed they were naked that day in paradise. From then on, shame or shyness is needed to restrain us. Shameless people have no respect for their own bodies or that of others. They have no boundaries or brakes. God expects from us to have a healthy dose of shyness, in order to know our place before Him and others.

# Sharing Is Caring

Moreover, brethren, we make known to you the grace of God bestowed on the churches of Macedonia: that in a great trial of affliction the abundance of their joy and their deep poverty abounded in the riches of their liberality.
**2 Corinthians 8:1-2 NKJV**

You will be enriched in every way to be generous in every way, which through us will produce thanksgiving to God.
**2 Corinthians 9:11 ESV**

In Him we have redemption through His blood, the forgiveness of sins, in accordance with the riches of God's grace. **Ephesians 1:7 NIV**

Don't forget to do good and to share with those in need. These are the sacrifices that please God.
**Hebrews 13:16 NLT**

Since the children have flesh and blood, He too shared in their humanity so that by His death He might break the power of him who holds the power of death – that is, the devil.
**Hebrews 2:14 NIV**

Command them to do good, to be rich in good deeds, and to be generous and willing to share.
**1 Timothy 6:18 NIV**

God is generous. He abounds in grace and goodness. There are no limits to His generosity. People, who are touched by His Spirit, are also generous. Their time, money and their hearts and hands are open to God's work to lighten the load of people in need. Such people know that their possessions belong to God; therefore they offer it back to Him in various ways.

# Our Heavenly Inheritance

If children, then heirs – heirs of God and joint heirs with Christ, if indeed we suffer with Him, that we may also be glorified together.
**Romans 8:17 NKJV**

So then you are no longer strangers and aliens, but you are fellow citizens with the saints and members of the household of God.
**Ephesians 2:19 ESV**

He died for us so that, whether we are awake or asleep, we may live together with Him.
**1 Thessalonians 5:10 NIV**

Because God's children are human beings – made of flesh and blood – the Son also became flesh and blood. For only as a human being could He die, and only by dying could He break the power of the devil, who had the power of death.
**Hebrews 2:14 NLT**

John answered, "Anyone who has two shirts should share with the one who has none, and anyone who has food should do the same."
**Luke 3:11 NIV**

"It is more blessed to give than to receive."
**Acts 20:35 ESV**

To share something means others are present to share in it with me. We are already sharing with our fellow believers in Christ the gifts of grace. He lets us fully partake in everything that He has established for us on the cross. We are co-heirs of His heavenly glory. His grace and abundance also belong to us. What a privilege to share in such a heavenly inheritance!

# The Good Shepherd

The LORD is my shepherd; I shall not want.
**Psalm 23:1 ESV**

"The one who enters by the gate is the shepherd of the sheep. The gatekeeper opens the gate for him, and the sheep listen to his voice. He calls his own sheep by name and leads them out."
**John 10:2-3 NIV**

"My sheep listen to My voice; I know them, and they follow Me. I give them eternal life, and they will never perish. No one can snatch them away from Me."
**John 10:27-28 NLT**

But He made His own people go forth like sheep, and guided them in the wilderness like a flock; and He led them on safely, so that they did not fear; but the sea overwhelmed their enemies.
**Psalm 78:52-53 NKJV**

"I am the good shepherd. The good shepherd lays down His life for the sheep."
**John 10:11 ESV**

"The Lamb who is in the midst of the throne will shepherd them and lead them to living fountains of waters. And God will wipe away every tear from their eyes."
**Revelation 7:17 NKJV**

We all know the popular Psalm 23. Or Jesus' words in John 10 that He is the Good Shepherd that laid down His life for His sheep. Sheep are not very brave animals. And neither are they risk-takers. Sheep need a shepherd. We are called to be the Lord's sheep, not lions or elephants or rhinos. We follow Him to green pastures. We follow Him. He knows the way, and He knows the best grazing fields.

# A Fight until Death

The next day John saw Jesus coming toward him and said, "Look, the Lamb of God, who takes away the sin of the world!"
**John 1:29 NIV**

For all have sinned and fall short of the glory of God.
**Romans 3:23 NKJV**

When Adam sinned, sin entered the world. Adam's sin brought death, so death spread to everyone, for everyone sinned.
**Romans 5:12 NLT**

For our sake He made Him to be sin who knew no sin, so that in Him we might become the righteousness of God. **2 Corinthians 5:21 ESV**

"I am sending you to open their eyes, so they may turn from darkness to light and from the power of Satan to God. Then they will receive forgiveness for their sins and be given a place among God's people, who are set apart by faith in me."
**Acts 26:17-18 ESV**

I am writing to you, little children, because your sins are forgiven for His name's sake.
**1 John 2:12 ESV**

Remember, it is sin to know what you ought to do and then not do it.
**James 4:17 NLT**

Sins are rebellion against God. It is disobeying His will. To sin is not to let God be God. It is not to stand in a relationship with Him. Sin is a destructive force. Things like murder, theft, greed, and gossip are such sinful symptoms. We trust Jesus to deliver us from the power of the symptoms and the sins. We're no longer slaves to this. He breaks the bonds of sin in our lives.

# All for His Glory

He who walks righteously and speaks uprightly, who despises the gain of oppressions, who shakes his hands, lest they hold a bribe, who stops his ears from hearing of bloodshed and shuts his eyes from looking on evil.
**Isaiah 33:15 ESV**

Let love be without hypocrisy. Abhor what is evil. Cling to what is good.
**Romans 12:9 NKJV**

For I want you to understand what really matters, so that you may live pure and blameless lives until the day of Christ's return.
**Philippians 1:10 NLT**

Now that you have purified yourselves by obeying the truth so that you have sincere love for each other, love one another deeply, from the heart.
**1 Peter 1:22 NIV**

"The glory which You gave Me I have given them, that they may be one just as We are one."
**John 17:22 NKJV**

So whether you eat or drink or whatever you do, do it all for the glory of God.
**1 Corinthians 10:31 NIV**

To be genuine and sincere is to synchronize your heart, thoughts, emotions, habits, words and deeds with each other. Such sincerity is always visible to others. Unfortunately the same is true of insincerity or hypocrisy as we often call it. God looks at our hearts. He tests our motives … He knows why we do certain things. Make sure your heart is pure. Let the Spirit renew and purify your life today. Allow Him to be in control of your life for His glory.

# Sing a New Song

Around midnight Paul and Silas were praying and singing hymns to God, and the other prisoners were listening.
**Acts 16:25 NLT**

Do not be drunk with wine, in which is dissipation; but be filled with the Spirit, speaking to one another in psalms and hymns and spiritual songs, singing and making melody in your heart to the Lord.
**Ephesians 5:18-19 NKJV**

Let everything that has breath praise the LORD. Praise the LORD.
**Psalm 150:6 NIV**

Sing to Him, sing psalms to Him; talk of all His wondrous works!
**Psalm 105:2 NKJV**

Come, let us sing to the LORD! Let us shout joyfully to the Rock of our salvation.
**Psalm 95:1 NLT**

Let the word of Christ dwell in you richly, singing psalms and hymns and spiritual songs, with thankfulness in your hearts to God.
**Colossians 3:16 ESV**

Rejoice in the Lord always. I will say it again: Rejoice!
**Philippians 4:4 NIV**

Music is prominent in the Bible. Some groups and people were always singing. When the people felt afraid or happy; when they were sorry or when they were celebrating, people sang. Most Psalms are musical phrases communicating with God in song. In heaven people also sing. Let's train our voices today for the eternal choir of celebration. Let's praise God with our voices and our song. He created and transformed us for this.

# Sinners and Saints

For while we were still weak, at the right time Christ died for the ungodly. For one will scarcely die for a righteous person – though perhaps for a good person one would dare even to die – but God shows His love for us in that while we were still sinners, Christ died for us.
**Romans 5:6-8 ESV**

This is a faithful saying and worthy of all acceptance, that Christ Jesus came into the world to save sinners, of whom I am chief.
**1 Timothy 1:15 NKJV**

For everyone has sinned; we all fall short of God's glorious standard. **Romans 3:23 NLT**

On hearing this, Jesus said to them, "It is not the healthy who need a doctor, but the sick. I have not come to call the righteous, but sinners."
**Mark 2:17 NIV**

If we confess our sins, He is faithful and just to forgive us. **1 John 1:9 ESV**

Indeed, there is no one on earth who is righteous, no one who does what is right and never sins.
**Ecclesiastes 7:20 NIV**

Though our outer self is wasting away, our inner self is being renewed day by day.
**2 Corinthians 4:16 ESV**

The term sinner is an indication of status or identity in the New Testament. Sinners are lost people. Never once did God call His people that, not even in 1 Timothy 1:15. There Paul speaks about His own past as a sinner. But he was saved and became a servant of God. It's also true for us. We're still doing sinful things, but we're children of God regarding our status and position before Him.

# A Servant's Heart

"When a servant comes in from plowing or taking care of sheep, does his master say, 'Come in and eat with me'? No, he says, 'Prepare my meal, put on your apron, and serve me while I eat. Then you can eat later.' And does the master thank the servant for doing what he was told to do? Of course not. In the same way, when you obey Me you should say, 'We are unworthy servants who have simply done our duty.'"
**Luke 17:7-10 NLT**

Paul, a servant of Christ Jesus, called to be an apostle and set apart for the gospel of God.
**Romans 1:1 NIV**

Though He was in the form of God, did not count equality with God a thing to be grasped, but emptied Himself, by taking the form of a servant, being born in the likeness of men.
**Philippians 2:6-7 ESV**

For the one who was a slave when called to faith in the Lord is the Lord's freed person; similarly, the one who was free when called is Christ's slave.
**1 Corinthians 7:22 NIV**

Having been set free from sin, you became slaves of righteousness.
**Romans 6:18 NKJV**

Slaves were at the bottom of the social ladder in biblical times. Slaves were human farming tools and talking dogs, one philosopher said. Paul called himself a servant of Christ many times. Day and night he was in service of the Lord. Christ was the Head, He was the servant. He waited expectantly for every command from Christ and performed it enthusiastically. We are also servants of Christ. His wishes are our command.

# Get Enough Sleep

You shall teach them diligently to your children, and shall talk of them when you sit in your house, when you walk by the way, when you lie down, and when you rise up.

**Deuteronomy 6:7 NKJV**

It is useless for you to work so hard from early morning until late at night, anxiously working for food to eat; for God gives rest to His loved ones."

**Psalm 127:2 NLT**

If you lie down, you will not be afraid; when you lie down, your sleep will be sweet.

**Proverbs 3:24 ESV**

The fear of the LORD leads to life; then one rests content, untouched by trouble.

**Proverbs 19:23 NIV**

Having hope will give you courage. You will be protected and will rest in safety. You will lie down unafraid, and many will look to you for help.

**Job 11:18-19 NLT**

In peace I will both lie down and sleep; for You alone, O LORD, make me dwell in safety.

**Psalm 4:8 ESV**

I lie down and sleep; I wake again, because the LORD sustains me.

**Psalm 3:5 NIV**

Sleep is something that our bodies need very much. Without sleep we get sick. Without healthy sleeping patterns our immune system is put under immense pressure. Sleep often. God will give you what you need in your sleep when you live for Him during your waking hours. Trust Him for a good night's rest so that you can live for His glory when you're awake.

# A Lovely Aroma

"You shall make an altar to burn incense on; you shall make it of acacia wood."
**Exodus 30:1 NKJV**

"Every morning when Aaron maintains the lamps, he must burn fragrant incense on the altar. And each evening when he lights the lamps, he must again burn incense in the LORD's presence. This must be done from generation to generation." **Exodus 30:7-8 NLT**

All Your garments are scented with myrrh and aloes and cassia, out of the ivory palaces, by which they have made You glad.
**Psalm 45:8 NKJV**

But thanks be to God, who always leads us as captives in Christ's triumphal procession and uses us to spread the aroma of the knowledge of Him everywhere. For we are to God the pleasing aroma of Christ among those who are being saved and those who are perishing.
**2 Corinthians 2:14-15 NIV**

Walk in love, as Christ loved us and gave Himself up for us, a fragrant offering and sacrifice to God.
**Ephesians 5:2 ESV**

You will offer special gifts as a pleasing aroma to the LORD. **Numbers 15:3 NLT**

Scents and smells are part of our faith. In the temple, Israel burnt incense as offerings. Paul said in 2 Corinthians 2 that followers of Christ should be His sweet-smelling aroma. We are a pleasant smell for His glory. We are the incense glorifying God. Others must smell His sweet aroma on us. They should be drawn to Him through the lovely smell of our faith. Then our scent is pleasing to Him.

# Armed for Battle

Stand your ground, putting on the belt of truth and the body armor of God's righteousness. For shoes, put on the peace that comes from the Good News so that you will be fully prepared. In addition to all of these, hold up the shield of faith to stop the fiery arrows of the devil. Put on salvation as your helmet, and take the sword of the Spirit, which is the word of God.
**Ephesians 6:14-17 NLT**

You believe that God is one; you do well.
**James 2:19 ESV**

The weapons we fight with are not the weapons of the world. On the contrary, they have divine power to demolish strongholds. We demolish arguments and every pretension that sets itself up against the knowledge of God, and we take captive every thought to make it obedient to Christ.
**2 Corinthians 10:4-5 NIV**

For You have armed me with strength for the battle; You have subdued under me those who rose up against me.
**Psalm 18:39 NKJV**

Soldiers are trained for battle. Jesus' soldiers too. We are His army and we're armed and ready to fight. Our weapons are ready: Faith is our shield with which we can extinguish all the flaming arrows of the evil one. The helmet and the sword of the Spirit assure our salvation. And put on your feet the shoes of readiness to proclaim the Good News.

# Soul and Spirit

So is it with the resurrection of the dead. What is sown is perishable; what is raised is imperishable. It is sown in dishonor; it is raised in glory. It is sown in weakness; it is raised in power. It is sown a natural body; it is raised a spiritual body. If there is a natural body, there is also a spiritual body.
**1 Corinthians 15:42-44 ESV**

That is why we never give up. Though our bodies are dying, our spirits are being renewed every day.
**2 Corinthians 4:16 NLT**

Oh, how my soul praises the Lord. **Luke 1:46 NLT**

When He opened the fifth seal, I saw under the altar the souls of those who had been slain for the word of God and for the testimony which they held.
**Revelation 6:9 NKJV**

Jesus replied: "'Love the Lord your God with all your heart and with all your soul and with all your mind.' This is the first and greatest commandment."
**Matthew 22:37-38 NIV**

And the dust returns to the earth as it was, and the spirit returns to God who gave it.
**Ecclesiastes 12:7 ESV**

During my childhood the pastor always referred to the people as the souls in the congregation. I found it amusing. Only later did I find out that our soul, according to the Bible, refers to our most inner part, and our bodies are the outward part. Outwardly we are wasting away, but our souls live forever. Yet, at the Second Coming we will receive brand-new bodies. We will be whole, body and spirit!

NOVEMBER

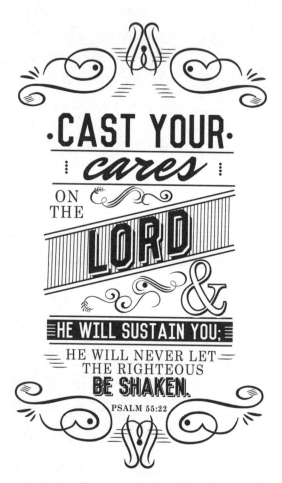

CAST YOUR·

*cares*

ON THE

LORD

&

HE WILL SUSTAIN YOU;

HE WILL NEVER LET
THE RIGHTEOUS
BE SHAKEN.

PSALM 55:22

# Sowing and Reaping

"But others fell on good ground and yielded a crop: some a hundredfold, some sixty, some thirty."
**Matthew 13:8 NKJV**

Here is another illustration Jesus used: "The Kingdom of Heaven is like a mustard seed planted in a field."
**Matthew 13:31 NLT**

The point is this: whoever sows sparingly will also reap sparingly, and whoever sows bountifully will also reap bountifully.
**2 Corinthians 9:6 ESV**

Those who are peacemakers will plant seeds of peace and reap a harvest of righteousness.
**James 3:18 NLT**

"Therefore I say to you, do not worry about your life, what you will eat or what you will drink; nor about your body, what you will put on. Is not life more than food and the body more than clothing? Look at the birds of the air, for they neither sow nor reap nor gather into barns; yet your heavenly Father feeds them. Are you not of more value than they?"
**Matthew 6:25-26 NKJV**

The Bible often tells of sowers, harvesting, seeds and farmlands. Jesus often compared the kingdom of God with good soil. When good seeds fall in the soil, it will bear fruit hundredfold. Talk about a phenomenal harvest! That's how wide God's goodness is. He always has a good harvest in mind. He prepares the soil for good crops. Make sure your heart is prepared and ready for His seed.

# Talk Right, Live Right

"Talk no more so very proudly; let no arrogance come from your mouth, for the LORD is the God of knowledge; and by Him actions are weighed."
**1 Samuel 2:3 NKJV**

Take control of what I say, O LORD, and guard my lips.
**Psalm 141:3 NLT**

The tongue has the power of life and death, and those who love it will eat its fruit.
**Proverbs 18:21 NIV**

Let your speech always be gracious, seasoned with salt, so that you may know how you ought to answer each person.
**Colossians 4:6 ESV**

Let no corrupting talk come out of your mouths, but only such as is good for building up, as fits the occasion, that it may give grace to those who hear.
**Ephesians 4:29 ESV**

The wise are known for their understanding, and pleasant words are persuasive.
**Proverbs 16:21 NLT**

When words are many, sin is not absent, but he who holds his tongue is wise.
**Proverbs 10:19 NIV**

Gracious words are a honeycomb, sweet to the soul and healing to the bones.
**Proverbs 16:24 NIV**

Words are powerful. We all use words on a daily basis. New studies show that men and women talk equally much every day. We make ourselves heard and understood through our words. But every now and then we need to slow down … and put a guard at our mouths. Keeping quiet and considering our words carefully are part of healthy habits of communication. The kind the Bible often mentions. Master a few rules of good speech today. Talk right, and live right!

# Avoid Stagnation

A little sleep, a little slumber, a little folding of the hands to rest, and poverty will come upon you like a robber.
**Proverbs 6:10-11 ESV**

The way of the lazy man is like a hedge of thorns, but the way of the upright is a highway.
**Proverbs 15:19 NKJV**

We all, who with unveiled faces contemplate the Lord's glory, are being transformed into His image with ever-increasing glory, which comes from the Lord, who is the Spirit.
**2 Corinthians 3:18 NIV**

Let all who are spiritually mature agree on these things. If you disagree on some point, I believe God will make it plain to you. But we must hold on to the progress we have already made.
**Philippians 3:15-16 NLT**

Do not conform to the pattern of this world, but be transformed by the renewing of your mind. Then you will be able to test and approve what God's will is – His good, pleasing and perfect will. **Romans 12:2 NIV**

He who began a good work in you will carry it on to completion until the day of Christ Jesus. **Philippians 1:6 NIV**

Stagnation happens in your head before it happens in your body. The rusting starts firstly in your mind. Afterwards it infects the rest of the body. To stagnate means not to want to learn anything new. The same old ways, complaints, questions, solutions, and conversations are signs of stagnation. Don't get stuck in a rut. It steals your joy and your soul. Be eager to learn so that you can discover new treasures in the Lord's Word every day.

# Standing in the Gap

"Do not pray for this people nor offer any plea or petition for them; do not plead with Me, for I will not listen to you."
**Jeremiah 7:16 NIV**

Now He who searches the hearts knows what the mind of the Spirit is, because He makes intercession for the saints according to the will of God.
**Romans 8:27 NKJV**

Who is to condemn? Christ Jesus is the one who died – more than that, who was raised – who is at the right hand of God, who indeed is interceding for us.
**Romans 8:34 ESV**

Therefore He is able, once and forever, to save those who come to God through Him. He lives forever to intercede with God on their behalf.
**Hebrews 7:25 NLT**

I urge you, first of all, to pray for all people. Ask God to help them; intercede on their behalf, and give thanks for them. Pray this way for kings and all who are in authority so that we can live peaceful and quiet lives marked by godliness and dignity. This is good and pleases God our Savior.
**1 Timothy 2:1-3 NLT**

To intercede for others is to give up your place in the prayer queue for someone else. It is to take their needs and wants on your shoulders, and bring them to the throne of God's grace. The best news ever is that Christ and the Holy Spirit are continuously interceding on our behalf. And we are the ones they plead for day and night. Their heavenly prayers keep us on the right course.

# Grow Towards God

At that time the disciples came to Jesus and asked, "Who, then, is the greatest in the kingdom of heaven?" He called a little child to Him, and placed the child among them. And He said: "Truly I tell you, unless you change and become like little children, you will never enter the kingdom of heaven. Therefore, whoever takes the lowly position of this child is the greatest in the kingdom of heaven. And whoever welcomes one such child in My name welcomes Me." Matthew 18:1-5 NIV

If anyone is in Christ, the new creation has come: The old has gone, the new is here! 2 Corinthians 5:17 NIV

Grow in the grace and knowledge of our Lord and Savior Jesus Christ. To Him be glory both now and forever! 2 Peter 3:18 NIV

My health may fail, and my spirit may grow weak, but God remains the strength of my heart; He is mine forever.
Psalm 73:26 NLT

My brethren, count it all joy when you fall into various trials, knowing that the testing of your faith produces patience. But let patience have its perfect work, that you may be perfect and complete, lacking nothing.
James 1:2-4 NKJV

If you don't change and grow backwards away from self and toward God, you become a victim of … yourself! If you don't change and become like a child, then you're going to be left with many hang-ups. Or worse, if you don't become like a child, you'll never see the kingdom of God – as simple as that. Growing backwards is growing in Jesus' direction. Smaller is greater. Less of yourself. More vulnerability and awe, less control.

# A Spirit of Hope

May the God of hope fill you with all joy and peace as you trust in Him, so that you may overflow with hope by the power of the Holy Spirit.
**Romans 15:13 NIV**

Faith shows the reality of what we hope for; it is the evidence of things we cannot see.
**Hebrews 11:1 NLT**

Blessed be the God and Father of our Lord Jesus Christ! According to His great mercy, He has caused us to be born again to a living hope through the resurrection of Jesus Christ from the dead.
**1 Peter 1:3 ESV**

But sanctify the Lord God in your hearts, and always be ready to give a defense to everyone who asks you a reason for the hope that is in you, with meekness and fear.
**1 Peter 3:15 NKJV**

Now may our Lord Jesus Christ Himself, and our God and Father, who has loved us and given us everlasting consolation and good hope by grace.
**2 Thessalonians 2:16 NKJV**

No one is established by wickedness, but the root of the righteous will never be moved.
**Proverbs 12:3 ESV**

We read about hope often in the Bible. Our hope is found in the Lord. Hope and steadfastness flow from a deep knowledge that God is who He says He is. It is extended from the breeding ground of His love, care and closeness. Steadfastness isn't vested in ourselves, but in our great God. We trust in Him and we put our hope in Him. He is our safe refuge and strength. Praise His name!

# Manage God's Assets Well

"Who then is the faithful and wise manager, whom his master will set over his household, to give them their portion of food at the proper time? Blessed is that servant whom his master will find so doing when he comes." Luke 12:42-43 ESV

If you instruct the brethren in these things, you will be a good minister of Jesus Christ, nourished in the words of faith and of the good doctrine which you have carefully followed.
1 Timothy 4:6 NKJV

Moreover it is required in stewards that one be found faithful.
1 Corinthians 4:2 NKJV

Each of you should use whatever gift you have received to serve others, as faithful stewards of God's grace in its various forms.
1 Peter 4:10 NIV

"The servant to whom he had entrusted the five bags of silver came forward with five more and said, 'Master, you gave me five bags of silver to invest, and I have earned five more.' The master was full of praise. 'Well done, my good and faithful servant. You have been faithful in handling this small amount, so now I will give you many more responsibilities. Let's celebrate together!'"
Matthew 25:20-21 NLT

We need to be good stewards of God's assets. He appointed us as managers of His earthly home. No, we can't do with God's things what we want. They don't belong to us. We need to invest it correctly and use it to make the maximum impact for His Kingdom. Each penny that we own, grow in God's hand. No single cent that we give away with a glad heart is ever wasted in His service.

# Mr. Stingy?

Every day they continued to meet together in the temple courts. They broke bread in their homes and ate together with glad and sincere hearts.
**Acts 2:46 NIV**

In a great trial of affliction the abundance of their joy and their deep poverty abounded in the riches of their liberality.
**2 Corinthians 8:2 NKJV**

You must each decide in your heart how much to give. And don't give reluctantly or in response to pressure. "For God loves a person who gives cheerfully."
**2 Corinthians 9:7 NLT**

You will be enriched in every way to be generous in every way, which through us will produce thanksgiving to God.
**2 Corinthians 9:11 ESV**

Tell them to use their money to do good. They should be rich in good works and generous to those in need, always being ready to share with others.
**1 Timothy 6:18 NLT**

Have I been stingy with my food and refused to share it with orphans? No, from childhood I have cared for orphans like a father, and all my life I have cared for widows.
**Job 31:17-18 NLT**

God doesn't like stingy people. He is endlessly generous. He also expects His children to be and do the same. The way we should follow is generosity, not greediness. Before trying to save a penny, we should rather give it away. Before clinging to our so-called hard-earned money, rather share it with people in need. After all, we have a Heavenly Father who cares for us in all things.

# Just Stop …

"Do not judge, or you too will be judged."
Matthew 7:1 NIV

"So don't be afraid, little flock. For it gives your Father great happiness to give you the Kingdom."
Luke 12:32 NLT

Do not get drunk with wine, for that is debauchery, but be filled with the Spirit.
Ephesians 5:18 ESV

Do not love the world or the things in the world. If anyone loves the world, the love of the Father is not in him.
1 John 2:15 NKJV

Therefore, change your hearts and stop being stubborn.
Deuteronomy 10:16 NLT

My child, listen to me and do as I say, and you will have a long, good life.
Proverbs 4:10 NLT

Therefore, I urge you, brothers and sisters, in view of God's mercy, to offer your bodies as a living sacrifice, holy and pleasing to God – this is your true and proper worship.
Romans 12:1 NIV

See to it, brothers and sisters, that none of you has a sinful, unbelieving heart that turns away from the living God. Hebrews 3:12 NIV

There are a couple of things that we need to stop doing in our lives. We must stop being afraid. We must stop busying ourselves with the sinful things of this world. We must stop giving in to alcohol and food, and allow the Spirit to fill us with His presence instead. We must stop judging others and leave that part to God. Then we're on the right track. Then we are free in Christ.

# His Power at Work

"This is My command – be strong and courageous! Do not be afraid or discouraged. For the LORD your God is with you wherever you go."
**Joshua 1:9 NLT**

The LORD your God is in your midst, a mighty one who will save; He will rejoice over you with gladness; He will quiet you by His love; He will exult over you with loud singing.
**Zephaniah 3:17 ESV**

LORD, be merciful to us, for we have waited for you. Be our strong arm each day and our salvation in times of trouble.
**Isaiah 33:2 NLT**

Therefore take up the whole armor of God, that you may be able to withstand in the evil day, and having done all, to stand.
**Ephesians 6:13 NKJV**

I can do all this through Him who gives me strength.
**Philippians 4:13 NIV**

Now to Him who is able to do far more abundantly than all that we ask or think, according to the power at work within us, to Him be glory in the church and in Christ Jesus throughout all generations, forever and ever. Amen.
**Ephesians 3:20-21 ESV**

Power is great. Everyone loves power. Men want to be strong. That is why there are so many strong man competitions. The Lord calls us to be strong; to be strong in the Lord, and to find your strength in Him. He alone is our strength. He is our refuge and help in trouble. Even when we feel powerless, we are strong in Him. His strength never diminishes. He is always and forever in control.

# Following in His Footsteps

"Stand at the crossroads and look; ask for the ancient paths, ask where the good way is, and walk in it, and you will find rest for your souls. But you said, 'We will not walk in it.'"
**Jeremiah 6:16 NIV**

Then Jesus, looking at him, loved him, and said to him, "One thing you lack: Go your way, sell whatever you have and give to the poor, and you will have treasure in heaven; and come, take up the cross, and follow Me." **Mark 10:21 NKJV**

"Go and walk through the land in every direction, for I am giving it to you."
**Genesis 13:17 NLT**

With the Lord's authority I say this: Live no longer as the Gentiles do, for they are hopelessly confused.
**Ephesians 4:17 NLT**

Yet you have still a few names in Sardis, people who have not soiled their garments, and they will walk with me in white, for they are worthy.
**Revelation 3:4 ESV**

God called you to do good, even if it means suffering, just as Christ suffered for you. He is your example, and you must follow in His steps.
**1 Peter 2:21 NLT**

A strong image in the Bible is walking or strolling. We walk in faith. We turn our heart's confessions into actions. We walk in Jesus' way. We sidestep the ways of sin and death. Jesus' footsteps are right in front of us, guiding the way. His way of the cross is our direction. We walk in His steps all the time.

# Dealing with Struggles

Count it all joy, my brothers, when you meet trials of various kinds, for you know that the testing of your faith produces steadfastness. And let steadfastness have its full effect, that you may be perfect and complete, lacking in nothing. **James 1:2-4 ESV**

For we do not wrestle against flesh and blood, but against the rulers, against the authorities, against the cosmic powers over this present darkness, against the spiritual forces of evil in the heavenly places. **Ephesians 6:12 ESV**

After all, you have not yet given your lives in your struggle against sin. **Hebrews 12:4 NLT**

The disciples were astonished at His words. But Jesus answered again and said to them, "Children, how hard it is for those who trust in riches to enter the kingdom of God!" **Mark 10:24 NKJV**

"I have told you all this so that you may have peace in Me. Here on earth you will have many trials and sorrows. But take heart, because I have overcome the world." **John 16:33 NLT**

We have put our hope in the living God, who is the Savior of all people, and especially of those who believe. **1 Timothy 4:10 NIV**

Struggles are a normal part of faith. We are in a battle against the evil forces of hell. People's eternal salvation is at stake. Our spiritual growth is also on the line. Struggles are therefore part of our daily existence when we're followers of the Lord. We keep our eyes fixed on Christ while we're fighting the good fight. We remain standing. He is our Anchor and safe Refuge.

# More Than Conquerors

"But whoever causes one of these little ones who believe in Me to stumble, it would be better for him if a millstone were hung around his neck, and he were thrown into the sea. If your hand causes you to sin, cut it off. It is better for you to enter into life maimed, rather than having two hands, to go to hell, into the fire that shall never be quenched."
**Mark 9:42-43 NKJV**

So, dear brothers and sisters, work hard to prove that you really are among those God has called and chosen. Do these things, and you will never fall away.
**2 Peter 1:10 NLT**

We all stumble in many ways. Anyone who is never at fault in what they say is perfect, able to keep their whole body in check. **James 3:2 NIV**

Jesus answered, "Are there not twelve hours in the day? If anyone walks in the day, he does not stumble, because he sees the light of this world. But if anyone walks in the night, he stumbles, because the light is not in him." **John 11:9-10 ESV**

The LORD directs the steps of the godly. He delights in every detail of their lives. Though they stumble, they will never fall, for the LORD holds them by the hand.
**Psalm 37:23-24 NLT**

We all stumble on our faith journey. The road is sometimes just too hard. We fall over our own words. We stumble over our sinful deeds. We stumble over our foolish behavior. During such times we must allow the Lord to bind up our wounds. When we put others at a disadvantage in the process, we need to clear the air. Stumbling should never become a habit or a dwelling place in our lives. Those who stumble and fall down, must get up in the name of the Lord.

# Submit to One Another

"However, do not rejoice that the spirits submit to you, but rejoice that your names are written in heaven." Luke 10:20 NIV

To one another in the fear of God. Wives, submit to your own husbands, as to the Lord.
Ephesians 5:21-22 NKJV

Remember your leaders, those who spoke to you the word of God. Consider the outcome of their way of life, and imitate their faith.
Hebrews 13:7 ESV

Submit yourselves, then, to God. Resist the devil, and he will flee from you.
James 4:7 NIV

The women should keep silent in the churches. For they are not permitted to speak, but should be in submission, as the Law also says. 1 Corinthians 14:34 ESV

Submit to God and be at peace with Him; in this way prosperity will come to you.
Job 22:21 NIV

Do not be stubborn, as they were, but submit yourselves to the LORD.
2 Chronicles 30:8 NLT

The mind governed by the flesh is hostile to God; it does not submit to God's law, nor can it do so.
Romans 8:7 NIV

To subject yourself to something is to be submissive. Many husbands have misused Bible verses on the topic of submission to dominate their wives. Listen to this, Paul commanded all of us in Ephesians 5:21 to submit to one another (although many Bible translations excluded this part of Paul's words on marriages incorrectly!). Husbands and wives need to submit to each other. Paul doesn't speak of a master-slave relationship; he refers to the language of love, caring and service!

# Success Is Living God's Way

Keep this Book of the Law always on your lips; meditate on it day and night, so that you may be careful to do everything written in it. Then you will be prosperous and successful. **Joshua 1:8 NIV**

Observe the requirements of the LORD your God, and follow all His ways. Keep the decrees, commands, regulations, and laws written in the Law of Moses so that you will be successful in all you do and wherever you go. **1 Kings 2:3 NLT**

Believe in the LORD your God, and you will be able to stand firm. Believe in His prophets, and you will succeed. **2 Chronicles 20:20 NLT**

So this Daniel prospered in the reign of Darius and in the reign of Cyrus the Persian. **Daniel 6:28 NKJV**

Then I replied to them, "The God of heaven will make us prosper, and we His servants will arise and build, but you have no portion or right or claim in Jerusalem." **Nehemiah 2:20 ESV**

His master saw that the LORD was with him and that the LORD caused all that he did to succeed in his hands. **Genesis 39:3 ESV**

May He give you the desire of your heart and make all your plans succeed. **Psalm 20:4 NIV**

Everybody strives for success. Success naturally means different things to different people. For God's people success is equal to a life lived closely to Him. Success is to live according to His will. A life dedicated to Him is expressed through our love for Him and others. Then it flows over to all other areas of life, as Daniel experienced. God's success is contagious; it always pulls people closer to Him.

# Suffering and Hardships

"I have said these things to you, that in Me you may have peace. In the world you will have tribulation. But take heart; I have overcome the world."
**John 16:33 ESV**

Since we are His children, we are His heirs. In fact, together with Christ we are heirs of God's glory. But if we are to share His glory, we must also share His suffering. **Romans 8:17 NLT**

All this is evidence that God's judgment is right, and as a result you will be counted worthy of the kingdom of God, for which you are suffering. **2 Thessalonians 1:5 NIV**

Because you have kept My command to persevere, I also will keep you from the hour of trial which shall come upon the whole world, to test those who dwell on the earth.
**Revelation 3:10 NKJV**

Resist him, steadfast in the faith, knowing that the same sufferings are experienced by your brotherhood in the world. But may the God of all grace, who called us to His eternal glory by Christ Jesus, after you have suffered a while, perfect, establish, strengthen, and settle you.
**1 Peter 5:9-10 NKJV**

Suffering is a reality. At one point or another we all endure suffering and hardships. It is part of life, and also part of the Gospel message. Because the Good News of Christ goes against the principles of the world, His people will always experience resistance. Jesus Himself said that it will happen to us. Yet He, as our risen Lord and Savior, is always with us to carry us through every storm.

# Become a Spiritual Supporter

"Don't be afraid, for I am with you. Don't be discouraged, for I am your God. I will strengthen you and help you. I will hold you up with My victorious right hand."
**Isaiah 41:10 NLT**

"In everything I did, I showed you that by this kind of hard work we must help the weak, remembering the words the Lord Jesus Himself said: 'It is more blessed to give than to receive.'"
**Acts 20:35 NIV**

Your words have supported those who were falling; You encouraged those with shaky knees.
**Job 4:4 NLT**

For they have gone out for the sake of the name. Therefore we ought to support people like these, that we may be fellow workers for the truth.
**3 John 7-8 ESV**

"Listen to Me, O house of Jacob, and all the remnant of the house of Israel, who have been upheld by Me from birth, who have been carried from the womb: Even to your old age, I am He, and even to gray hairs I will carry you! I have made, and I will bear; even I will carry, and will deliver you."
**Isaiah 46:3-4 NKJV**

Our greatest supporter is God. With His mighty hand He keeps us standing. We should do the same with each other. To support someone is to assist them in a special way. It means that a specific person needs help, and that the person receives it from us. We help where we can, and do it despite our own needs and wants. We offer ourselves to the service of God and others.

# Absolute Surrender

Thus says the LORD, the God of hosts, the God of Israel: "If you surely surrender to the king of Babylon's princes, then your soul shall live; this city shall not be burned with fire, and you and your house shall live."
**Jeremiah 38:17 NKJV**

"How can I give you up, O Ephraim? How can I hand you over, O Israel? How can I make you like Admah? How can I treat you like Zeboiim? My heart recoils within Me; My compassion grows warm and tender."
**Hosea 11:8 ESV**

Then, when our dying bodies have been transformed into bodies that will never die, this Scripture will be fulfilled: "Death is swallowed up in victory."
**1 Corinthians 15:24 NLT**

If I give all I possess to the poor and give over my body to hardship that I may boast, but do not have love, I gain nothing. **1 Corinthians 13:3 NIV**

Going a little farther, He fell on the ground and prayed that, if it were possible, the hour might pass from Him. And He said, "Abba, Father, all things are possible for you. Remove this cup from Me. Yet not what I will, but what You will."
**Mark 14:35-36 ESV**

To surrender is to lay down your weapons. Surrender usually means that you lose something, but not when it comes to the Lord. To surrender your life to Him is to gain life for all eternity. Also when Jesus surrenders all power to God at the end of time, He is acknowledging that all power and might belongs to the Triune God. And that He once more chooses to share it with His Father.

# A Taste for Life

Oh, taste and see that the LORD is good; blessed is the man who trusts in Him!
**Psalm 34:8 NKJV**

Like the finest apple tree in the orchard is my lover among other young men. I sit in his delightful shade and taste his delicious fruit.
**Song of Songs 2:3 NLT**

"For I tell you, none of those men who were invited shall taste My banquet."
**Luke 14:24 ESV**

Like newborn babies, crave pure spiritual milk, so that by it you may grow up in your salvation, now that you have tasted that the Lord is good. **1 Peter 2:2-3 NIV**

"Salt is good for seasoning. But if it loses its flavor, how do you make it salty again? Flavorless salt is good neither for the soil nor for the manure pile. It is thrown away. Anyone with ears to hear should listen and understand!"
**Luke 14:34-35 NLT**

Who have tasted the goodness of the word of God and the power of the age to come.
**Hebrews 6:5 NLT**

How sweet are Your words to my taste, sweeter than honey to my mouth!
**Psalm 119:103 NIV**

Taste is an important part of our senses. When we have flu, and can't smell or taste anything we appreciate our senses again. God says He is so close to us that we can taste and see His goodness. We also taste His goodness when we break bread together in Holy Communion. Then we taste and smell godly grace and love.

# Teach to Change Lives

The things that you have heard from me among many witnesses, commit these to faithful men who will be able to teach others also.
2 Timothy 2:2 NKJV

Preach the word of God. Be prepared, whether the time is favorable or not. Patiently correct, rebuke, and encourage your people with good teaching.
2 Timothy 4:2 NLT

Not many of you should become teachers, my brothers, for you know that we who teach will be judged with greater strictness.
James 3:1 ESV

An angel of the Lord came at night, opened the gates of the jail, and brought them out. Then he told them, "Go to the Temple and give the people this message of life!" So at daybreak the apostles entered the Temple, as they were told, and immediately began teaching. When the high priest and his officials arrived, they convened the high council – the full assembly of the elders of Israel. Then they sent for the apostles to be brought from the jail for trial.
Acts 5:19-21 NLT

The Lord's servant must be kind to everyone, able to teach, not resentful.
2 Timothy 2:24 NIV

Christianity is about faith that is constantly learning and teaching. We learn from beginning to end … from early in the morning until late at night. We should never stop learning. And for that to happen we need skilled teachers. Paul knew this, and that is why he made a big effort to train clergy; people who could convey God's Word correctly and purely. Make sure you do the same when you teach others about God. Stick to the Word, and surround yourself with such people.

# Through the Valley of Tears

Then he set his countenance in a stare until he was ashamed; and the man of God wept. **2 Kings 8:11 NKJV**

Therefore, I will mourn and lament. I will walk around barefoot and naked. I will howl like a jackal and moan like an owl. **Micah 1:8 NLT**

The LORD said, "The outcry against Sodom and Gomorrah is so great and their sin so grievous." **Genesis 18:20 NIV**

Be wretched and mourn and weep. Let your laughter be turned to mourning and your joy to gloom. **James 4:9 ESV**

Let, I pray, Your merciful kindness be for my comfort, according to Your word to Your servant. Let Your tender mercies come to me, that I may live; for Your law is my delight. **Psalm 119:76-77 NKJV**

"Blessed are those who mourn, for they will be comforted." **Matthew 5:4 NIV**

Rejoice with those who rejoice; mourn with those who mourn. **Romans 12:15 NIV**

Those who sow in tears shall reap with shouts of joy! **Psalm 126:5 ESV**

Sadness and grief are genuine human emotions. As men we are allowed to experience such emotions, and we are also allowed to show them! You are not made of stone. We are not emotionless icebergs. God created us to experience our emotions deeply and intensely. That is why we cry when we're sad. That is why we express our emotions when we, our friends, or family members suffer hardship. We also know that God will wipe every tear from our eyes. He comforts us when our hearts are breaking.

# The Testing of Your Faith

Blessed is the man who endures temptation; for when he has been approved, he will receive the crown of life which the Lord has promised to those who love Him. Let no one say when he is tempted, "I am tempted by God"; for God cannot be tempted by evil, nor does He Himself tempt anyone. James 1:12-13 NKJV

Fire tests the purity of silver and gold, but the LORD tests the heart. Proverbs 17:3 NLT

Beloved, do not believe every spirit, but test the spirits to see whether they are from God, for many false prophets have gone out into the world.
1 John 4:1 ESV

Search me, O God, and know my heart; test me and know my anxious thoughts.
Psalm 139:23 NLT

Let us behave decently, as in the daytime, not in carousing and drunkenness, not in sexual immorality and debauchery, not in dissension and jealousy.
Romans 13:13 NIV

Consider it pure joy, my brothers and sisters, whenever you face trials of many kinds, because you know that the testing of your faith develops perseverance. Let perseverance finish its work so that you may be mature and complete, not lacking anything. James 1:2-4 NIV

Life puts us through tests. Don't say that God orchestrates the testing, because He doesn't. He trusts His good work in our lives. He trusts His Son's salvation enough so that He doesn't need to put us through a test to find out if we're really His children. But life comes with testing. Since sin and evil entered the world, it's our lot. Yet God wants to see what we do with the tests of life. Will it pull us closer ever closer, or away from Him?

# Following Jesus' Example

There is a way that appears to be right, but in the end it leads to death.
**Proverbs 14:12 NIV**

"In the wilderness prepare the way of the LORD; make straight in the desert a highway for our God."
**Isaiah 40:3 ESV**

"You can enter God's Kingdom only through the narrow gate. The highway to hell is broad, and its gate is wide for the many who choose that way."
**Matthew 7:13 NLT**

We can make our plans, but the LORD determines our steps. **Proverbs 16:9 NLT**

God called you to do good, even if it means suffering, just as Christ suffered for you. He is your example, and you must follow in His steps.
**1 Peter 2:21 NLT**

Jesus said to him, "I am the way, the truth, and the life. No one comes to the Father except through Me."
**John 14:6 NKJV**

Let the word of Christ dwell in you richly, teaching and admonishing one another in all wisdom, singing psalms and hymns and spiritual songs, with thankfulness in your hearts to God.
**Colossians 3:16 ESV**

Our lives are often compared to a road in the Bible. We must make sure we are on the right way when we're heading for a certain destination. Jesus assures us in John 14:6 that He is the only Way to our final destination. To follow Him is to know when we've reached our destination, but also to keep walking and living on the narrow path.

# Thirsty for God

"For I was hungry and you gave Me food, I was thirsty and you gave Me drink, I was a stranger and you welcomed Me."
**Matthew 25:35 ESV**

"But those who drink the water I give will never be thirsty again. It becomes a fresh, bubbling spring within them, giving them eternal life." **John 4:14 NLT**

On the last and greatest day of the festival, Jesus stood and said in a loud voice, "Let anyone who is thirsty come to Me and drink."
**John 7:37 NIV**

The Spirit and the bride say, "Come!" And let him who hears say, "Come!" And let him who thirsts come. Whoever desires, let him take the water of life freely."
**Revelation 22:17 NKJV**

Come, everyone who thirsts, come to the waters; and he who has no money, come, buy and eat! Come, buy wine and milk without money and without price.
**Isaiah 55:1 ESV**

God is our refuge and strength, a very present help in trouble.
**Psalm 46:1 ESV**

Thirsty people urgently need water. Spiritually thirsty ones seek living water. Jesus is the only Living Water to quench our thirst forever. He is True Life. He is abundance. God invites us to drink from the living water found in Him alone, freely. His Living Water will never let us thirst for anything ever again. Quench your thirst with Jesus. Surrender your life to Him.

# Fill Your Thoughts with God

"For I know the plans I have for you," says the LORD. "They are plans for good and not for disaster, to give you a future and a hope."
**Jeremiah 29:11 NLT**

For I say, through the grace given to me, to everyone who is among you, not to think of himself more highly than he ought to think, but to think soberly, as God has dealt to each one a measure of faith.
**Romans 12:3 NKJV**

Therefore, holy brothers and sisters, who share in the heavenly calling, fix your thoughts on Jesus, whom we acknowledge as our apostle and high priest.
**Hebrews 3:1 NIV**

Finally, brothers and sisters, whatever is true, whatever is noble, whatever is right, whatever is pure, whatever is lovely, whatever is admirable – if anything is excellent or praiseworthy – think about such things.
**Philippians 4:8 NIV**

What is man that You are mindful of him, and the son of man that You care for him?
**Psalm 8:4 ESV**

As for me, since I am poor and needy, let the LORD keep me in His thoughts. You are my helper and my savior. O my God, do not delay.
**Psalm 40:17 NLT**

To think doesn't happen as often as we thought. Most people prefer not to think too much. That is why we daydream almost 50% of the time. But God is thinking all the time, and He is thinking about us. Therefore we should learn to constantly think about Him. We must fill our thoughts with everything that is lovely, praiseworthy, pure and admirable. Our thoughts must bring glory to God. Then our lives will become what we think – pleasing to the Lord.

# Make Time for God

For I consider that the sufferings of this present time are not worthy to be compared with the glory which shall be revealed in us.
**Romans 8:18 NKJV**

This is why it is said: "Wake up, sleeper, rise from the dead, and Christ will shine on you." Be very careful, then, how you live – not as unwise but as wise, making the most of every opportunity, because the days are evil.
**Ephesians 5:14-16 NIV**

Let the hearts of those who seek the LORD rejoice! Seek the LORD and His strength; seek His presence continually!
**1 Chronicles 16:10-11 ESV**

Do not waste time arguing over godless ideas and old wives' tales. Instead, train yourself to be godly. "Physical training is good, but training for godliness is much better, promising benefits in this life and in the life to come."
**1 Timothy 4:7-8 NLT**

Let us then approach God's throne of grace with confidence, so that we may receive mercy and find grace to help us in our time of need.
**Hebrews 4:16 NIV**

Times of refreshment will come from the presence of the Lord.
**Acts 3:20 NLT**

Time, among other things, is divided up into 24-hour time zones. There are 86400 seconds in a day. How we use our time depends on ourselves. None of us are passive victims of time. We can choose what we think, feel and how we live within our 24-hour time zone that God has given us. We can and should live with hearts filled with Him, otherwise time will not be kind to us.

# Tired of Trying?

Then they got rid of the foreign gods among them and served the LORD. And he could bear Israel's misery no longer.
**Judges 10:16 NIV**

They who wait for the LORD shall renew their strength; they shall mount up with wings like eagles; they shall run and not be weary; they shall walk and not faint.
**Isaiah 40:31 ESV**

So let's not get tired of doing what is good. At just the right time we will reap a harvest of blessing if we don't give up.
**Galatians 6:9 NLT**

He makes me to lie down in green pastures; He leads me beside the still waters. He restores my soul; He leads me in the paths of righteousness for His name's sake.
**Psalm 23:2-3 NKJV**

He gives strength to the weary and increases the power of the weak.
**Isaiah 40:29 NIV**

As for you, brethren, do not grow weary in doing good.
**2 Thessalonians 3:13 NKJV**

"Come to Me, all you who are weary and burdened, and I will give you rest."
**Matthew 11:28 NIV**

We all feel exhausted and weary at some point. Work pressure, too much stuff to do and too little time to get everything done – all these things add to our tiredness. Rest helps. But it doesn't fix the problem. Resting in faith is what is needed. We need to find rest in God. He never gets tired. He gives rest to every weary traveler. You can find eternal and temporary rest in Him, despite the hustle and bustle that tires us out.

# Be a Tolerant Person

Then Laban said to Jacob, "See this heap and the pillar, which I have set between you and me. This heap is a witness, and the pillar is a witness, that I will not pass over this heap to you, and you will not pass over this heap and this pillar to me, to do harm. The God of Abraham and the God of Nahor, the God of their father, judge between us." So Jacob swore by the Fear of his father Isaac.
**Genesis 31:51-53 ESV**

Be completely humble and gentle; be patient, bearing with one another in love.
**Ephesians 4:2 NIV**

Make allowance for each other's faults, and forgive anyone who offends you. Remember, the Lord forgave you, so you must forgive others.
**Colossians 3:13 NLT**

Therefore receive one another, just as Christ also received us, to the glory of God.
**Romans 15:7 NKJV**

Whoever resists the authority resists the ordinance of God, and those who resist will bring judgment on themselves.
**Romans 13:2 NKJV**

To tolerate someone is the first step in restoring a relationship. Jacob and his father-in-law for example, agreed not to attack each other if they were to run into each other. At least it was a step in the right direction. Always start with "bear with one another" as the first step to reconcile people. That is how you build the right kind of bridges, little by little. From that point on, people can at least look each other in the eye.

# Tenacity in Tough Times

Therefore put on the full armor of God, so that when the day of evil comes, you may be able to stand your ground, and after you have done everything, to stand.
**Ephesians 6:13 NIV**

Resist him, firm in your faith, knowing that the same kinds of suffering are being experienced by your brotherhood throughout the world.
**1 Peter 5:9 ESV**

Fight the good fight of the faith. Take hold of the eternal life to which you were called and about which you made the good confession in the presence of many witnesses. **1 Timothy 6:12 ESV**

Therefore submit to God. Resist the devil and he will flee from you.
**James 4:7 NKJV**

We desire each one of you to show the same earnestness to have the full assurance of hope until the end, so that you may not be sluggish, but imitators of those who through faith and patience inherit the promises.
**Hebrews 6:11-12 ESV**

God has said, "Never will I leave you; never will I forsake you."
**Hebrews 13:5 NIV**

"The one who endures to the end will be saved."
**Matthew 24:13 NLT**

Sometimes we give in to the demands of life. Other times we give up, as we read in Lamentations happened to the Israelites when they returned from exile. But through His Spirit He adds a bit of tenacity to each of our hearts. We know how to get up after we've stumbled and fell. We know how to encourage each other after we've given up hope. Never will the Lord forsake us. We fight with Him until the bitter end for His glory.

# Taming the Tongue

The tongue of the righteous is choice silver; the heart of the wicked is of little worth.
**Proverbs 10:20 ESV**

Death and life are in the power of the tongue, and those who love it will eat its fruit.
**Proverbs 18:21 NKJV**

For their tongues shoot lies like poisoned arrows. They speak friendly words to their neighbors while scheming in their heart to kill them. **Jeremiah 9:8 NLT**

If you claim to be religious but don't control your tongue, you are fooling yourself, and your religion is worthless. **James 1:26 NIV**

Wise words bring many benefits, and hard work brings rewards. Some people make cutting remarks, but the words of the wise bring healing.
**Proverbs 12:14, 18 NLT**

You have searched me, Lord, and You know me. You know when I sit and when I rise; You perceive my thoughts from afar. Before a word is on my tongue You, Lord, know it completely. Such knowledge is too wonderful for me, too lofty for me to attain.
**Psalm 139:1-2, 4, 6 NIV**

Over and over again the Bible tells us that the tongue is not neutral. We must choose to use it correctly and wisely. Only then can it be an instrument of great blessing to the Lord. Tongues in the mouths of wise people are like fine silver. The words that flow from their mouths are gentle. It brings healing to other people's lives. It is like ointment for wounds. That is why we must yield our tongues to the Lord's control. He teaches us to use it wisely.

DECEMBER

NOTHING CAN EVER SEPARATE US FROM GOD'S LOVE

ROMANS 8:38

# Christel Makes us New

"Blessed are you when men hate you, and when they exclude you, and revile you, and cast out your name as evil, for the Son of Man's sake." Luke 6:22 NKJV

Do not be conformed to this world, but be transformed by the renewal of your mind, that by testing you may discern what is the will of God, what is good and acceptable and perfect.
Romans 12:2 ESV

"I will give you a new heart, and a new spirit I will put within you. And I will remove the heart of stone from your flesh and give you a heart of flesh."
Ezekiel 36:26 NIV

Therefore, if anyone is in Christ, He is a new creation. The old has passed away; behold, the new has come. All this is from God, who through Christ reconciled us to Himself and gave us the ministry of reconciliation. 2 Corinthians 5:17-18 ESV

We all, who with unveiled faces contemplate the Lord's glory, are being transformed into His image with ever-increasing glory, which comes from the Lord, who is the Spirit. 2 Corinthians 3:18 NIV

It doesn't matter whether we have been circumcised or not. What counts is whether we have been transformed into a new creation. Galatians 6:15 NLT

Change is a big word in most businesses and companies. Everybody is talking about change, even the church, but few people are willing to face the implications it brings. Change requires new ways of thinking, courage and purposeful deeds. Change needs to happen the right way, otherwise we're heading for the edge. My motto is: "I change for God and others. Otherwise, it's all about me."

# The Christian Backpacker

When the camp is to set out, Aaron and his sons shall go in and take down the veil of the screen and cover the ark of the testimony with it.
**Numbers 4:5 ESV**

You shall teach them to your children, speaking of them when you sit in your house, when you walk by the way, when you lie down, and when you rise up.
**Deuteronomy 11:19 NKJV**

"The people of one city will say to the people of another, 'Come with us to Jerusalem to ask the LORD to bless us. Let's worship the LORD of Heaven's Armies. I'm determined to go.'"
**Zechariah 8:21 NLT**

"Today or tomorrow we will go to this or that city, spend a year there, carry on business and make money."
**James 4:13 NIV**

The LORD your God may show us the way in which we should walk and the thing we should do.
**Jeremiah 42:3 NKJV**

"Do not be afraid; do not be discouraged, for the LORD your God will be with you wherever you go."
**Joshua 1:9 NIV**

Whether you turn to the right or to the left, your ears will hear a voice behind you, saying, "This is the way; walk in it." **Isaiah 30:21 NIV**

To get from Point A to Point B, we need to move. Standing still won't bring us anywhere, not even when we are on the right path. We need to shift from neutral gear and get moving if we want to get somewhere. To travel supposes that we know where we're going. Or that we are taking the best traveling companions to successfully end the journey. Christ assures us that He will walk with us each step of the way. Never once will we ever walk alone.

# Treasures in Heaven

"Store your treasures in heaven, where moths and rust cannot destroy, and thieves do not break in and steal. Wherever your treasure is, there the desires of your heart will also be. Your eye is like a lamp that provides light for your body. When your eye is healthy, your whole body is filled with light."

Matthew 6:20-22 NLT

"Again, the kingdom of heaven is like a merchant seeking beautiful pearls, who, when he had found one pearl of great price, went and sold all that he had and bought it."

Matthew 13:45-46 NKJV

"Sell your possessions and give to the poor. Provide purses for yourselves that will not wear out, a treasure in heaven that will never fail, where no thief comes near and no moth destroys. For where your treasure is, there your heart will be also."

Luke 12:33-34 NIV

"But seek first the kingdom of God and His righteousness, and all these things will be added to you."

Matthew 6:33 NKJV

"Where your treasure is, there your heart will be also."

Matthew 6:21 NIV

Jesus' timeless words are the greatest truth ever. Eternal words, but also words to belief and live by. You'll quickly discover where your treasures are at when you think about conversations, about what you fight over, reflect on and worry about the most. That's where your treasures lie. Your energy, and most of your time also. Ask Christ to reinvest your life with Him, if you're storing up treasure somewhere else at the moment.

# The Courage to Trust

Every word of God proves true. He is a shield to all who come to Him for protection. **Proverbs 30:5 NLT**

"Therefore I tell you, whatever you ask for in prayer, believe that you have received it, and it will be yours." **Mark 11:24 NIV**

"Let not your hearts be troubled. Believe in God; believe also in Me." **John 14:1 ESV**

Command those who are rich in this present age not to be haughty, nor to trust in uncertain riches but in the living God, who gives us richly all things to enjoy. **1 Timothy 6:17 NKJV**

Trust in Him at all times, you people; pour out your hearts to Him, for God is our refuge. Surely the lowborn are but a breath, the highborn are but a lie. If weighed on a balance, they are nothing; together they are only a breath. **Psalm 62:8-9 NIV**

I pray that God, the source of hope, will fill you completely with joy and peace because you trust in Him. Then you will overflow with confident hope through the power of the Holy Spirit. **Romans 15:13 NLT**

Put your trust in the LORD. **Psalm 4:5 NKJV**

I set my heart on it!" Have you heard this saying? It means that someone puts their trust and hope in a certain thing. Well, before you set your heart on anything, you need to first focus it on God. He is the Source of your trust. He is the origin of all goodness. To trust Him with the detail of your life, is to make the best decision ever!

# Washed Clean

"Woe to me!" I cried. "I am ruined! For I am a man of unclean lips, and I live among a people of unclean lips, and my eyes have seen the King, the LORD Almighty." Isaiah 6:5 NIV

Its prophets are arrogant liars seeking their own gain. Its priests defile the Temple by disobeying God's instructions. Zephaniah 3:4 NLT

For from within, out of the heart of man, come evil thoughts, sexual immorality, theft, murder, adultery. Mark 7:21 ESV

"God blesses those whose hearts are pure, for they will see God." Matthew 5:8 NLT

To the pure all things are pure, but to those who are defiled and unbelieving nothing is pure; but even their mind and conscience are defiled. Titus 1:15 NKJV

Now that you have purified yourselves by obeying the truth so that you have sincere love for each other, love one another deeply, from the heart.
1 Peter 1:22 NIV

Create in me a clean heart, O God, and renew a right spirit within me. The sacrifices of God are a broken spirit; a broken and contrite heart, O God, You will not despise.
Psalm 51:10, 17 ESV

Impurity was a cultic concept of the Jewish world while Jesus was on earth. Unclean people or objects were not allowed to enter the temple and to serve God there. Jesus moved these laws out of the way. He had a compassionate heart for unclean people. He declared people clean and pure. He grants us access to the throne of God's grace. That is why we should never categorize people as clean or unclean. A friend of Jesus is also a friend of us.

# A Matter of the Heart

The ox knows its master, the donkey its owner's manger, but Israel does not know, my people do not understand.
Isaiah 1:3 NIV

Let every man be swift to hear, slow to speak, slow to wrath. James 1:19 NKJV

Let those who are wise understand these things. Let those with discernment listen carefully. The paths of the LORD are true and right, and righteous people live by walking in them.
Hosea 14:9 NLT

When you read this, you can perceive my insight into the mystery of Christ.
Ephesians 3:4 ESV

You are great in counsel and mighty in work, for Your eyes are open to all the ways of the sons of men, to give everyone according to his ways and according to the fruit of his doings.
Jeremiah 32:19 NKJV

Wisdom will enter your heart, and knowledge will fill you with joy. Wise choices will watch over you. Understanding will keep you safe.
Proverbs 2:10-11 NLT

The human heart is the most deceitful of all things, and desperately wicked. Who really knows how bad it is?
Jeremiah 17:9 NLT

To understand is to have insight into a matter. In other words, to have insight into the matters concerning the Lord. To understand is to believe the right way. It is to bow down before God to serve Him with your whole heart. Understanding is not the same as head knowledge. Understanding also refers to matters of the heart. It is to move from ignorance to faith in action.

# Be Faithful to God

"The whole assembly of the LORD says: 'How could you break faith with the God of Israel like this? How could you turn away from the LORD and build yourselves an altar in rebellion against Him now?'"
**Joshua 22:16 NIV**

The LORD is good to everyone. He showers compassion on all His creation. All of Your works will thank You, LORD, and Your faithful followers will praise You.
**Psalm 145:9-10 NLT**

A faithful person will be richly blessed, but one eager to get rich will not go unpunished.
**Proverbs 28:20 NIV**

"If you are faithful in little things, you will be faithful in large ones. But if you are dishonest in little things, you won't be honest with greater responsibilities."
**Luke 16:10 NLT**

Let love and faithfulness never leave you; bind them around your neck, write them on the tablet of your heart.
**Proverbs 3:3 NIV**

"His master said to him, 'Well done, good and faithful servant. You have been faithful over a little; I will set you over much. Enter into the joy of your master.'"
**Matthew 25:21 ESV**

Throughout the history of Israel, unfaithfulness to God was the order of the day. From the desert to Jerusalem, unfaithfulness characterized their relationship with God many times. God didn't tolerate this. Time after time the people were called to return to Him. His calls for obedience apply to us as well. We are God's ambassadors on earth. We represent Him everywhere we go on earth. Therefore, we must be faithful and obedient to Him all the time.

# You're One of a Kind

The LORD has declared today that you are His people, His own special treasure, just as He promised, and that you must obey all His commands.
**Deuteronomy 26:18 NLT**

For I too was a son to my father, still tender, and cherished by my mother.
**Proverbs 4:3 NIV**

"I gave them My Sabbath days of rest as a sign between them and Me. It was to remind them that I am the LORD, who had set them apart to be holy."
**Ezekiel 20:12 NLT**

As each one has received a gift, minister it to one another, as good stewards of the manifold grace of God.
**1 Peter 4:10 NKJV**

For You formed my inward parts; You knitted me together in my mother's womb. I praise You, for I am fearfully and wonderfully made. Wonderful are Your works; my soul knows it very well. My frame was not hidden from You, when I was being made in secret, intricately woven in the depths of the earth.
**Psalm 139:13-15 ESV**

In his book *The Arithmetic of Life and Death*, George Shaffner calculated the possibility of you getting your specific 23 chromosomes from your mom, to be one in ten million. The same goes for the 23 chromosomes from your dad. Multiply it and you find that for you to be you, the mathematical probability is 1 in 100 trillion. Moreover, your pair of 23 chromosomes binds in 8 388 608 ways. You are absolutely unique in every way!

# Upside-Down in His Presence

The LORD watches over the strangers; He relieves the fatherless and widow; but the way of the wicked He turns upside down.
**Psalm 146:9 NKJV**

Behold, the LORD will empty the earth and make it desolate, and He will twist its surface and scatter its inhabitants.
**Isaiah 24:1 ESV**

You turn things upside down, as if the potter were thought to be like the clay! Shall what is formed say to the one who formed it, "You did not make me"? Can the pot say to the potter, "You know nothing"?
**Isaiah 29:16 NIV**

Not finding them there, they dragged out Jason and some of the other believers instead and took them before the city council. "Paul and Silas have caused trouble all over the world," they shouted, "and now they are here disturbing our city, too.
**Acts 17:6 NLT**

"But many who are first will be last, and many who are last will be first."
**Matthew 19:30 NIV**

"The Son of Man did not come to be served, but to serve, and to give His life as a ransom for many."
**Matthew 20:28 NIV**

Acts 17:6 is one the most compelling Scripture verses in the Bible. A group of people accused Paul and his people in Thessalonica of turning the world upside-down. Isn't that exactly what Christianity is all about? To Jesus the first will be last, and whoever is behind will be in front. The weak is strong and disgraced people will be honorable. Everything is turned upside-down in Christ's presence. He cares about losers, broken people and outcasts. We need to do the same.

# A Godly Urgency

Most people are motivated to success because they envy their neighbors. But this, too, is meaningless – like chasing the wind. Ecclesiastes 4:4 NLT

So teach us to number our days that we may get a heart of wisdom. Psalm 90:12 ESV

For He says: "In an acceptable time I have heard you, and in the day of salvation I have helped you." Behold, now is the accepted time; behold, now is the day of salvation. 2 Corinthians 6:2 NKJV

"But seek first the kingdom of God and His righteousness, and all these things will be added to you." Matthew 6:33 ESV

Let our people learn to devote themselves to good works, so as to help cases of urgent need, and not be unfruitful. Titus 3:14 ESV

Preach the word; be prepared in season and out of season; correct, rebuke and encourage – with great patience and careful instruction. 2 Timothy 4:2 NIV

See then that you walk circumspectly, not as fools but as wise, redeeming the time, because the days are evil. Therefore do not be unwise, but understand what the will of the Lord is. Ephesians 5:15-17 NKJV

Urgency mustn't be confused with hurriedness. People who are always in a hurry are chasing around after the wind. They are always busy without really getting anything done. People with a sense of urgency, however, are focused. They know why God put them on earth, and they busy themselves with their purpose. People with urgency build on the dreams that God put in their hearts. They don't wait until tomorrow when they can do the right thing for the Lord today. Such people seize the moment, and use their time wisely to honor God.

# Victory in Christ

The horse is made ready for the day of battle, but the victory belongs to the LORD.
**Proverbs 21:31 ESV**

Thanks be to God! He gives us the victory through our Lord Jesus Christ.
**1 Corinthians 15:57 NIV**

"Death is swallowed up in victory. O Death, where is your sting? O Hades, where is your victory?" The sting of death is sin, and the strength of sin is the law. But thanks be to God, who gives us the victory through our Lord Jesus Christ.
**1 Corinthians 15:54-57 NKJV**

The LORD your God is the one who goes with you to fight for you against your enemies to give you victory.
**Deuteronomy 20:4 NIV**

Thanks be to God, who in Christ always leads us in triumphal procession, and through us spreads the fragrance of the knowledge of Him everywhere.
**2 Corinthians 2:14 ESV**

"Here on earth you will have many trials and sorrows. But take heart, because I have overcome the world."
**John 16:33 NLT**

Victory is guaranteed for a child of God. Christ has triumphed over our greatest enemy, death, once and for all. He walked through the gates of Hades, and emerged triumphant on the third day. This is how He broke the bonds of death forever. Now Jesus guarantees this victory over death for each of us fighting on His side. Death is swallowed up by Christ's victory.

# A Righteous Judge

Now the earth was corrupt in God's sight, and the earth was filled with violence. **Genesis 6:11 ESV**

The mouth of the righteous is a well of life, but violence covers the mouth of the wicked. **Proverbs 10:11 NKJV**

Again, I observed all the oppression that takes place under the sun. I saw the tears of the oppressed, with no one to comfort them. The oppressors have great power, and their victims are helpless. **Ecclesiastes 4:1 NLT**

Whoever sows injustice will reap calamity, and the rod of his fury will fail. **Proverbs 22:8 ESV**

Since we know that Christ is righteous, we also know that all who do what is right are God's children. **1 John 2:29 NLT**

Righteous are You, O LORD, and upright are Your judgments. **Psalm 119:137 NKJV**

Because of the violence against your brother Jacob, you will be covered with shame; you will be destroyed forever. **Obadiah 1:10 NIV**

He has cast the lot for them, and His hand has divided it among them with a measuring line. They shall possess it forever; from generation to generation they shall dwell in it. **Isaiah 34:17 NKJV**

Violence is a daily reality in our broken and sinful world. People rob and steal from each other. Not to mention the senseless murders. It grieves God. Enough blood has been shed – His Son's was enough. That is why God can't stand ruthless and violent people. He will deal with them. Even if they fall through the cracks of the world's justice system, we can count on God to give them what they deserve. We can trust Him to keep us safe.

# Virtues for Everyday Living

But select from all the people some capable, honest men who fear God and hate bribes. Appoint them as leaders over groups of one thousand, one hundred, fifty, and ten.
**Exodus 18:21 NLT**

A wife of noble character who can find? She is worth far more than rubies.
**Proverbs 31:10 NIV**

And let us not grow weary while doing good, for in due season we shall reap if we do not lose heart. Therefore, as we have opportunity, let us do good to all, especially to those who are of the household of faith.
**Galatians 6:9-10 NKJV**

His divine power has granted to us all things that pertain to life and godliness, through the knowledge of Him who called us to His own glory and excellence, by which He has granted to us His precious and very great promises, so that through them you may become partakers of the divine nature, having escaped from the corruption that is in the world because of sinful desire. For this very reason, make every effort to supplement your faith with virtue, and virtue with knowledge. **2 Peter 1:3-5 ESV**

Fire tests the purity of silver and gold, but a person is tested by being praised.
**Proverbs 27:21 NLT**

A virtue is a characteristic that you can use to glorify God and for the benefit of other people. Godly virtues are shaped by the Spirit in our lives. It becomes visible in our lives through our kindness, servitude, humility and gentleness. Virtuous men and women are living blessings to others in the community. They draw people to the Lord like a moth to a flame. Their faithfulness to Him and their loyalty to others inspire people to live good lives.

# He Cares for the Vulnerable

Finally, Samson shared his secret with her. "My hair has never been cut," he confessed, "for I was dedicated to God as a Nazirite from birth. If my head were shaved, my strength would leave me, and I would become as weak as anyone else."
**Judges 16:17 NLT**

"Beat your plowshares into swords and your pruning hooks into spears; let the weak say, 'I am strong.'"
**Joel 3:10 NKJV**

Immediately the boy's father exclaimed, "I do believe; help me overcome my unbelief!"
**Mark 9:24 NIV**

On that day the LORD will protect the inhabitants of Jerusalem, so that the feeblest among them on that day shall be like David, and the house of David shall be like God, like the angel of the LORD, going before them.
**Zechariah 12:8 ESV**

And those who know Your name will put their trust in You; for You, LORD, have not forsaken those who seek You. Sing praises to the LORD, who dwells in Zion! Declare His deeds among the people.
**Psalm 9:10-11 NKJV**

We are weak, but you are strong. **1 Corinthians 4:10 NIV**

To feel vulnerable is not a nice feeling. It is a complete feeling of helplessness when you are supposed to be doing something. Being helpless or defenseless is when you see the wickedness in the world, and not being able to do anything about it. Well, the good news is: God notices the defenseless. He has a heart for outsiders and outcasts. He will push the wicked and haughty from their self-made thrones.

# Waiting Is the Hardest Part

Wait for the LORD; be strong and take heart and wait for the LORD. **Psalm 27:14 NIV**

Those who wait on the LORD shall renew their strength; they shall mount up with wings like eagles, they shall run and not be weary, they shall walk and not faint.
**Isaiah 40:31 NKJV**

Our citizenship is in heaven, and from it we await a Savior, the Lord Jesus Christ.
**Philippians 3:20 ESV**

Wait on the LORD, and keep His way, and He shall exalt you to inherit the land; when the wicked are cut off, you shall see it.
**Psalm 37:34 NKJV**

But we are looking forward to the new heavens and new earth He has promised, a world filled with God's righteousness. **2 Peter 3:13 NLT**

The LORD is good to those who wait for Him, to the soul who seeks Him.
**Lamentations 3:25 ESV**

I will wait for God of my salvation; my God will hear me.
**Micah 7:7 ESV**

The Lord is not slow to fulfill His promise as some count slowness, but is patient toward you, not wishing that any should perish, but that all should reach repentance.
**2 Peter 3:9 ESV**

To wait on the Lord means to actively linger in His presence. It is not passively sitting around doing nothing. To wait on the Lord is a lifelong spiritual discipline where we learn to subject our plans to Him. Waiting on Him means synchronizing our lives with the will of the living God. We are therefore not waiting to be served, but we're waiting on God Himself.

# Walk in His Steps

So now there is no condemnation for those who belong to Christ Jesus.
**Romans 8:1 NLT**

So I say, walk by the Spirit, and you will not gratify the desires of the flesh.
**Galatians 5:16 NIV**

For we are His workmanship, created in Christ Jesus for good works, which God prepared beforehand, that we should walk in them.
**Ephesians 2:10 ESV**

Blessed are those who keep His testimonies, who seek Him with their whole heart, who also do no wrong, but walk in His ways!
**Psalm 119:2-3 ESV**

As you therefore have received Christ Jesus the Lord, so walk in Him.
**Colossians 2:6 NKJV**

In everything set them an example by doing what is good. In your teaching show integrity, seriousness and soundness of speech that cannot be condemned, so that those who oppose you may be ashamed because they have nothing bad to say about us.
**Titus 2:7-8 NIV**

Follow God's example, therefore, as dearly loved children and walk in the way of love, just as Christ loved us and gave Himself up for us as a fragrant offering and sacrifice to God. **Ephesians 5:1-2 NIV**

Walking as an image of the Christian life is often neglected. But it's used over and over in the New Testament to indicate how we should follow Jesus by walking in His steps. We follow Jesus on His road of discipleship. We imitate Him and walk behind Him all the time. That's why we must consider our "walking" before the Lord. We need to do it with integrity. We must walk with dignity and purity of heart, as the Lord expects from us.

# Walking in Grace

Even when I walk through the darkest valley, I will not be afraid, for You are close beside me. Your rod and Your staff protect and comfort me. **Psalm 23:4 NLT**

I therefore, a prisoner for the Lord, urge you to walk in a manner worthy of the calling to which you have been called.
**Ephesians 4:1 ESV**

So then, just as you received Christ Jesus as Lord, continue to live your lives in Him. **Colossians 2:6 NIV**

"Small is the gate and narrow the road that leads to life, and only a few find it." **Matthew 7:14 NIV**

For we are His workmanship, created in Christ Jesus for good works, which God prepared beforehand that we should walk in them. **Ephesians 2:10 NKJV**

"I know your works, your toil and your patient endurance, and how you cannot bear with those who are evil, but have tested those who call themselves apostles and are not, and found them to be false." **Revelation 2:2 ESV**

"My grace is sufficient for you, for My strength is made perfect in weakness." **2 Corinthians 12:9 NKJV**

Walking is an often forgotten but an essential image of the Christian life. Paul often used it in his letters to depict how we should follow Christ. We as believers don't walk the way of unbelief anymore. Jesus' footsteps are our guiding light and direction. We put our feet where His footsteps are imprinted in front of us on our journey through life. With Him we walk and live on the path leading to life.

# The Unseen War

For we are not fighting against flesh-and-blood enemies, but against evil rulers and authorities of the unseen world, against mighty powers in this dark world, and against evil spirits in the heavenly places. **Ephesians 6:12 NLT**

I have fought the good fight, I have finished the race, I have kept the faith. **2 Timothy 4:7 NKJV**

You will hear of wars and rumors of wars. See that you are not alarmed, for this must take place, but the end is not yet. **Matthew 24:6 ESV**

For though we walk in the flesh, we are not waging war according to the flesh. **2 Corinthians 10:3 ESV**

You therefore must endure hardship as a good soldier of Jesus Christ. No one engaged in warfare entangles himself with the affairs of this life, that he may please him who enlisted him as a soldier. **2 Timothy 2:3-4 NKJV**

Praise be to the Lord my Rock, who trains my hands for war, my fingers for battle. **Psalm 144:1 NIV**

He shall judge between the nations, and rebuke many people; they shall beat their swords into plowshares, and their spears into pruning hooks; nation shall not lift up sword against nation, neither shall they learn war anymore. **Isaiah 2:4 NKJV**

War is life threatening. It takes lives. We as Christians are also involved in a war with the evil spirit at work. Yet we are armed and ready. Our armor is given to us by Christ, and allows us to remain standing until the end of days. We also know that He fights with us. His victorious power is available to us.

# God Hates Lukewarmness

What does the LORD your God require of you? He requires only that you fear the LORD your God, and live in a way that pleases Him, and love Him and serve Him with all your heart and soul.
**Deuteronomy 10:12 NLT**

"I know your works, that you are neither cold nor hot. I could wish you were cold or hot. So then, because you are lukewarm, and neither cold nor hot, I will vomit you out of My mouth."
**Revelation 3:15-16 NKJV**

May your hearts be fully committed to the LORD our God, to live by His decrees and obey His commands.
**1 Kings 8:61 NIV**

Only fear the LORD and serve Him faithfully with all your heart. For consider what great things He has done for you.
**1 Samuel 12:24 ESV**

To Timothy, my true child in the faith: Grace, mercy, and peace from God the Father and Christ Jesus our Lord.
**1 Timothy 1:2 ESV**

If one of you says to them, "Go in peace; keep warm and well fed," but does nothing about their physical needs, what good is it? In the same way, faith by itself, if it is not accompanied by action, is dead.
**James 2:16-17 NIV**

It's not pleasant to feel cold. We want to feel warm and cozy, especially in winter. We put on our winter clothes: thick jerseys, scarves, jackets – everything to protect us from the cold. When the wind blows we don't want to be dressed in "medium warm" clothes. We also don't want to drink lukewarm tea or coffee. In the same way, God can't stand people who are neither hot nor cold. He can still do something for a cold person, but He will spit lukewarm people out of His mouth.

# Warn People in Love

"But I will show you whom you should fear: fear Him who, after your body has been killed, has authority to throw you into hell. Yes, I tell you, fear Him." Luke 12:5 NIV

Do not regard him as an enemy, but warn him as a brother. 2 Thessalonians 3:15 ESV

For I testify to everyone who hears the words of the prophecy of this book: if anyone adds to these things, God will add to him the plagues that are written in this book. Revelation 22:18 NKJV

For this command is a lamp, this teaching is a light, and correction and instruction are the way to life. Proverbs 6:23 NIV

So we tell others about Christ, warning everyone and teaching everyone with all the wisdom God has given us. We want to present them to God, perfect in their relationship to Christ. Colossians 1:28 NLT

Whoever heeds life-giving correction will be at home among the wise. Those who disregard discipline despise themselves, but the one who heeds correction gains understanding. Proverbs 15:31-32 NIV

Let the godly strike me! It will be a kindness! If they correct me, it is soothing medicine. Don't let me refuse it.
Psalm 141:5 NLT

Each of us has a calling on our lives to warn those who have lost their way. The Lord expects it from us. No, we don't have to insult, threaten or hit them over the head. We must guide and ask them to return to the way of the Lord with the love of Christ in our hearts. We should plead with them to live right. If we don't correct and reprimand in love, we will get in trouble with the Lord.

# The Christian Warrior

He said, "Let Me go, for the day breaks." But he said, "I will not let You go unless You bless me!" So He said to him, "What is your name?" He said, "Jacob." And He said, "Your name shall no longer be called Jacob, but Israel; for you have struggled with God and with men, and have prevailed." Then Jacob asked, saying, "Tell me Your name, I pray." And He said, "Why is it that you ask about My name?" And He blessed him there. Genesis 32:26-29 NKJV

We use God's mighty weapons, not worldly weapons, to knock down the strongholds of human reasoning and to destroy false arguments.
2 Corinthians 10:4 NLT

In Your majesty ride out victoriously for the cause of truth and meekness and righteousness; let Your right hand teach you awesome deeds! Your arrows are sharp in the heart of the king's enemies; the peoples fall under You. Psalm 45:4-5 ESV

Put on the full armor of God, so that you can take your stand against the devil's schemes. Ephesians 6:11 NIV

The LORD your God is with you, the Mighty Warrior who saves. He will take great delight in you; in His love He will no longer rebuke you, but will rejoice over you with singing.
Zephaniah 3:17 NIV

Warriors are fighters. Jacob was one. After he wrestled with the message from the Lord for a whole night, and won, God changed his name to Israel. It means "the one who wrestled with God." Jacob was allowed by God to wrestle with the messenger. He even allows us to wrestle with Him. He lets us fight and argue, and win, if it's His will.

# Embrace Your Weaknesses

We are fools for Christ, but you are so wise in Christ! We are weak, but you are strong! You are honored, we are dishonored!
**1 Corinthians 4:10 NIV**

Each time He said, "My grace is all you need. My power works best in weakness." So now I am glad to boast about my weaknesses, so that the power of Christ can work through me. That's why I take pleasure in my weaknesses, and in the insults, hardships, persecutions, and troubles that I suffer for Christ. For when I am weak, then I am strong.
**2 Corinthians 12:9-10 NLT**

The Holy Spirit helps us in our weakness. For example, we don't know what God wants us to pray for. But the Holy Spirit prays for us with groanings that cannot be expressed in words. And the Father who knows all hearts knows what the Spirit is saying, for the Spirit pleads for us believers in harmony with God's own will. **Romans 8:26-27 NLT**

He is not weak in dealing with you, but is powerful among you. For to be sure, He was crucified in weakness, yet He lives by God's power. Likewise, we are weak in Him, yet by God's power we will live with Him in our dealing with you.
**2 Corinthians 13:3-4 NIV**

Weakness is a building block of the Christian faith … Really? Paul had to learn it the hard way. Three times Paul asked God to take the thorn of his weakness, suffering and opposition away in 2 Corinthians 6 and 11. Then he heard that God's grace is more than enough for him. God's power becomes visible when His children are weak. We aren't power sources, we are carriers of great heavenly strength and power.

# Bless Others with Your Wealth

Honor the LORD with your wealth and with the best part of everything you produce.

**Proverbs 3:9 NLT**

Better a little with the fear of the LORD than great wealth with turmoil.

**Proverbs 15:16 NIV**

But this is gain for a land in every way: a king committed to cultivated fields.

**Ecclesiastes 5:9 ESV**

"Do not lay up for yourselves treasures on earth, where moth and rust destroy and where thieves break in and steal."

**Matthew 6:19 NKJV**

You will be enriched in every way to be generous in every way, which through us will produce thanksgiving to God.

**2 Corinthians 9:11 ESV**

Command them to do good, to be rich in good deeds, and to be generous and willing to share.

**1 Timothy 6:18 NIV**

"Give, and it will be given to you. A good measure, pressed down, shaken together and running over, will be poured into your lap. For with the measure you use, it will be measured to you."

**Luke 6:38 NIV**

Wealth is never neutral. If money is your master then you'll never have enough, says Ecclesiastes. On the other hand, wealth is a blessing in the hands of the righteous. Such people have a caring heart for others. They don't spend all their money on themselves. God is generous, and His people should be too. We should never wait until tomorrow if we can help someone today.

# Finish Well

Don't you realize that in a race everyone runs, but only one person gets the prize? So run to win! All athletes are disciplined in their training. They do it to win a prize that will fade away, but we do it for an eternal prize. **1 Corinthians 9:24-25 NLT**

Yet indeed I also count all things loss for the excellence of the knowledge of Christ Jesus my Lord, for whom I have suffered the loss of all things, and count them as rubbish, that I may gain Christ. **Philippians 3:8 NKJV**

An athlete is not crowned unless he competes according to the rules.
**2 Timothy 2:5 ESV**

Those who are victorious will inherit all this, and I will be their God and they will be My children.
**Revelation 21:7 NIV**

Therefore we also, since we are surrounded by so great a cloud of witnesses, let us lay aside every weight, and the sin which so easily ensnares us, and let us run with endurance the race that is set before us, looking unto Jesus, the author and finisher of our faith, who for the joy that was set before Him endured the cross, despising the shame, and has sat down at the right hand of the throne of God.
**Hebrews 12:1-2 NKJV**

We all like to win. That's why the Bible has such good news: Each one of us who participate in Christ's team and plays by His rules is a winner. We stand on the podium next to Jesus. We share in His eternal victory. We should run the race in such a way as to win the eternal prize of salvation.

# Wisdom Starts with God

And this is what He says to all humanity: "The fear of the LORD is true wisdom; to forsake evil is real understanding." **Job 28:28 NLT**

The fear of the LORD is the beginning of wisdom, and the knowledge of the Holy One is insight. **Proverbs 9:10 ESV**

It is because of Him that you are in Christ Jesus, who has become for us wisdom from God – that is, our righteousness, holiness and redemption. **1 Corinthians 1:30 NIV**

If any of you lacks wisdom, let him ask of God, who gives to all liberally and without reproach, and it will be given to him. **James 1:5 NKJV**

The fear of the LORD is the beginning of wisdom; a good understanding have all those who do His commandments. His praise endures forever.
**Psalm 111:10 NKJV**

You have been taught the holy Scriptures from childhood, and they have given you the wisdom to receive the salvation that comes by trusting in Christ Jesus. All Scripture is inspired by God and is useful to teach us what is true and to make us realize what is wrong in our lives. It corrects us when we are wrong and teaches us to do what is right.
**2 Timothy 3:15-16 NLT**

Wisdom is not to speak a few right words at the right time. Wisdom is a full-time way of living in God's presence. Wisdom is to be humble in His presence. Wise people know their place before the Lord. Their words are precious and have healing power. Their hearts overflow with compassion for other people. They sidestep sin because they know how to walk in the Lord's way.

# Share Your Faith

This day I call the heavens and the earth as witnesses against you that I have set before you life and death, blessings and curses. Now choose life, so that you and your children may live.
Deuteronomy 30:19 NIV

But none of these things move me; nor do I count my life dear to myself, so that I may finish my race with joy, and the ministry which I received from the Lord Jesus, to testify to the gospel of the grace of God.
Acts 20:24 NKJV

And you also will bear witness, because you have been with Me from the beginning.
John 15:27 ESV

"Everyone who acknowledges Me publicly here on earth, I will also acknowledge before My Father in heaven." Matthew 10:32 NLT

"You will receive power when the Holy Spirit comes on you; and you will be My witnesses in Jerusalem, and in all Judea and Samaria, and to the ends of the earth." Acts 1:8 NIV

And He said to them, "Go into all the world and proclaim the gospel to the whole creation. Whoever believes and is baptized will be saved, but whoever does not believe will be condemned."
Mark 16:15-16 ESV

We are Christ's witnesses. No, we're not His advocates or arrest officers. We give good testimonies of who He is and what He has done to deliver us. We should never feel ashamed of Christ. We also know that the Spirit is Jesus' true witness. Only the Holy Spirit can defend Jesus and convince people about their sins and God's righteousness.

# Work Hard for the Lord

Then the LORD God took the man and put him in the garden of Eden to tend and keep it. **Genesis 2:15 NKJV**

The heavens proclaim the glory of God. The skies display His craftsmanship. **Psalm 19:1 NLT**

"Do not work for the food that perishes, but for the food that endures to eternal life, which the Son of Man will give to you. For on Him God the Father has set His seal." **John 6:27 ESV**

As for you, always be sober-minded, endure suffering, do the work of an evangelist, fulfill your ministry. **2 Timothy 4:5 ESV**

Therefore, my dear brothers and sisters, stand firm. Let nothing move you. Always give yourselves fully to the work of the Lord, because you know that your labor in the Lord is not in vain. **1 Corinthians 15:58 NIV**

Now at just the right time He has revealed this message, which we announce to everyone. It is by the command of God our Savior that I have been entrusted with this work for Him. **Titus 1:3 NLT**

The one who plants and the one who waters work together with the same purpose. And both will be rewarded for their own hard work. **1 Corinthians 3:8 NLT**

Working hard is a biblical requirement. We aren't called to sit around idly, and to expect others to take care of us. But we should also not become workaholics. What does it help when the whole world knows us, but our family and loved ones are strangers to us? We work in order to live, not to die. In other words, we shouldn't work ourselves to death. We work for God and we live for Him. Balance is key.

# Worry Destroys Faith

"That is why I tell you not to worry about everyday life – whether you have enough food and drink, or enough clothes to wear. Isn't life more than food, and your body more than clothing?" Matthew 6:25 NLT

"Are not five sparrows sold for two pennies? Yet not one of them is forgotten by God." Luke 12:6 NIV

Be anxious for nothing, but in everything by prayer and supplication, with thanksgiving, let your requests be made known to God. Philippians 4:6 NKJV

Give all your worries and cares to God, for He cares about you. 1 Peter 5:7 NLT

Worry weighs a person down; an encouraging word cheers a person up. Proverbs 12:25 NLT

Remove vexation from your heart, and put away pain from your body, for youth and the dawn of life are vanity. Ecclesiastes 11:10 ESV

"Don't worry about tomorrow, for tomorrow will bring its own worries." Matthew 6:34 NLT

"Let not your heart be troubled; you believe in God, believe also in Me." John 14:1 NKJV

Worry is a dangerous thing. It destroys our faith. It shifts the focus away from God and to our problems. It changes our lives into a dark pit of sorrow and suffering. Worst of all – to worry brings you nowhere. Therefore, we need to take God's offering of grace and make it our own, by bringing all our worries and burdens to Him. He will carry it on our behalf. Then we can live carefree lives.

# You Are Precious

"Since you were precious in My sight, you have been honored, and I have loved you."
**Isaiah 43:4 NKJV**

"See, I have engraved you on the palms of My hands; your walls are ever before Me."
**Isaiah 49:16 NIV**

Your beauty should not come from outward adornment, such as elaborate hairstyles and the wearing of gold jewelry or fine clothes. Rather, it should be that of your inner self, the unfading beauty of a gentle and quiet spirit, which is of great worth in God's sight.
**1 Peter 3:3-4 NIV**

If you call on the Father, who without partiality judges according to each one's work, conduct yourselves throughout the time of your stay here in fear; knowing that you were not redeemed with corruptible things, like silver or gold, from your aimless conduct received by tradition from your fathers, but with the precious blood of Christ, as of a lamb without blemish and without spot.
**1 Peter 1:17-19 NKJV**

However, I consider my life worth nothing to me; my only aim is to finish the race and complete the task the Lord Jesus has given me – the task of testifying to the good news of God's grace. **Acts 20:24 NIV**

Everything has its price. Everything has a value determined by supply and demand. If something is scarce, it costs more. Paul knew how to determine his worth. He regarded himself so shockingly insignificant that he was willing to lose his own life. But he regarded Christ's worth very highly, and was willing to offer his life exclusively to Him. Christ alone has eternal worth. To lose ourselves in Him, is to gain life.

# When You Get it Wrong

"Do not seek revenge or bear a grudge against a fellow Israelite, but love your neighbor as yourself. I am the LORD." **Leviticus 19:18 NLT**

Then Zerubbabel son of Shealtiel, Joshua son of Jozadak, the high priest, and the whole remnant of the people obeyed the voice of the LORD their God and the message of the prophet Haggai, because the LORD their God had sent him. And the people feared the LORD. **Haggai 1:12 NIV**

But in that land of exile, they might turn to You in repentance and pray, "We have sinned, done evil, and acted wickedly." **1 Kings 8:47 NLT**

All Scripture is breathed out by God and profitable for teaching, for reproof, for correction, and for training in righteousness. **2 Timothy 3:16 ESV**

Blessed are those whose way is blameless, who walk in the law of the LORD! Blessed are those who keep His testimonies, who seek Him with their whole heart, who also do no wrong, but walk in His ways! **Psalm 119:1-3 ESV**

Then Peter came to Him and said, "Lord, how often shall my brother sin against me, and I forgive him? Up to seven times?" **Matthew 18:21 NKJV**

It's not a nice feeling to be wrong. If you got the facts wrong, or travelled in the wrong direction, then you're mad at yourself and a bit embarrassed. Fortunately God's grace is for all people who acknowledge their wrongs in His presence. He sets them straight. He puts our feet back on the right track. He starts over. He gives second chances, hundreds of chances ... ten thousand chances.

# Passion Like a Consuming Fire

Jesus Christ, who gave Himself for us to redeem us from all lawlessness and to purify for Himself a people for His own possession who are zealous for good works.
**Titus 2:13-14 ESV**

His disciples remembered that it was written, "Zeal for your house will consume Me." **John 2:17 ESV**

Do not let your heart envy sinners, but always be zealous for the fear of the LORD.
**Proverbs 23:17 NIV**

Since you are zealous for spiritual gifts, let it be for the edification of the church that you seek to excel.
**1 Corinthians 14:12 NKJV**

Now who is there to harm you if you are zealous for what is good? But even if you should suffer for righteousness' sake, you will be blessed. **1 Peter 3:13-14 ESV**

Thank God! He has given Titus the same enthusiasm for you that I have. Titus welcomed our request that he visit you again. In fact, he himself was very eager to go and see you.
**2 Corinthians 8:16-17 NLT**

Be devoted to one another in love. Honor one another above yourselves. Never be lacking in zeal, but keep your spiritual fervor, serving the Lord.
**Romans 12:10-11 NIV**

Zeal is the overwhelming passion with which some people take on a task. When we have such zeal for the Lord, then He alone is the center of your world. Then His love is like a consuming fire. Only God's approval matters. Zealous people always perform for an audience of One – God Himself. He is the oxygen; their breath, their life. Become zealous again for the work of the Lord!

# Thematic Index

# Other Books in This Range

366 powerful reflections with
Scripture verses on relevant topics.

The Pocket Bible
Devotional for
Women

The Pocket Bible
Devotional for
Guys

The Pocket Bible
Devotional for
Girls

ISBN 978-1-4321-1925-6

ISBN 978-1-4321-2415-1

ISBN 978-1-4321-1926-3

# About the Author

Stephan Joubert is a renowned speaker, pastor, leadership consultant and acclaimed author. He is an Extraordinary Professor in Theology at the University of the Free State. Stephan is a research fellow in Theology at the Radboud University in Nijmegen, Netherlands and is also the editor of echurch, an online community of followers of Jesus, with more than 55,000 members worldwide. He is married to Marietjie and they have two daughters, Tarien and Elani.